A Cézanne Sketchbook

FIGURES, PORTRAITS, LANDSCAPES and STILL LIFES

by

PAUL CÉZANNE

DOVER PUBLICATIONS, INC., NEW YORK

Published in Canada by General Publishing Company, Ltd., 30 Lesmill Road, Don Mills, Toronto, Ontario.

This Dover edition, first published in 1985, is an unabridged, slightly corrected republication of the work originally published in two volumes by Curt Valentin, New York, in 1951 under the title *Paul Cézanne/Sketch Book/Owned by The Art Institute of Chicago*, in an edition limited to 1500 copies. The introductory text is by Carl O. Schniewind, who was Curator of Prints and Drawings at the time.

Manufactured in the United States of America
Dover Publications, Inc., 31 East 2nd Street, Mineola, N.Y. 11501

Library of Congress Cataloging in Publication Data

Cézanne, Paul, 1839–1906.
A Cézanne sketchbook.

Rev. ed. of: Sketch book. 1951.
Sketches owned by the Art Institute of Chicago.
1. Cézanne, Paul, 1839–1906. I. Cézanne, Paul, 1839–1906. Sketch book. II. Art Institute of Chicago. III. Title. IV. Title: Cézanne sketch book.
NC248.C37A4 1985 741.944 84-21195
ISBN 0-486-24790-2

PAUL CEZANNE

BORN AIX-EN-PROVENCE, 1839

DIED AIX-EN-PROVENCE, 1906

A SKETCH BOOK BY PAUL CEZANNE

PURCHASED BY THE ART INSTITUTE OF CHICAGO

THROUGH THE ARTHUR HEUN FUND, 1951

THE SKETCH BOOK here reproduced in full was one of five books which came to the United States late in 1950. This group was owned by M. Maurice Renou of Lyon, France, and was known as "The Lyon Sketch Books." M. Renou was a close friend of Renoir, Cézanne and his family and we are told it was from Cézanne's family that he acquired the group. Our book is here published for the first time.

This book, which is of the same size as the four others, measures 5 x 8¾ inches. It is bound in a stiff unbleached linen cover. At one side there is a pencil holder and at one end a linen tape has been bound in which could be looped over the opposite cover to hold it firmly closed. As the tape became looser during the many years Cézanne used the book, the artist tied a knot into the center of the loop. The book is of a kind readily obtainable from art supply shops to this day.

The paper is uniformly white, of a good quality "wove" and shows no watermarks.

There are fifty leaves, or one hundred pages in all, not counting the white inside surfaces of the covers. One of the former owners of the book numbered one side of each leaf with a Roman numeral (I-L). Since these numerals appear in the reproductions we have made use of them in describing the book's contents. The page on the reverse of the one with a numeral is described as its *back*, thus: p. XX and p. XX back.

The cover shows numerous oil paint spots and a large dark brown oil stain has penetrated the top edge of almost all the pages. It appears almost black in the reproductions. There are also some water color spots (p. XLI). These spots and stains indicate that the artist must have kept this and other note books close at hand while painting.

A particularly interesting aspect of our book is the fact that the artist's only child, his son Paul, was permitted to draw and write in it on many occasions. These efforts of the artist's son are often important clues in identifying or dating certain subjects, as will be shown later.

The subject matter may be loosely classified as follows:

Figure studies, not including those after sculpture
Drawings of the sculpture known as *L'Ecorché*
Portraits of Cézanne and his family
Landscapes
Objects

It might be helpful for the reader to keep in mind the above general classification which we have used in discussing and analyzing the book's contents. At the same time the question of dates will develop more logically.

FIGURE STUDIES

THE earliest work of Cézanne was largely devoted to compositions with figures. While there are a certain number of landscapes in the earlier years they became of much more importance to him as he progressed. Following the traditional precepts of art training, his teachers at Aix encouraged him in rendering the human figure. His early work, therefore, is after the living model or plaster casts. When he decided to give up his studies of law at the University of Aix in 1861 he moved to Paris in the same year, having briefly gone to the capital for the first time in 1858. Cézanne visited the Luxembourg and the Louvre frequently, studying such great masters of figure composition as Rubens, Poussin and Delacroix, whom he admired particularly. Awkward in the extreme, as many of his early figure studies are, the influence of Poussin in particular, may be noticed (pp. XXXIII, XXXIV and XXXV). Cézanne shows a peculiar emotionalism strongly tinged with eroticism and violence in this early phase. It is of considerable interest in tracing the artist's development that our sketch book contains three figure studies for the man in the painting known as "The Strangler" or "Rape" (V. 123*, about 1870) on pp. XIII back, XXXIII and XXXVIII. Even earlier than these studies must be the one on p. XLII back, the figure of a seated man who appears in an early painting and a drawing (V. 118 and 1198, between 1869 and 1870). This sketch and the others on the same page appear to be the earliest drawings in our book. They are hesitating, conventional and do not indicate any of the mastery achieved by Cézanne in his landscapes and portraits.

Compare the drawings for "The Strangler" with the figure composition "Fauns Attacking a Woman" (p. XLVI back) which is strongly reminiscent of Rubens. In every figure of the latter composition the plastic qualities have been thoroughly studied, the lines consolidated into a well coördinated form. The earlier drawings lack these qualities (cf. also p. XXXIII). The studies for "The Strangler" and the composition on p. XXXIII are a confusing web of agitated lines which delineate the figure but hardly attempt to render anatomy. They give no feeling of a third dimension. A further step is achieved in the composition "Two Women" (p. XXX back) where a tranquility rarely shown by Cézanne in previous drawings, seems to predominate. A tentative date assigned by Venturi for a similar composition is 1872 to 1877, whereas "The Strangler" is about 1870. In the drawing "Two Women" elements of a landscape have been introduced as an integral part of the composition.

*Reference is made to the numbers and dates assigned to Cézanne's works in Lionello Venturi: Cézanne, Son Art—Son Oeuvre. Paris, Paul Rosenberg, 1936, two volumes.

An important series of drawings occurs in the sketch book which are studies of bathers. They are invariably drawings of a single male figure and no attempt was made to use several figures as a composition. Our studies are mainly of one bather with his right arm raised. Some of these drawings, particularly the one on p. XXIII, show a preoccupation with the sculptural qualities of the figure. On p. XXVIII a landscape is indicated in the background. All of these studies are closely linked with oil sketches (V. 259, 262 and 271, the latter between 1875 and 1877). Stylistically they conform to the period of the "Two Women" (p. XXX back) discussed above.

On p. IV we find a careful and masterly study after a figure in a painting by Delacroix which caught Cézanne's attention in the Louvre. Though following Delacroix' concept very closely, Cézanne has translated the brushwork and color of the painting into a terse formula of pencil lines. There is a minimum of elaboration, light and shade follow with a precision which he had hardly ever before achieved.

L'ECORCHE

CÉZANNE owned a number of small plaster casts of sculpture which he used again and again in his drawings as a convenient means of study of the human figure. Though much weight is given to the plastic values in these studies, they all show Cézanne concerned with the play of light and shade over a three dimensional surface. Our book contains nine studies after one such cast known as *L'Ecorché* (Flayed Man). This cast was made after a wax model which was kept in the Berlin Museum. The model was formerly attributed to Michelangelo but is now generally believed to be a copy of a figure which may have been a bronze. It is also doubtful that the lost original was a work of Michelangelo. Dürer knew it and incorporated it in an etching. Cézanne made use of the cast in his studies of human anatomy but he was also constantly absorbed by the effects of sharp lighting and resulting deep shadows on the surface of the sculpture. The angle of his vision was changed in every drawing, sometimes only slightly, sometimes drastically. The figure was rotated and studied from all sides and at times appears to be seen more from above. The artist accentuated the distortions of the cast's familiar appearance caused by changing the figure's position and lighting. In these studies Cézanne shows growing confidence in his draughtsmanship. The drawing on p. XI still seems hesitant, the possibilities of the sculpture hardly explored. The series seems to culminate in the study on p. XXIII back. Without hesitation Cézanne applies patches of shading, accentuating here, giving full play of light through the white paper there, but all according to a precisely mapped out plan. He renders and interprets the *exact topography* of the figure. A system of lines has been found which will easily be detected in the mature landscapes.

The dates of these studies and their consequent relationship to other studies in our book are not easily established. The drawings of *L'Ecorché* certainly reveal increasing maturity within the series. If they were made at very short intervals it might seem logical to expect them in close sequence in the book. However, they are scattered between pp. XI and XXXVII back. We might conclude that there was an interval of some length between each sketch. This seems further substantiated by the gradual development of the drawings' style. It might be safe to guess that these studies follow those of the bathers but are previous to the landscapes of L'Estaque (which may all be dated between 1882 and 1885). Thus they may be between 1877, the last date given for the bathers and 1882, the earliest date given for the studies of L'Estaque.

PORTRAITS

IN presenting the contents of the sketch book in some sort of chronological sequence we come to another group of studies, the portraits. The most important and interesting of these are the five self portraits which occur on pp. VII back, XXI, XXII, XXXVII and XXXIX. The earliest of these is undoubtedly the one on p. XXII. The sequence of the others might be thus: pp. XXI, VII back, XXXVII and XXXIX.

Cézanne was a man who seems to have aged rather early in life. At the age of thirty-five or six he was quite bald and a heavy beard made him look older than his years. The constant wearing, nagging worry on his conscience whether or not his talent could measure up to the high standard he had set for himself, the disappointments, public rejections of his work, the scorn he met with, all weighed heavily on his sensitive nature. No human being can face such adversity without its leaving a telling mark on his appearance. His painful shyness must have proven a tremendous handicap in asserting himself in his work. Periods of the most profound depression and despair came all too often. How old was Cézanne when he did the self portrait on p. XXII? A photograph dated approximately 1875 is a good clue. Some painted self portraits of this period are equally important (V. 286, 288 and 290). They are dated between 1875 and 1877. These dates would be substantiated by the style of the drawing, which is still somewhat hesitant and tentative, as for instance the later versions of the bathers in our book. Cézanne appears sombre, critical, uncommunicative.

If the theoretical sequence of the self portraits is correct the next one would be the drawing on p. XXI. Appearing slightly older than in the previous drawing, the general mood of this portrait is about the same, though perhaps a little more pronounced. The expression of discouragement is poignant and Cézanne seems more careworn. The style of the drawing is more assured, it approaches the clear simplicity of the landscape drawings. The date of this study would be nearer to 1880, we suppose.

In the third drawing of our series (p. VII back) the artist appears more relaxed, introspective as always but less tense. The mood is freer and not as depressed. But again he seems slightly older. The treatment of the drawing is loose, very clear, almost tender. As in the drawing discussed before, only the head is shown. The succinct quality of the shading is reminiscent of the earlier versions of L'Estaque and appears to have developed beyond the heavier treatment of *L'Ecorché*. It seems logical to date this drawing between 1880 and 1882.

All of the happenings and struggles which made life so hard for Cézanne seem to be concentrated in the most profound of the self portraits in this book (p. XXXVII). A permanent veil of despondency seems to have descended over the artist's features. His eyes, though penetrating and analytical, carry an expression of bleak hopelessness. The mouth is compressed in a bitter line, the head seems bowed between his shoulders. It is an oppressive, relentless self-appraisal Cézanne has given us. A self-appraisal which despite his negative attitude he so gloriously repudiates through the great paintings, water colors and drawings. Was Cézanne under some new and painful strain when he made this drawing? Possibly. An event which was shattering to Cézanne was the final breaking up of his friendship with Zola in 1886. In this year the artist also lost his father. It is possible that we see him in this new phase of increased loneliness. The highly developed technique of the drawing would be in favor of this late date.

On p. XXXIX we find a quick, powerful though incomplete sketch of the artist's head.

His features appear more emaciated, bonier, still older. The aquiline nose is more pronounced. In a photograph taken in 1889 Cézanne had a smaller, pointed beard whereas all earlier photographs and self portraits show him with a rounded beard. While this self portrait does not show the shape of his beard, the four drawings discussed before show the full rounded beard of his earlier years.

Of the various portrait heads of women, two are definitely of the artist's wife, born Hortense Fiquet (1850 — ?). They are on pp. XLIX back and L back. The first of the two drawings is inscribed "*a Madame Cézanne*", the second, "*Madame Cézanne*" by the artist's son. The inscriptions are in the cramped hand of a child who has just learned to write. Cézanne's son Paul was born in 1872. Assuming that this is the writing of a six to seven year old, the two portraits of Madame Cézanne were probably done between 1878 and 1879. The style of the drawings would certainly bear out this approximate date. It may be added that the inscriptions on the two portraits should also disprove the doubts voiced by some authors as to whether the woman shown in sketches and in a series of paintings was actually Madame Cézanne.

There are three sketches of the artist's father in our book (pp. XIX back, XXIX, XXXVIII back). The order in which they come in the book may be their approximate chronological sequence. The last one shows Cézanne's father asleep. This drawing is more mature in style than the previous ones, though it is difficult to assign a logical date to it. Louis-Auguste Cézanne was born in 1798 at Saint-Zacharie, a short distance northeast of Marseille. He died in 1886. The portraits probably preceded the father's death by a few years.

Of the artist's son Paul, who was born in 1872, there are no less than twenty-nine drawings. Only six of these occur prior to p. XXXIX back. The remaining twenty-three are between pp. XXXIX back and XLIX. They show a boy not younger than four and not older than eight, if indeed the range in age is that much. Perhaps the earliest portrait, judging from the appearance of the child, is on p. XXIV back, the latest is perhaps the one on p. XXI. The latter drawing, showing more pronounced features, occurs on the same page as a self portrait by Cézanne. The style of drawing is the same in both heads and they were probably made at the same time. If our tentative dating of the self portrait is correct (about 1880) then the boy was about eight. Cézanne's attachment to his only child is well known and the affectionate handling of the boy's features is a vivid testimony of the artist's feelings for him. Constantly observing him, Cézanne shows his face from many angles, at times asleep but usually looking at the spectator with a bright, open look. We gain the impression of an alert, wholesome boy. His father permitted him to make free use of his sketch book and it is full of childish attempts to produce drawings of his own. In this Cézanne obviously encouraged him. Once we find the boy copying a landscape of his father's which was on the opposite page (pp. IV back and V). Frequently the boy's drawings are indiscriminately drawn over those of his father. In obvious delight at recognizing himself in a portrait he has proudly inscribed his name (p. XLVIII back).

What became of Cézanne's son? Having inherited a magnificent collection of his father's paintings, water colors and drawings, his financial future was assured once Cézanne's work became universally recognized, which was not long after his death. The great artist's son never developed any talent of his own. The major part of his life was spent in Paris where for a while he held a clerical position in a bank. But such comparatively unremunerative work became unnecessary with the fabulous rise of the prices of Cézanne's work. He was described to us as a modest, quiet, unassuming man. In later years he was a little portly and his appearance is said to have been that of a typical French *bourgeois*. He died in 1948 at the age of seventy-six. He is supposed to have been survived by a son still living in Paris.

LANDSCAPES

ARTISTICALLY, the landscapes together with the self portraits, form perhaps the most memorable portion of our book. They are outnumbered by many other subjects but the mastery of Cézanne's draughtsmanship is at its height in these. We have seen Cézanne struggle with the art of drawing, have examined the early figure studies in all their awkwardness and have then seen him gradually triumph over his own hesitations and fears. The landscapes are concise and assertive. They are statements of fact, yet subtly interpreted in the artist's way of seeing. They seem to draw the very quintessence from the *motif*, beyond which there is nothing to add. Every line, every little patch of shading has been scientifically arranged so that the removal of one small element would throw the whole delicate structure out of balance. The stresses and strains of the landscape drawings are in perfect equilibrium, yet the whole is permeated with lyrical rhythm. Brilliant sunlight, the sunlight of the South of France, quivers through the solid structure, as air visibly rises on a hot day. And it is reflected with blinding brilliance from the flat surface of the side of a house. Cézanne has learned to show color through black and white. His whole characteristic color scale is suggested in these drawings. Each color, each nuance seems to be rendered by a corresponding quality of shading. There is the clarity of Ingres, but more, there is color.

Of the sixteen landscapes, seven can be identified as various views of L'Estaque, two of the house at Bellevue near Aix-en-Provence which belonged to Cézanne's brother-in-law, Maxime Conil. The remaining seven are various views of gardens or houses and trees. These could not be definitely linked with any of the paintings or water colors though it may be a fair guess that some were made in the garden of his father's estate, Le Jas de Bouffan.

Maxime Conil, who married the artist's younger sister Rose, bought the house at Bellevue about 1885. It had become one of Cézanne's favorite *motifs* by that time. There are numerous paintings and drawings of it which Venturi dates between 1882 and 1885. These would coincide with the dates of our two drawings (pp. X and XXXII back). One end of the house is shown bathed in glaring sunlight. At the left, sketched more loosely and lightly, is a group of trees. In the first of the two drawings the house dominates the composition. With the utmost restraint Cézanne establishes the various planes which in their interrelationship create the volume of the house. A square, a triangle, a cube, a pyramid, these are the basic elements which constitute the house. Cézanne *emphasizes* these elements and therewith seems to anticipate what came a generation or so later: Cubism. Throughout the later years of his life Cézanne seems to have been conscious of the necessity of referring to the essential and elementary forms and the necessity of their revaluation. This tendency becomes ever more apparent, particularly in his drawings. Picasso approached these problems about 1909.

The seven studies of L'Estaque are some of the few sketches known to exist of this famous *motif*. Cézanne went there in 1870 to 1871 and then again at various intervals between 1882 and 1885. Our drawings are undoubtedly of the later period.

L'Estaque is a village at the northernmost point of the bay west of Marseille. From this vantage point we obtain a view of the coastline in the center of which lies Marseille itself. Opposite Marseille lies a group of islands and the view ends with the slopes of the Marseilleveyre massif south of Marseille. It was a perfect *motif* for Cézanne and he made the fullest use of it. The surroundings of L'Estaque are rugged and the intervening gullies and rocky slopes lent themselves as an introductory foreground to the placid bay and the horizontal line of hills beyond (pp. X back and XVII back).

All of the views of L'Estaque occur within a few pages of each other (pp. V back and XVII back), which might indicate the close sequence of the series. Stylistically they are all very closely related. On pp. XIII back and XIV Cézanne has given us a sweeping view of this *motif*, across both pages of the sketchbook. In the lower right corner appears, incongruously, the much earlier study for "The Strangler" which has been discussed previously, but here it may serve again to demonstrate Cézanne's extraordinary development as a draughtsman.

One of the great drawings of this book is a view of houses at the viaduct in L'Estaque (p. V back). It reminds us of the two drawings of Bellevue. We find again the almost mathematical precision, the mastery of elimination, the accents of small patches of shading dispersed in a staccato rhythm. A factory chimney drawn in with emphasis at the right not only establishes a new, more distant plane but also an important vertical, repeated in a milder form through the center of the buildings. One vertical plane succeeds the other and since these are parallel to the page's surface the spectator is drawn into the composition with irresistible force.

The trees are barely indicated, particularly at the right, and yet we are made fully aware of their round structure as against the cubes of the houses.

Scattered throughout the book are six other landscapes. Some of these seem to be a few years earlier than the drawings of L'Estaque (pp. V, VII, XXV). The others, views of gardens, groups of trees, probably come later but hardly after 1885.

OBJECTS

CÉZANNE, though eliminating details in his landscapes was always aware of the most insignificant objects around him. Thus, with equal intensity of observation he studied the shape of the base of a lamp or a sugar bowl (p. XXVII back), a glass carafe (p. XXVII) or a pitcher (p. XXIII). Each object presented its own structural problem and was therefore found worthy of his careful attention. With these studies he memorized their essential forms and when they became part of some painting or water color their appearance and presentation is authoritative because they have been fully understood.

AN interesting sidelight is shed on Cézanne's complex character by the draft of a letter which we find on the inside of the front cover, on p. I and p. I back. Although not completely decipherable, it shows the artist hard at work attempting to write a formal acknowledgment of a wedding announcement. One passage after another is mulled over, abandoned, deleted, only to be repeated with ever increasing stiffness and formality. His shyness becomes very apparent in this note.

In discussing the drawings in our sketch book we have attempted to give approximate dates wherever this seemed reasonably possible. It should be borne in mind, however, that Cézanne almost never dated his work. In the entire catalogue by Venturi where over sixteen hundred items are described and reproduced, only six (V. 22, 59, 101, 104, 138 and 139) are found to be actually dated. These are all fairly early works, that is from 1864 to 1873. Our sketch book is no exception for not a single date appears anywhere. We have had to rely, therefore, on biographical data, analysis of his drawing styles at various obvious periods and then attempting to fit into the general structure those drawings where the date was not too apparent. A general survey of the book's scope will establish its range between 1869 to 1870 (p. XLII back) and 1885 (L'Estaque) or the latest of the self portraits (pp. XXXVII and XXXIX) about 1886. The book, therefore, covers a period slightly over fifteen years of Cézanne's life, fifteen very important and critical years in his development.

Cézanne's fame rests largely today on his oils and water colors. His drawings are less known and too little attention has been paid to their importance in his entire work. Distortions and simplifications found chiefly in his oils are often, with superficial reasoning, attributed to a lack of draughtsmanship. On the contrary, Cézanne willfully deviated from the known form. He could do so in the interest of an intended result, because he was fully conscious of this form's composite elements. His incisive studies are the backbone of all of his paintings. The paintings are the fulfillment, his drawings the structure, his basic vision.

Carl O. Schniewind

For having kindly given me access to his preliminary notes on Cézanne's sketch books thanks are due John Rewald, New York. I am also indebted to Rachael Brenner, Hugh Edwards and Harold Joachim of the Department of Prints and Drawings of The Art Institute of Chicago for their help in preparing the manuscript.

Contents of the Sketchbook

NOTE: *All drawings are in pencil unless otherwise stated. Wherever other works by Cézanne are mentioned reference is made to the numbers and dates assigned to them in Lionello Venturi: Cézanne, Son Art—Son Oeuvre. Paris, Paul Rosenberg, 1936, two volumes.*

Inside of front cover (horizontal writing): Draft of a letter in which Cézanne acknowledges the receipt of a wedding announcement. The handwriting is often indistinct and there was much hesitation about the text. In the transcript below, words which could not be deciphered are indicated by a dotted line and the many passages which were crossed out by Cézanne are given in brackets. Asterisks indicate that at this point the lines of the draft extend onto the opposite page where they are partly obscured by a second draft of the same letter.

Mon (cher) Sauvan (?)

Vous nous avez fait l'honneur de nous—
*apprendre votre mariage avec Mlle la comtesse Gilette *de St. Joseph*
[nous ne saurions vous exprimer (?) *les sentiments] *C'est avec*
les plus vifs sentiments
*Nous avons [la] reçu la lettre *par laquelle*
*vous nous apprenez votre mariage avec Mlle la *comtesse Gilette de*
*St. Joseph; [c'est avec les sentiments plus vifs sentim *ents d'affection . . .*
*sentiments d'aff de la plus vive aff reconnaissance que *pour le . . . souvenir*
*C'est avec la plus gran] Nous ne saurions . . . *exprimer [la] notre reconnaissance*
*[et le pl] pour le plaisir et l'honneur que vous nous faites *. . . de nous avoir preservé a votre souvenir*
*aussi vous nous permettez de vous dire que nous *faisons les vœux les plus sincères*
*pour la prosperité et . . . bonheur de votre *union, et que nous[vous . . .]*
[union] *[Nous]*

Written vertically across the draft are a column of numerals in ink and a list of expenditures:

Mercredi	*matin*	*0.35—10*	Wednesday	morning	0.35—10
—	*soir*	*0.90*	—	evening	0.90
Vendredi	*soir*	*0.70*	Friday	evening	0.70
Samedi	*matin*	*rognon(?)payé*	Saturday	morning	kidneys(?) paid
Dimanche	*matin*	*.60—10*	Sunday	morning	.60—10
—	*soir*	*.60*	—	evening	.60
Lundi	*matin*	*.40*	Monday	morning	.40
	soir	*.35*		evening	.35
Mardi	*matin*	*0.60*	Tuesday	morning	0.60
	soir	*.40*		evening	.40

p. I: A small sketch of a vase and head and shoulders of a boy in uniform, the latter may be by the artist's son, reworked by Cézanne.

Horizontal writing: At left a continuation of the draft described before. Further to the right a second draft for the same letter:

[Nous som]
Nous ne saurions vous dire combien
nous sommes contents de . . . [vous av] de nous savoir
preservés a votre souvenir.
Vous nous permettez de vous
faire toutes nos félicitations pour votre
heureuse union et de vous presenter
. . . mariage de —
nos vœux les plus
vifs et les plus sincères
pour votre bonheur —

Vertical writing:

le sac (?)	the bag (?)
les tubes (?)	the tubes (?)
l'album	the album
le seau (?)	the pail (?)
Hotel du Gard	
. . . Nimes	

p. I: (back): Sketch of a seated old man with a beard. The writing seems to be a draft for the concluding sentence of the letter on the two preceding pages. Numerals also appear on this page.

Et bien que nous n'ayons pas l'honneur d'etre connus par Madame Sauvan (?) *vous voudrez bien etre auprês d'elle l'interprète des souhaits que nous faisons.*	And though we do not have the honor of being known to Madame Sauvan (?) will you please convey to her our best wishes.

p. II: Sketch of a glass tumbler and a head in profile, evidently the artist's son. The name "*Cézanne*" is written across the glass in a child's hand, apparently that of the artist's son. This inscription seems to have been made when the boy was just learning to write and was younger than when he did the inscriptions at the end of the sketch book (cf. pp. XLVIII back, XLIX back and L back). List of meals taken and their cost:

Janvier				January			
Mercredi	*matin*	*60^{c}*	*Boeuf plus rognons*	Wednesday	morning	60^{c}	Beef and kidneys
—	*soir*	*—50*	*cotelettes*		evening	—50	cutlets
Jeudi	*matin*	*.75*	*cotelettes*	Thursday	morning	.75	cutlets
	soir		*Six saucisses*		evening		six sausages
Vendredi	*matin*	*70*		Friday	morning	70	
	soir		*rien*		evening		nothing
Samedi	*matin*	*1^{fr}*	*Boeuf et rognon payés*	Saturday	morning	1^{fr}	Beef and kidney paid
Dimanche	*mat.*	*1*	*Boeuf et* (?) *Tranche*	Sunday	morning	1	Beef and (?) slice
	soir	*35^{c}*	*Boeuf*		evening	35^{c}	Beef
Lundi	—		—	Monday	—		—
Dimanche	*matin*	*1^{fr}*		Sunday	morning	1^{fr}	
Lundi	*matin*	*70^{c}*	*cotelette*	Monday	morning	70^{c}	cutlet

p. II: (back): Drawings by the artist's son.

p. III: Study of trees in a garden. At top a drawing of a sailboat by the son.

p. III: (back): Blank.

p. IV: Figure of a river god taken from Delacroix' ceiling in the Gallery of Apollo, The Louvre, Paris. The subject of the ceiling, painted in 1849-50, shows Apollo vanquishing the serpent Python. This drawing may have been made between 1874 and 1877, during which years Cézanne went to Paris several times. The figure was used in one version of "The Bathers" (V.275, between 1875 and 1877).

p. IV: (back): Copy by the artist's son of a drawing on the opposite page (p. V).

p. V: A country house surrounded by trees. A drawing in a rather broad manner, similar in style to the one after Delacroix (p. IV).

p. V: (back): View of houses at the viaduct in L'Estaque. A study for a painting (V. 402, between 1882 and 1885).

p. VI: Study for a composition, a servant carrying a platter to a reclining nude figure. This may be related to two paintings, both entitled "Afternoon at Naples" (V. 223 and 224, between 1872 and 1875) and to a water color (V. 822, between 1870 and 1872). In the center the head of a cat.

p. VI: (back): Head of a woman in profile.

p. VII: Group of trees, a rapid sketch.

p. VII: (back): Self portrait of the artist. There are four other self portraits in this sketch book on pp. XXI, XXII, XXXVII and XXXIX.

p. VIII: Head of a youth with eyes closed, possibly a sketch of Louis Guillaume, the son of a neighbor of Cézanne. There is a painting of this boy (V. 374, between 1879 and 1882).

p. VIII: (back): Drawing by the artist's son of a sailboat.

p. IX: Head of a man and drawing of a railroad train, the latter by the artist's son.

p. IX: (back): Three studies of bathers. They may be preliminary drawings for oil sketches (V. 259, 262 and 271, between 1875 and 1877). There are other studies for bathers in this sketch book on pp. XVII, XVIII back, XXII back, XXIII, XXVI and XXVIII.

p. X: The house at Bellevue near Aix-en-Provence. Cézanne's brother-in-law, Maxime Conil, lived here. This drawing, similar in style to the one on p. V back, is a study for the paintings of the same subject (V. 412, 651 and 652, the first of this series between 1882 and 1885).

p. X: (back): View of the Mediterranean coast near L'Estaque. Evidently a study for the right half of a painting (V. 404, between 1882 and 1885).

p. XI: Study of a sculpture known as *L'Ecorché* (Flayed Man) which was formerly attributed to Michelangelo. Cézanne owned a cast of this small sculpture which is about ten inches in height. He made numerous drawings of it, nine of which are in this sketch book (cf. also pp. XIX, XX, XXIII back, XXVIII back, XXXIII back, XXXIV back, XXXVI, and XXXVII back). There is also a painting after the same sculpture (V. 709, about 1895). Dates given for similar sketches are between 1888 and 1895. The general impression of the *Ecorché* sketches in the book is that they may have been made somewhat earlier than the dates assigned by Venturi.

p. XI: (back): Study of a horse's head with ornamental harness and head of a child or *putto*. This seems to be the head of another small cast Cézanne owned which was by the French sculptor, Puget. Cézanne did a series of sketches of this figure (V. 1457-1465, between 1888 and 1895). The style of this particular drawing, however, appears to be earlier and is probably simultaneous with the horse's head on the same page.

p. XII: Part of a landscape study. The page is torn in half, the left half is missing.

p. XII: (back): Study of a child's head, the upper part missing.

p. XIII: Portrait of the artist's son. He appears to be about six years old, which would give us an approximate date of 1878. Beneath the head are scribbles by the artist's son.

p. XIII: (back): At the top of the page is the right half of a large view of L'Estaque which is a continuation of the drawing on p. XIV. This drawing corresponds closely with a painting (V. 407, between 1882 and 1885). The figure is of a much earlier period. It is a study for the man in the composition known as "The Strangler," of about 1870 (V. 123). Thus it antedates the drawing of L'Estaque by more than ten years.

p. XIV: Left half of a landscape drawing of L'Estaque (cf. comments to the preceding page).

p. XIV: (back): Study of L'Estaque closely related to a painting (V. 408, between 1882 and 1885). In style it is comparable to the preceding drawing.

p. XV: A house surrounded by trees, drawn by the artist's son.

p. XV: (back): View of L'Estaque (cf. V. 407 and 408).

p. XVI: Head of a man in profile. Two figures by the artist's son.

p. XVI: (back): To the left a head of the artist's son and to the right a landscape of L'Estaque, similar to p. XIV back. In the center is a face which might be the artist's son, drawn with the guidance of his father.

p. XVII: Study of a bather (cf. note to p. IX back). Also two studies of a cat (cf. V. 1428, studies in a sketch book now in the museum of Basle, Switzerland).

p. XVII: (back): Rocky coastline at L'Estaque. Both this drawing and the one on p. X back are related to the painting V. 404.

p. XVIII: Study of a tree's foliage. Part of a house near right center. *This drawing should be viewed vertically with stitching of sketch book at bottom.*

p. XVIII: (back): Study of a bather (cf. note to p. IX back). To the left a figure of a bather drawn on a smaller scale.

p. XIX: Study of *L'Ecorché* (cf. note to p. XI) with the shadows accentuated.

p. XIX: (back): Portraits of the artist's father and of his son.

p. XX: Study of *L'Ecorché* (cf. note to p. XI) with very pronounced modeling.

p. XX: (back): Trees within a garden wall. Certainly one of the later drawings in the sketch book.

p. XXI: Self portrait of the artist and portrait of the artist's son. The boy is apparently a little older than in the portrait on p. XIII.

p. XXI: (back): Study of a hanging coat. *This drawing should be viewed vertically with stitching of sketch book at the bottom.*

p. XXII: Self portrait of the artist. Probably the earliest of the self portraits in the sketch book.

p. XXII: (back): Study of a bather similar to the one on p. IX back. Also studies of a hand and a shoe.

p. XXIII: Study of a bather, probably somewhat later than the other studies of bathers in the book (cf. note to p. IX back). To the left a pitcher and to the right a conical shaped object (a candle-snuffer).

p. XXIII: (back): Study of *L'Ecorché* (cf. note to p. XI). The front of the figure is deeply shaded.

p. XXIV: Study of a man in a broad brimmed hat sitting in an easy chair and reading a newspaper.

p. XXIV: (back): Slight sketch of a door or gate and head of the artist's son who appears to be about four years old (ca. 1876).

p. XXV: View of a garden with trees.

p. XXV: (back): Trunk and foliage of a large tree across which is drawn a study for a bather in a similar pose as the one on p. IX back.

p. XXVI: Study of a bather (cf. note to p. IX back) and a sugar bowl.

p. XXVI: (back): Three studies: at the left two objects which appear to be bellows; in the center a short wide-necked bottle or shaker, probably a table utensil; to the right an incomplete light sketch of a woman in profile.

p. XXVII: A carafe and a pitcher.

p. XXVII: (back): From left to right: an object which appears to be the base of a lamp, a sugar bowl and head of a woman in profile.

p. XXVIII: Study of a bather with arm raised above his head. Evidently a drawing for a painting (V. 261, between 1875 and 1877). A rough sketch of an object which appears to be a candlestick and two rapid studies of nudes.

p. XXVIII: (back): Study of *L'Ecorché* (cf. note to p. XI) seen from the back.

p. XXIX: Portrait of the artist's father.

p. XXIX: (back): Drawing of a boy or young man who is surrounded by rats. The drawing is strongly reminiscent of Daumier and Delacroix but no direct connection with any works by either of these two artists has been found.

p. XXX: Straight-backed chair with rush seat.

p. XXX: (back): Two women, the one to the left with a broad-brimmed straw hat. This composition is closely linked with another drawing (V. 1233, between 1872 and 1877) which shows approximately the same setting. There the two women are sitting in a flat bottom boat close to the shore.

p. XXXI: Study of cloth folds.

p. XXXI: (back): Landscape with large trees in foreground. In the background appears to be a river with a steep embankment topped by houses.

p. XXXII: Study of flowers and foliage.

p. XXXII: (back): The house at Bellevue (cf. note to p. X).

p. XXXIII: Composition with five figures. The style of the drawing indicates that it is early and the figure in the lower left corner appears to be another study for the painting entitled "The Strangler" (cf. notes to pp. XIII back and XXXVIII).

p. XXXIII: (back): Study of *L'Ecorché* (cf. note to p. XI) seen slightly from the left.

p. XXXIV: Studies of three figures which are apparently linked with the composition on p. XXXIII. They also are early in style. In the center is a study of cloth folds which is certainly later than the figures appearing on this page.

p. XXXIV: (back): Study of *L'Ecorché* (cf. note to p. XI) almost completely in outline.

p. XXXV: Large unfinished study of a woman's profile and smaller sketch of a figure resembling in style and gesture the drawings on pp. XXXIII and XXXIV.

p. XXXV: (back): Two studies of heads, probably the same head in different positions.

p. XXXVI: Study of *L'Ecorché* (cf. note to p. XI) seen from the right and back.

p. XXXVI: (back): Two studies of heads. The lower one is perhaps the same as the head on the right of p. XXXV back, and might be Madame Cézanne.

p. XXXVII: Self portrait of the artist.

p. XXXVII: (back): Study of *L'Ecorché* (cf. note to p. XI) seen from the right and back with plastic values accentuated.

p. XXXVIII: Studies of two figures. Both are evidently early drawings, approximately 1870 to 1872. The figure in the lower right is another study for "The Strangler" (V. 123), a painting which has already been discussed in connection with the drawings on pp. XIII back and XXXIII.

p. XXXVIII: (back): At the top of the sheet is a study of the artist's father asleep. Below, the head of a woman in profile.

p. XXXIX: Self portrait of the artist, incomplete study. To the right the head of a woman in profile, also incomplete.

p. XXXIX: (back): Two portrait studies of the artist's son at about the age of five or six (ca. 1877 to 1878).

p. XL: Head of the artist's son in profile and a drawing by the artist's son.

p. XL: (back): Incomplete studies of the artist's son and a woman's head.

p. XLI: Head of the artist's son. Splashes of water color in blue and green towards inside of the page.

p. XLI: (back): Portrait of the artist's son aged six or seven (1878 to 1879).

p. XLII: Practice in writing figures by the artist's son.

p. XLII: (back): A series of early drawings. To the left the head of a bearded man in broad-brimmed hat. This drawing is in pen and ink. At top right the head and bust of a young man seemingly in uniform, also in pen and ink. At right center the head of a man in profile. Center, a seated man seen from the back. The latter figure occurs in a painting and a drawing *Lecture chez Zola* (V. 118 and 1198,

1869-1870). Thus the drawing would probably be one of the earliest in the sketch book.

p. XLIII: Two studies of the head of the artist's son.

p. XLIII: (back): Two studies of the head of the artist's son.

p. XLIV: Head of the artist's son, drawing in pen and ink, and the head and bust of a woman.

p. XLIV: (back): Two studies of the artist's son wearing a cap.

p. XLV: The artist's son and below it a rapid sketch of a head wearing a cap.

p. XLV: (back): A woman seated on a straight-backed chair seen from the back (compare coiffure with that in the portrait of the artist's wife on p. XLIX back).

p. XLVI: Head of the artist's son.

p. XLVI: (back): A group of fauns or satyrs attacking a woman. This drawing is a combination of pencil and pen and ink. It is reminiscent of such bacchanalian scenes as the water color drawing V. 897, between 1875 and 1876.

p. XLVII: The artist's son asleep. The boy is evidently dressed in a similar blouse or jacket as shown on p. XLI back.

p. XLVII: (back): Head of the artist's son asleep and partial study of a cap or hat.

p. XLVIII: At the top, head of the artist's son. Below, head of the son asleep, similar to the drawing on p. XLVII.

p. XLVIII: (back): Two studies of the head of the artist's son who has written his name, "*Paul*", next to his portrait at the top. Since the boy was able to write he must have been about six or seven years old (ca. 1878 to 1879).

p. XLIX: Two studies of the head of the artist's son.

p. XLIX: (back): Portrait of Madame Cézanne leaning her head on her hand. This portrait is inscribed "*a Madame Cézanne*" in the childish hand of the artist's son.

p. L: Practice in printing letters of the alphabet by the artist's son.

p. L: (back): Portrait of the artist's wife also inscribed "*Madame Cézanne*" by the artist's son. Full figure of a boy or a young man with his hands in his pockets and very light sketch of the head of the artist's wife.

Inside of back cover: The entire sheet is taken up by a diagram which looks as though it might be a plan of properties. At the top is the inscription "*Nord*" (North). Calculations based on 100,000 and five times 100,000, possibly pertaining to the value or dimensions of parts of the diagram. Across the diagram is the following list in Cézanne's hand, written in pen and ink.

Pot de fleur 0.32 c	Flower pot 32 centimes
boite de fer blanc . . .	tin container—(last word illegible)
tricot pour Rose	sweater or knitted jacket for Rose (the artist's younger sister)
boite de fer blanc poivre	container or can of (or for) pepper
toile grise . . .	grey cloth or canvas—(last word illegible)
bottines femme (?)	woman's shoes (?)
Charbon pour chauferette	Coal for small stove
pincette	tweezers

A Cézanne Sketchbook

Mon [illegible]

Vous nous avez fait l'honneur de nous apprendre votre mariage avec Melle la comtesse [illegible]

~~[illegible]~~

les plus vifs sentiments.

Monsieur, [illegible]

[illegible] votre mariage [illegible]

[illegible]

~~[illegible]~~ reconnaissance

Nous [illegible]

et [illegible] pour le plaisir et l'honneur que vous nous avez fait

nous permettre de vous dire que nous

pour le ~~[illegible]~~ bonheur de votre

18
14
12
18
7
12
90

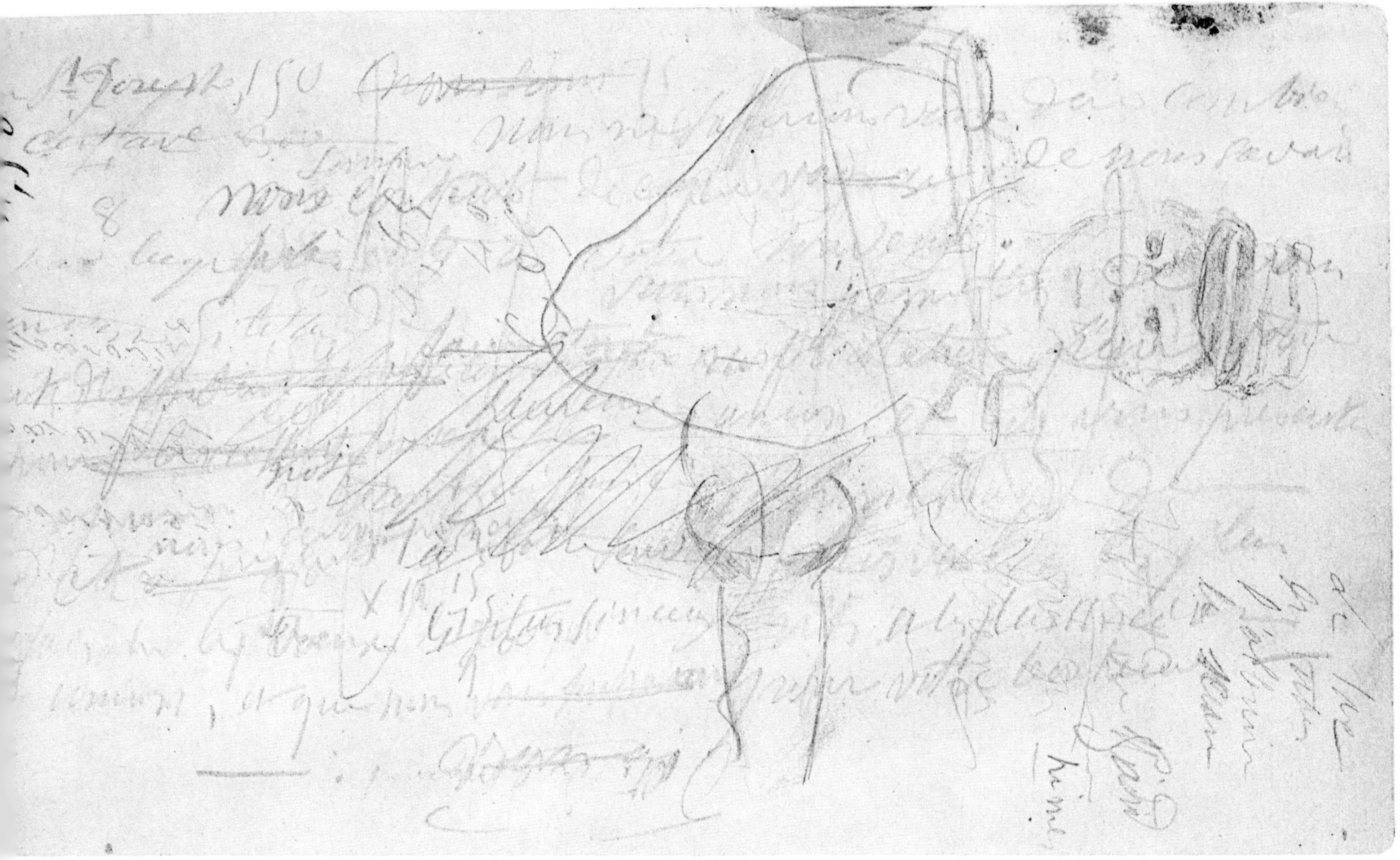

Mr [illegible], 150 [illegible] 15

[illegible] [illegible] de [illegible]

[illegible]

&

[illegible] de nous [illegible]

[illegible]

X 15 15

[illegible]

[illegible]

Et venger mon visage par l'honneur d'être connu par
madame Suivant qui voudrait bien être auprès d'elle
l'interprète des portraits que nous faisons

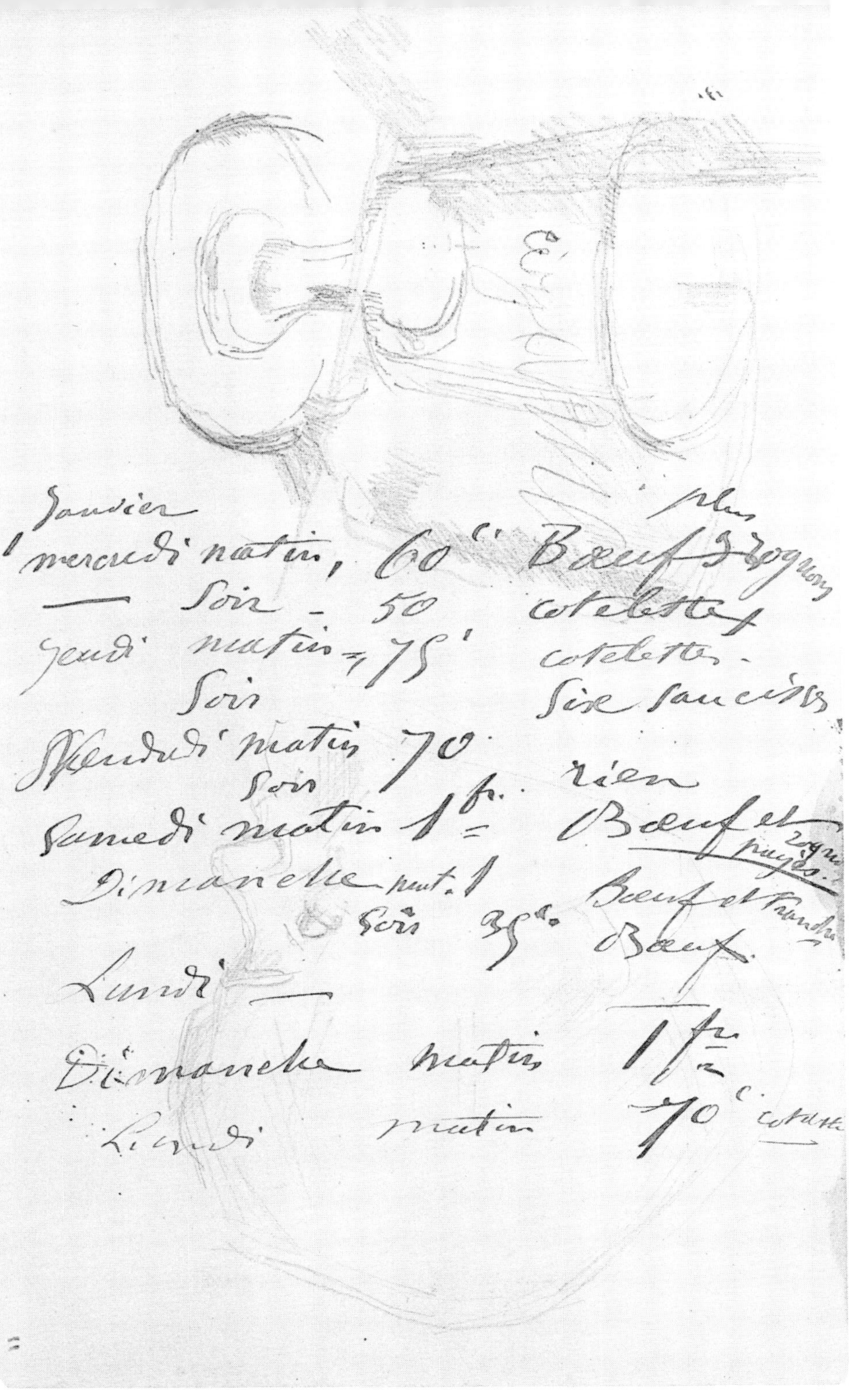

Janvier

1 mercredi matin, 60 c. plus Bœuf d'rognons

— Soir — 50 cotelettes

Jeudi matin — 75 c. cotelettes.

Soir six saucisses

Vendredi matin 70 c.

Soir rien

Samedi matin 1 f. Bœuf et rognons payés.

Dimanche mat. 1

Soir 35 c. Bœuf et viande

Bœuf.

Lundi

Dimanche matin 1 fr.

Lundi matin 70 c. cotelette

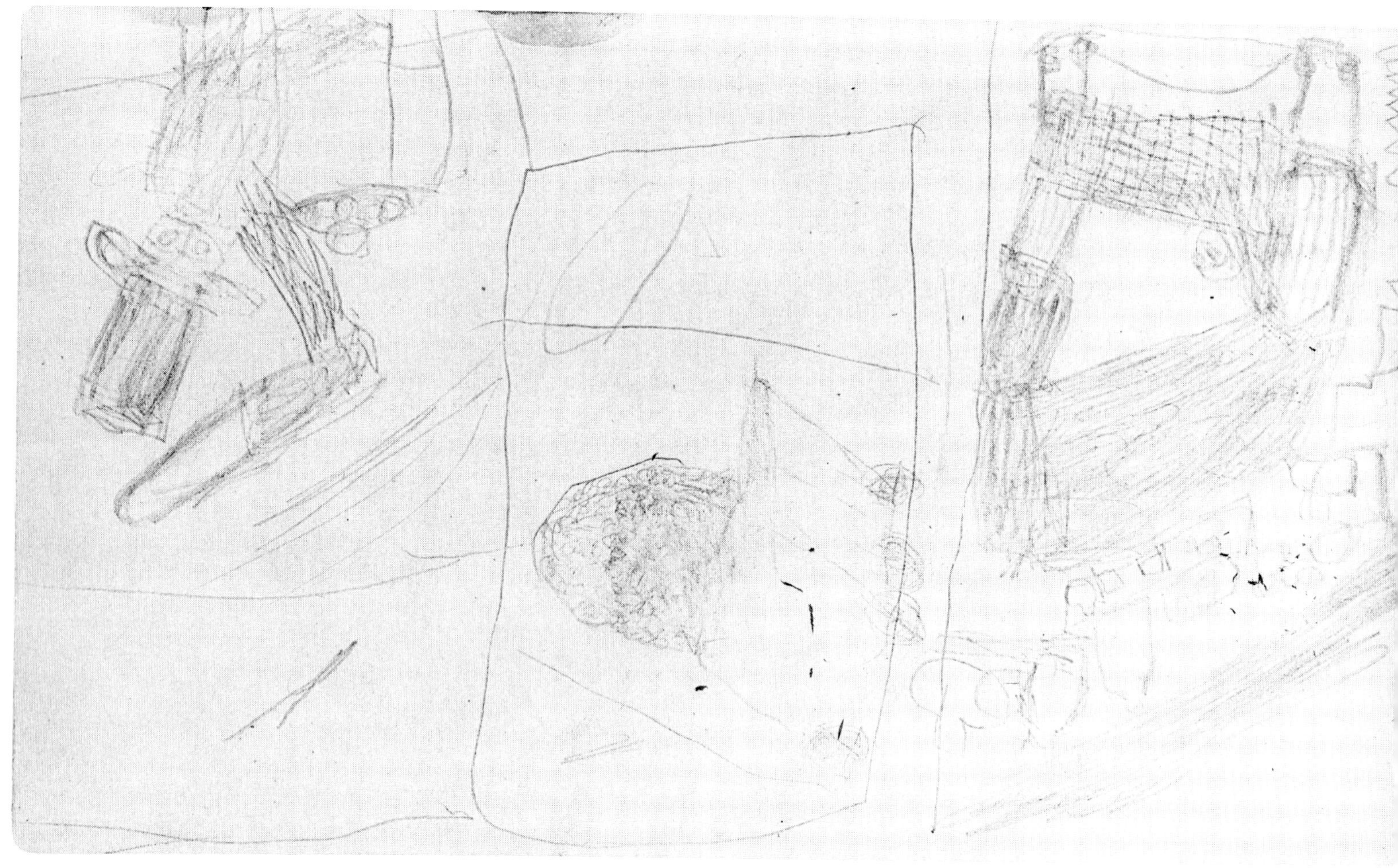

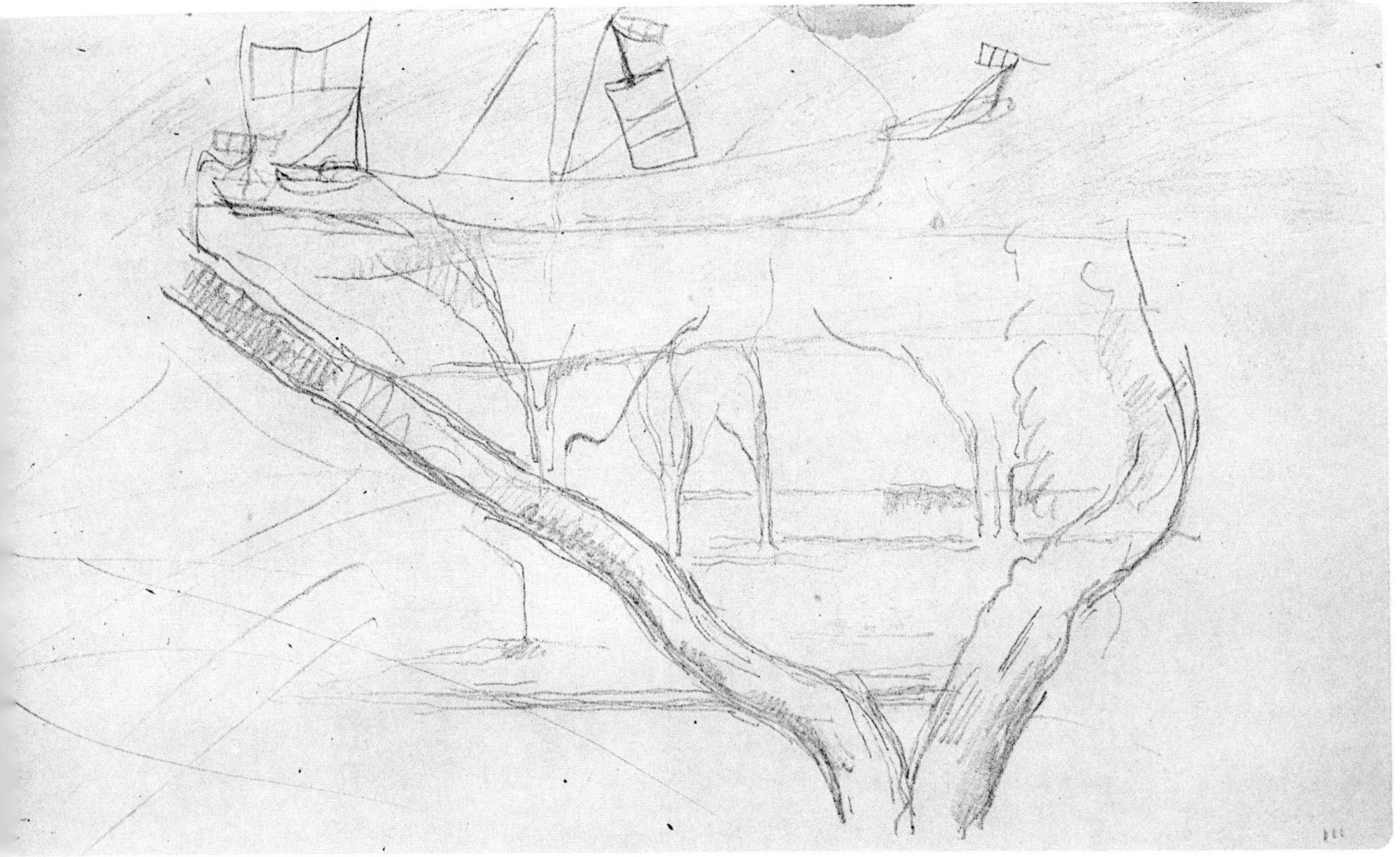

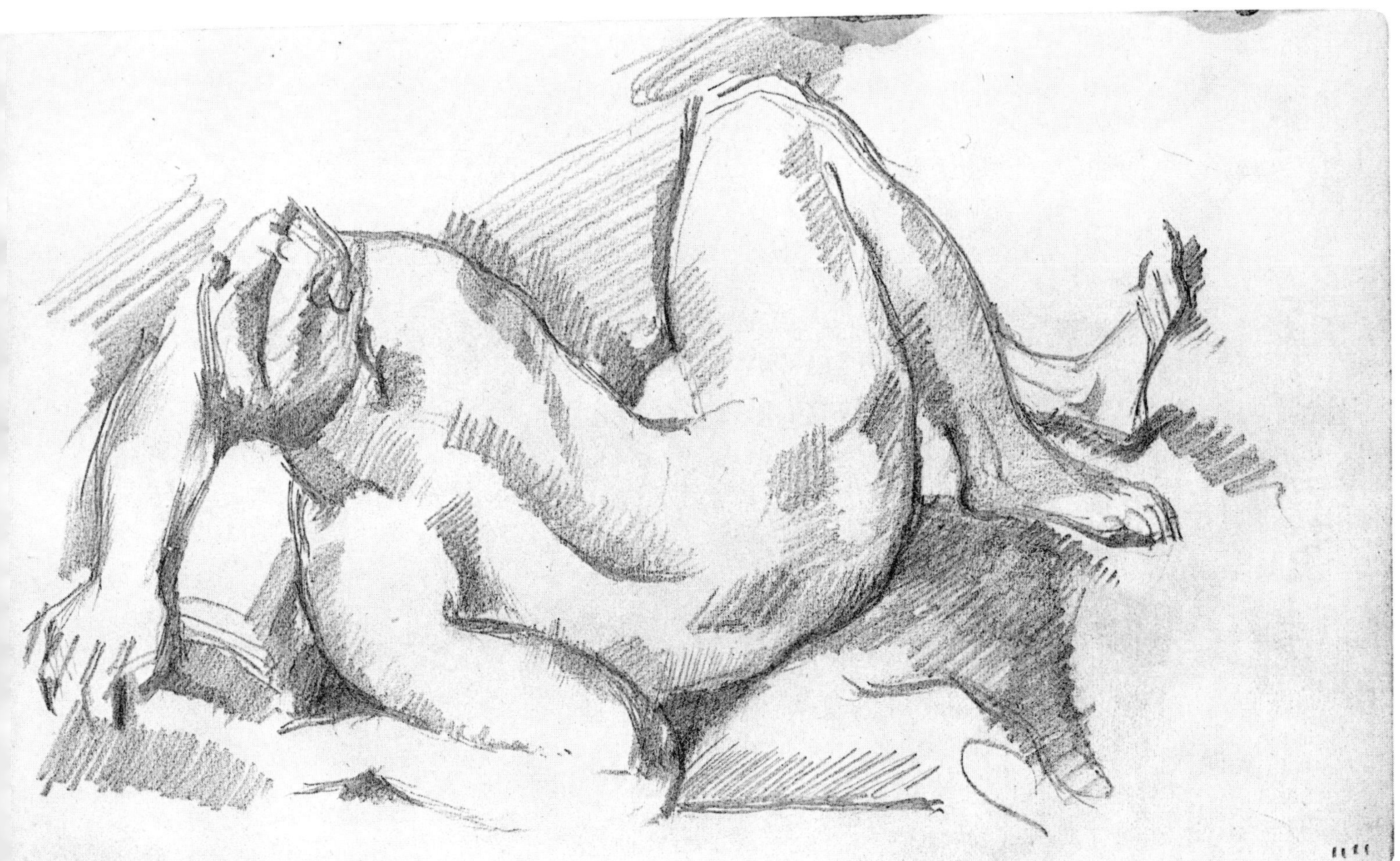

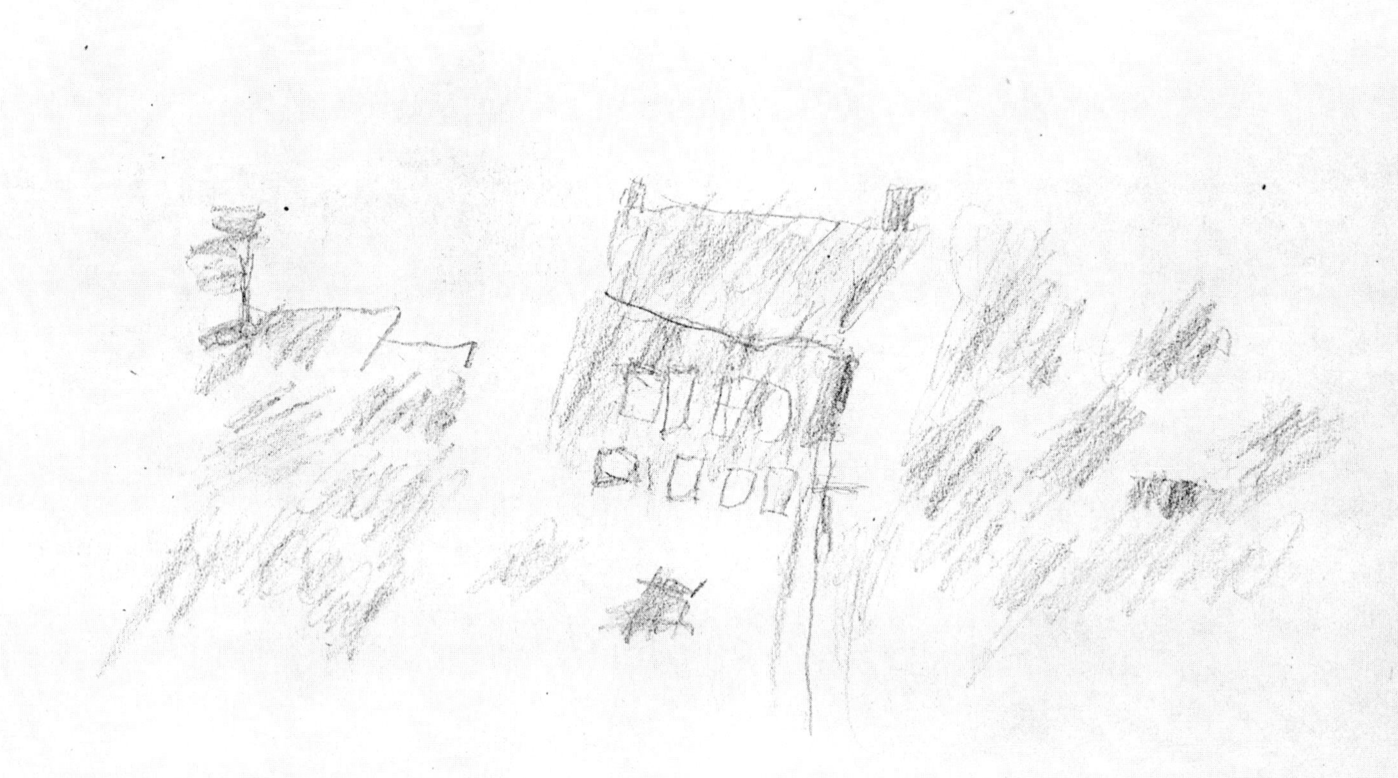

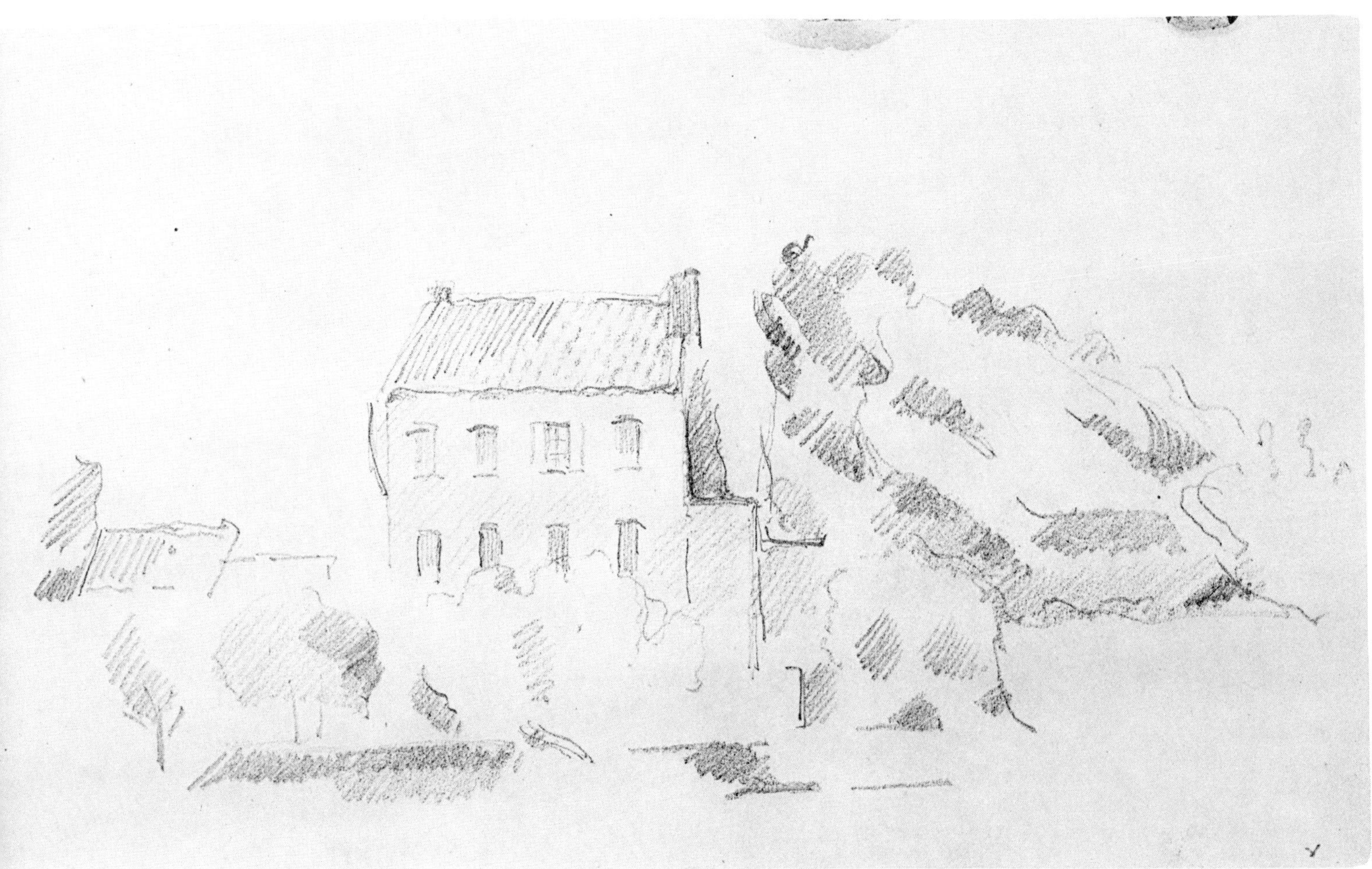

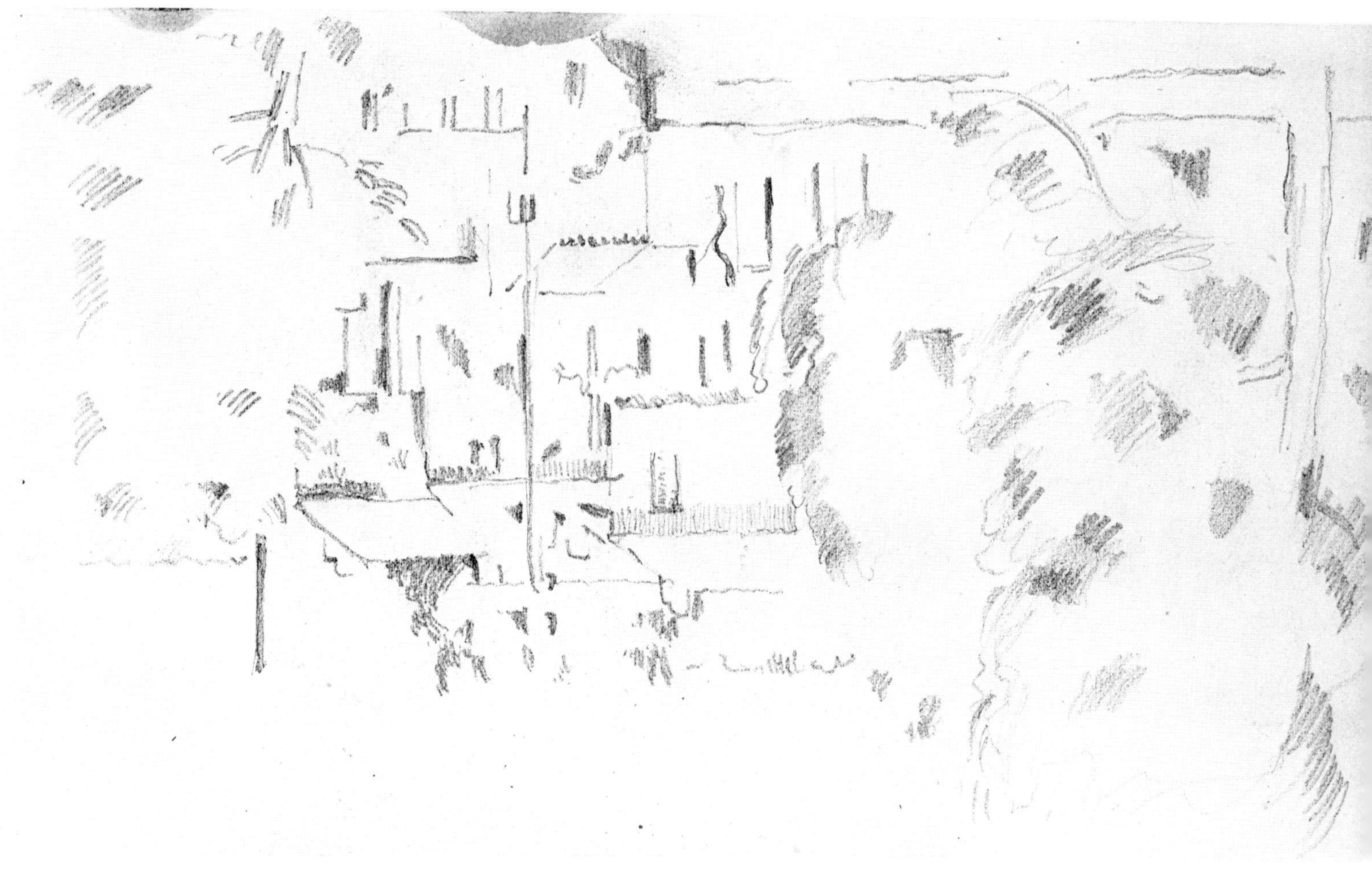

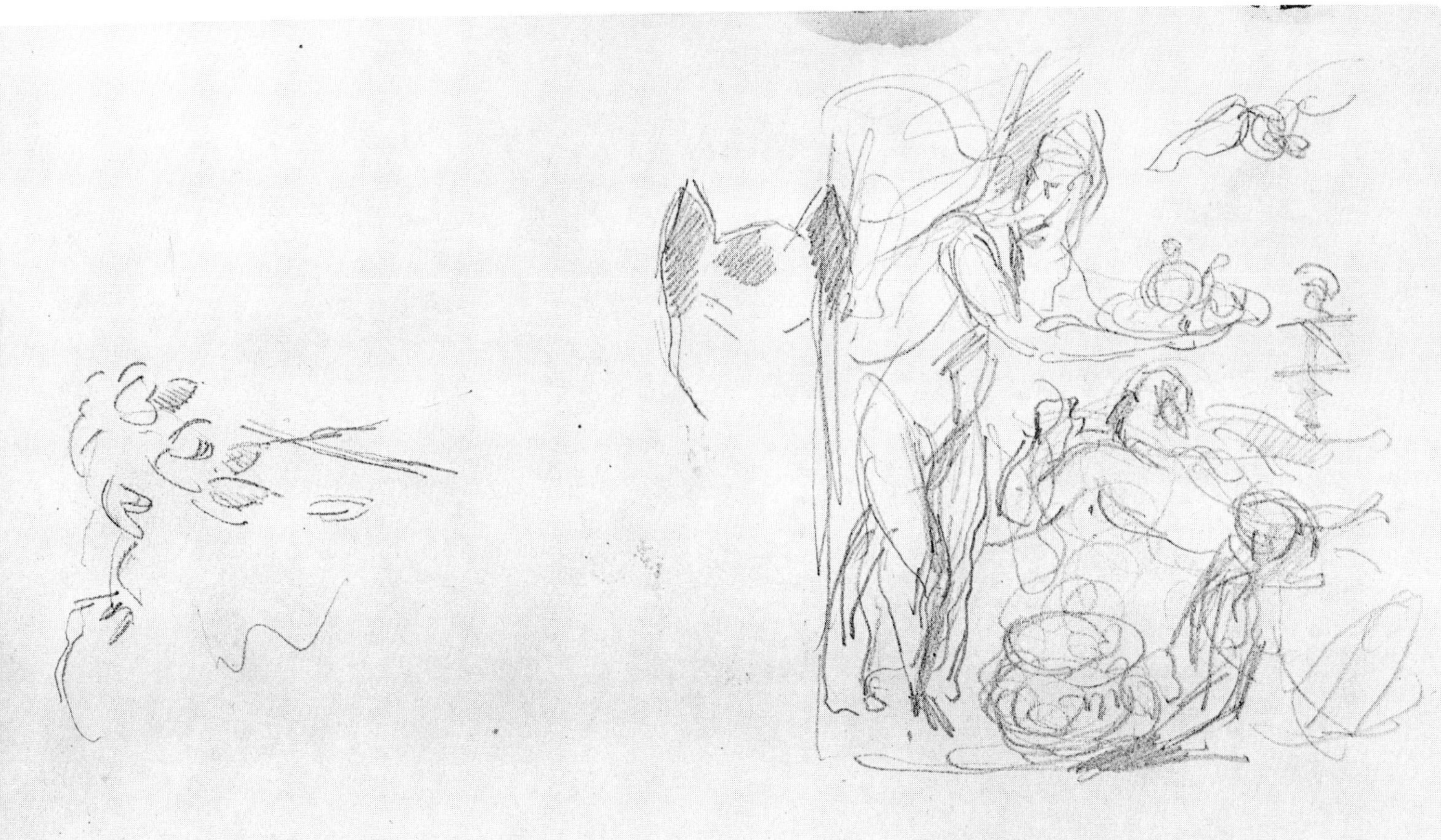

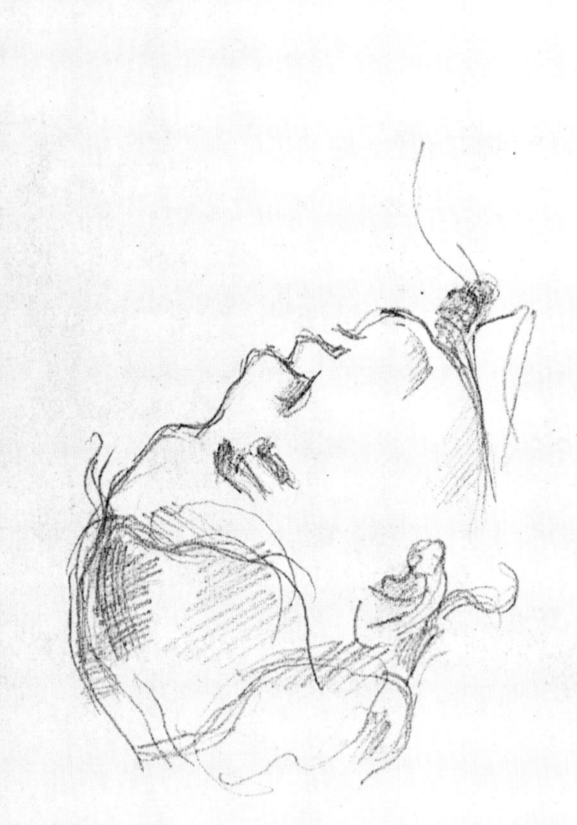

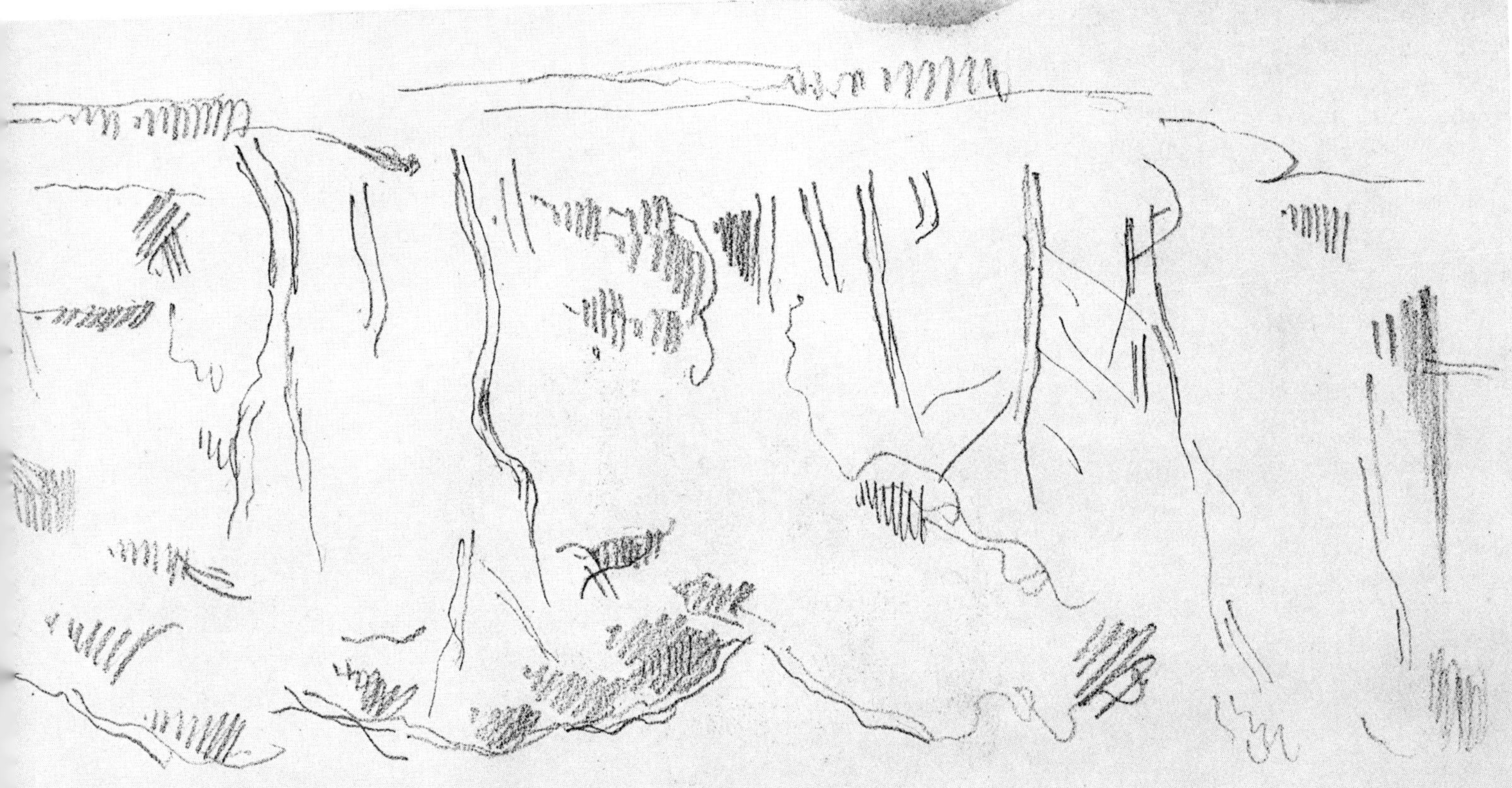

VII

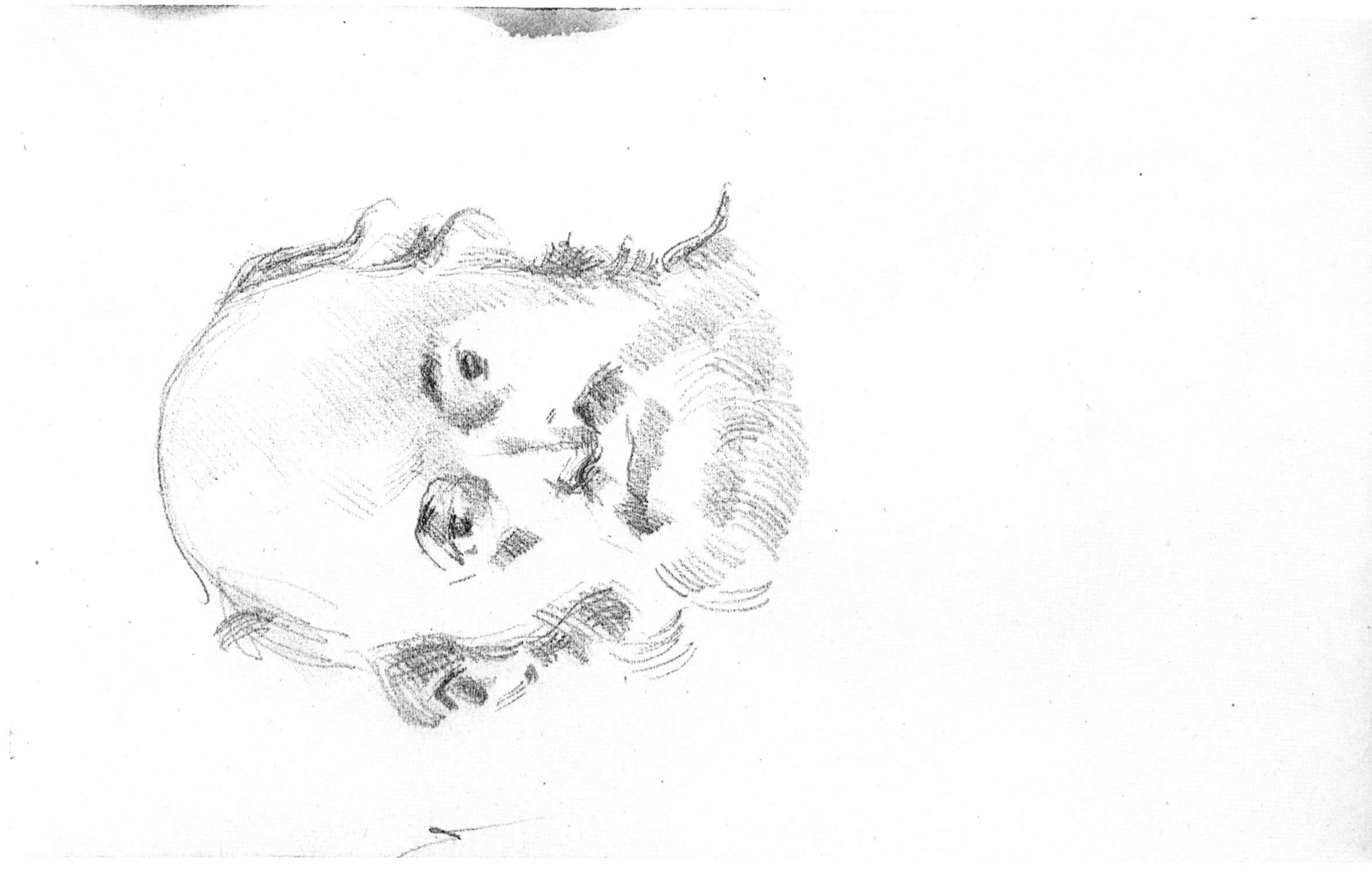

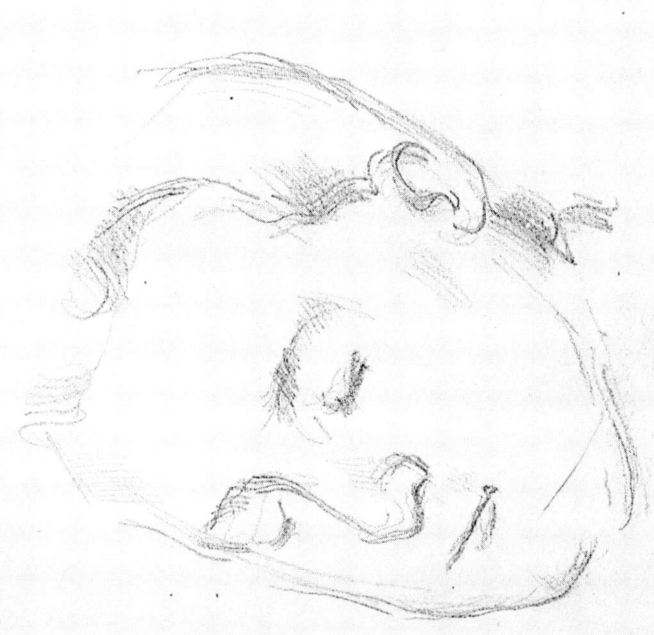

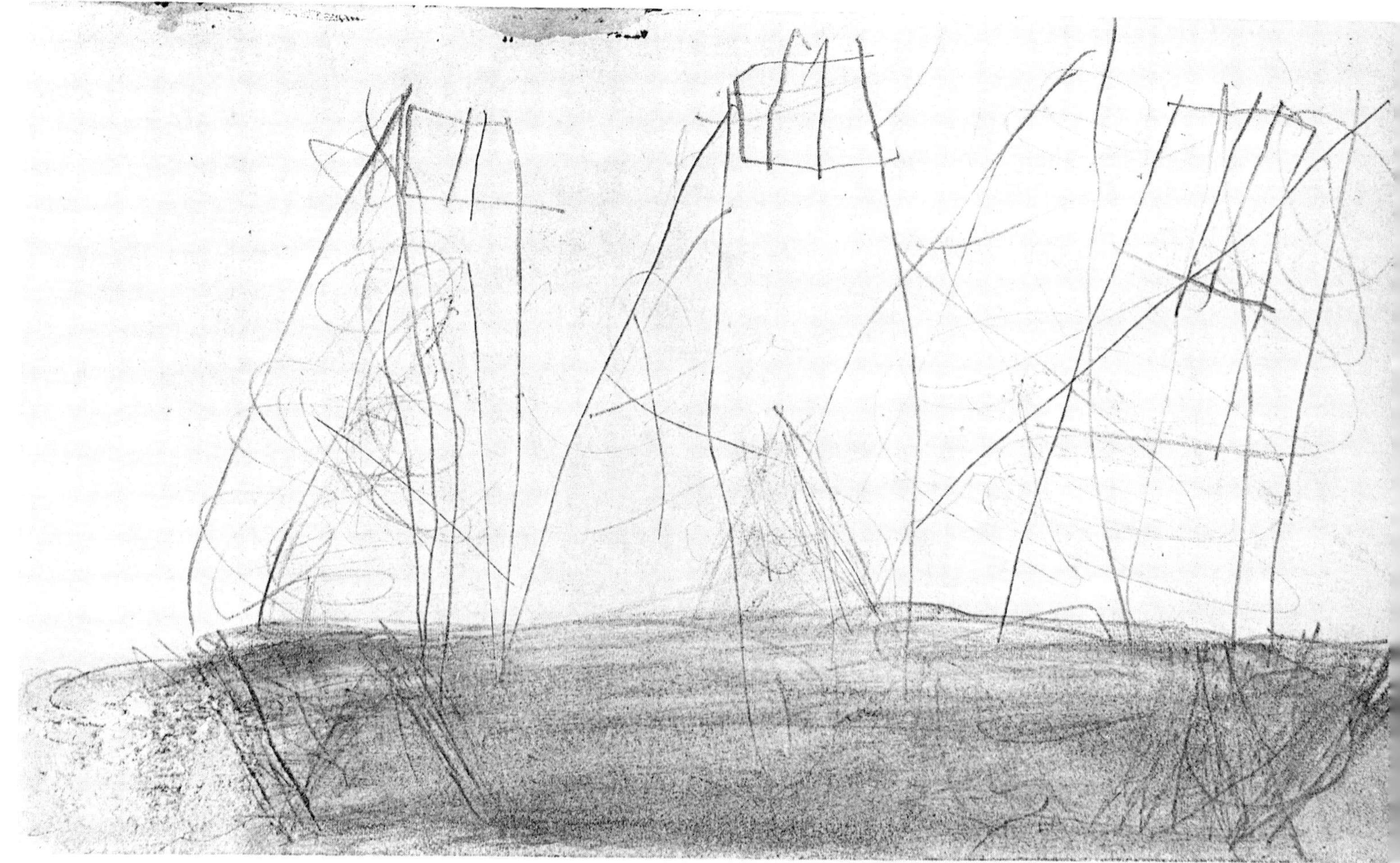

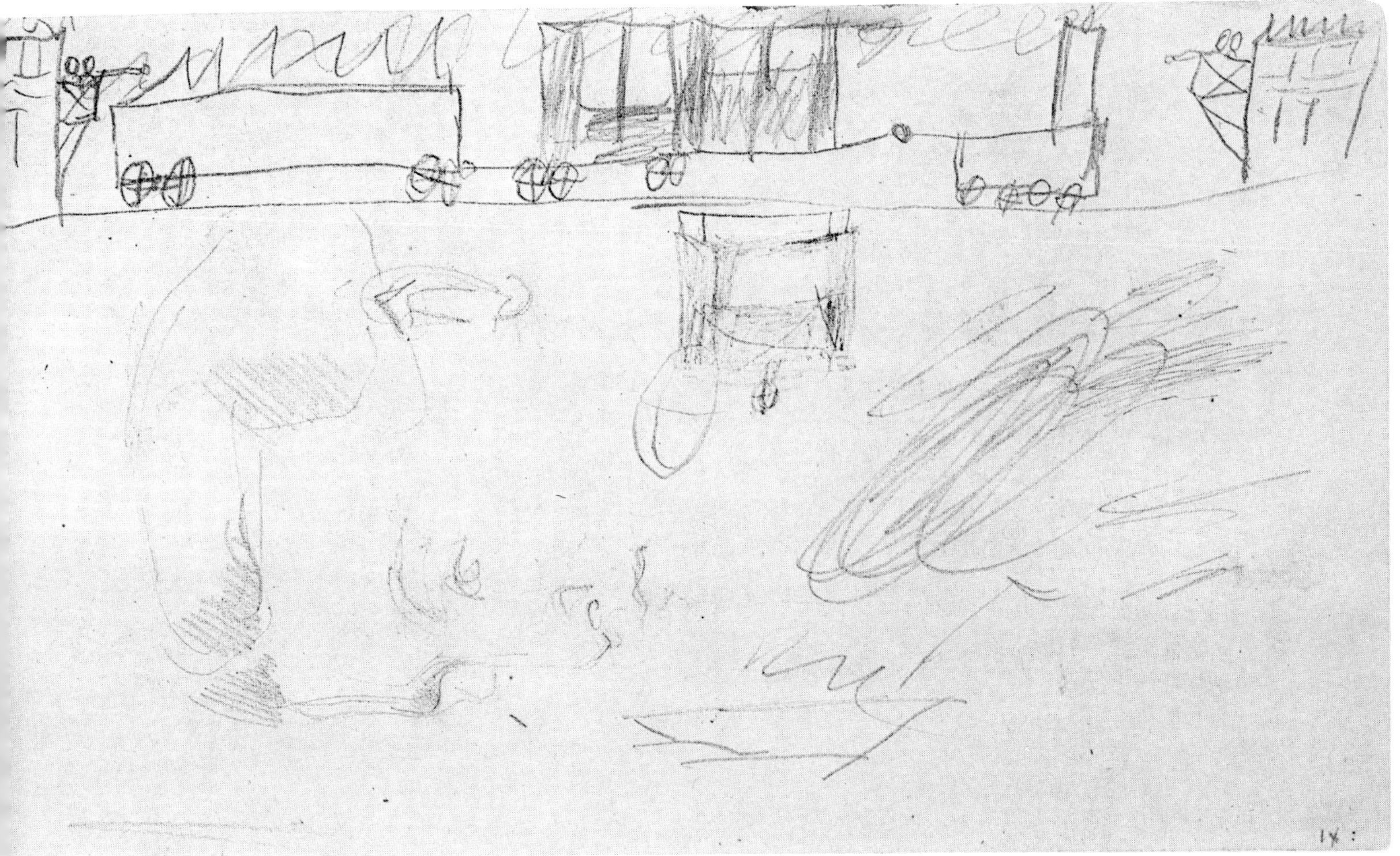

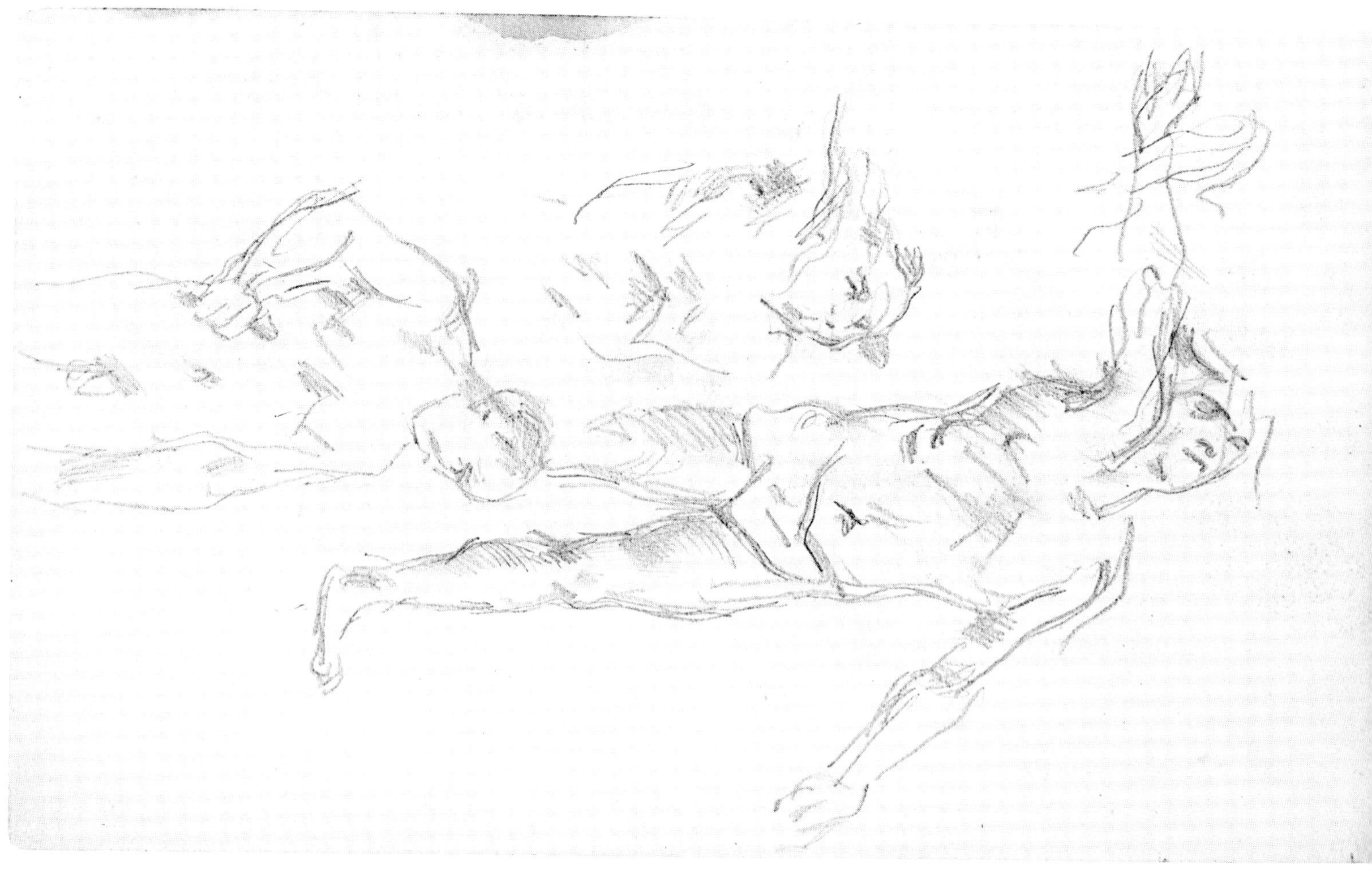

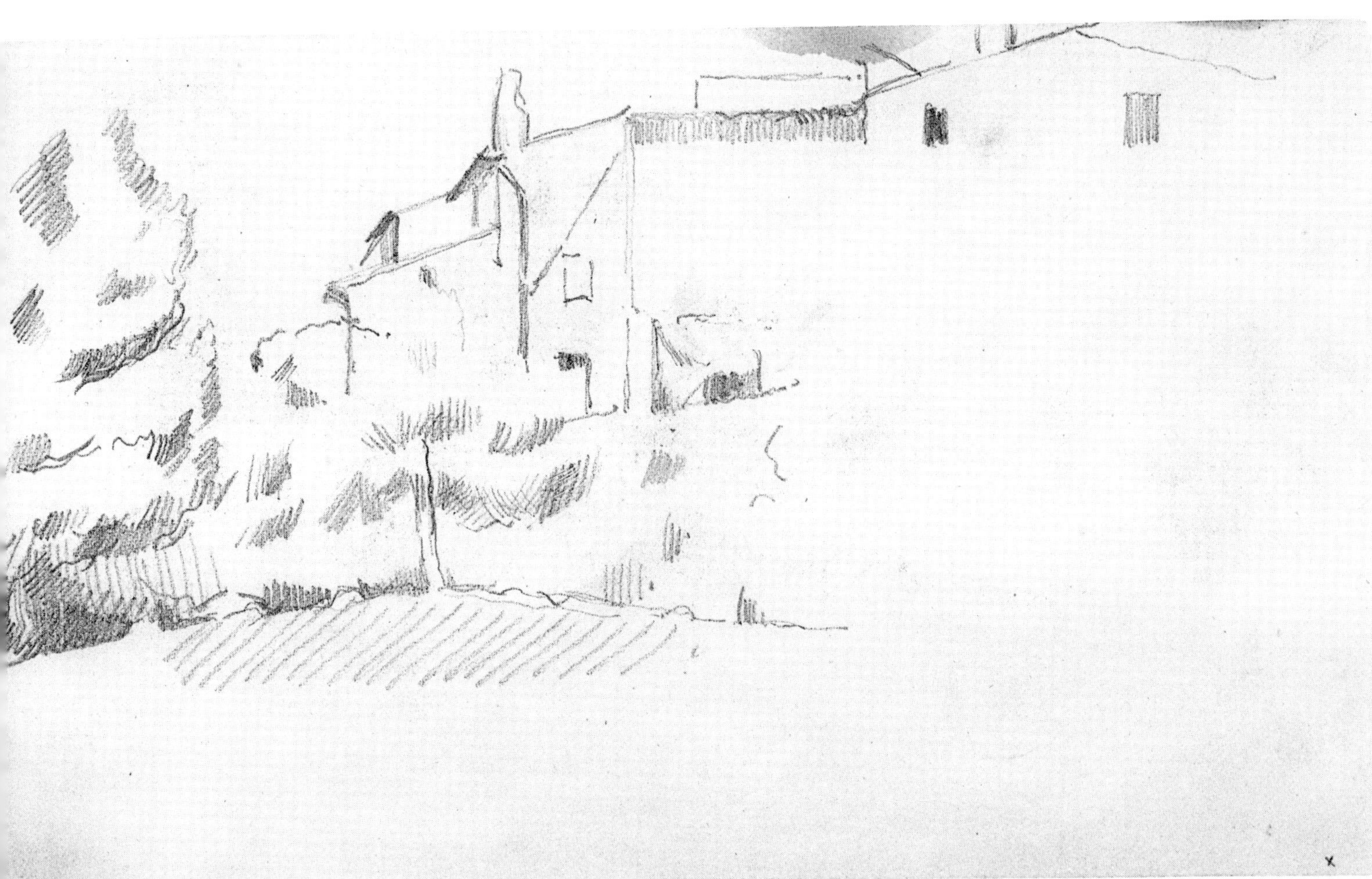

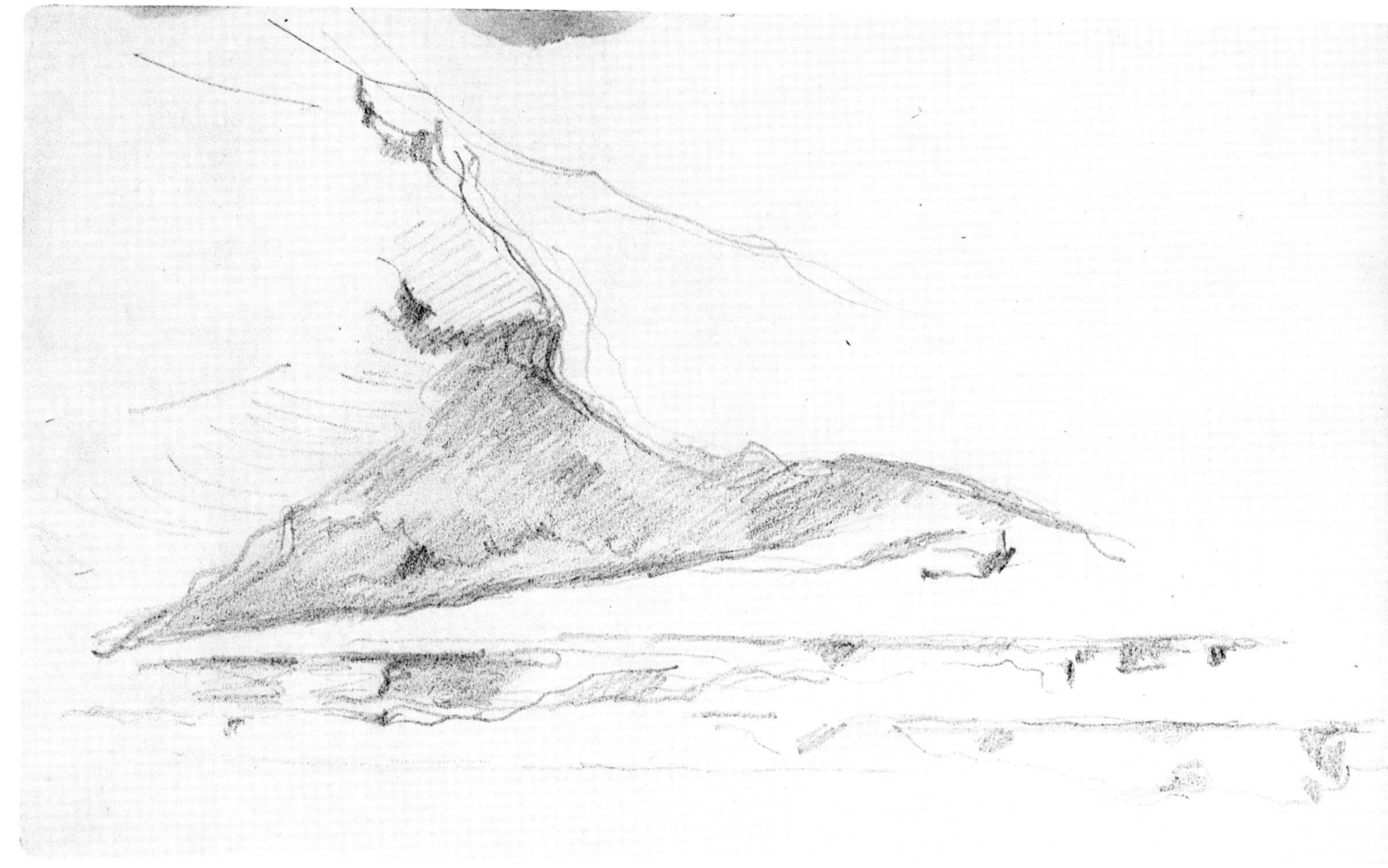

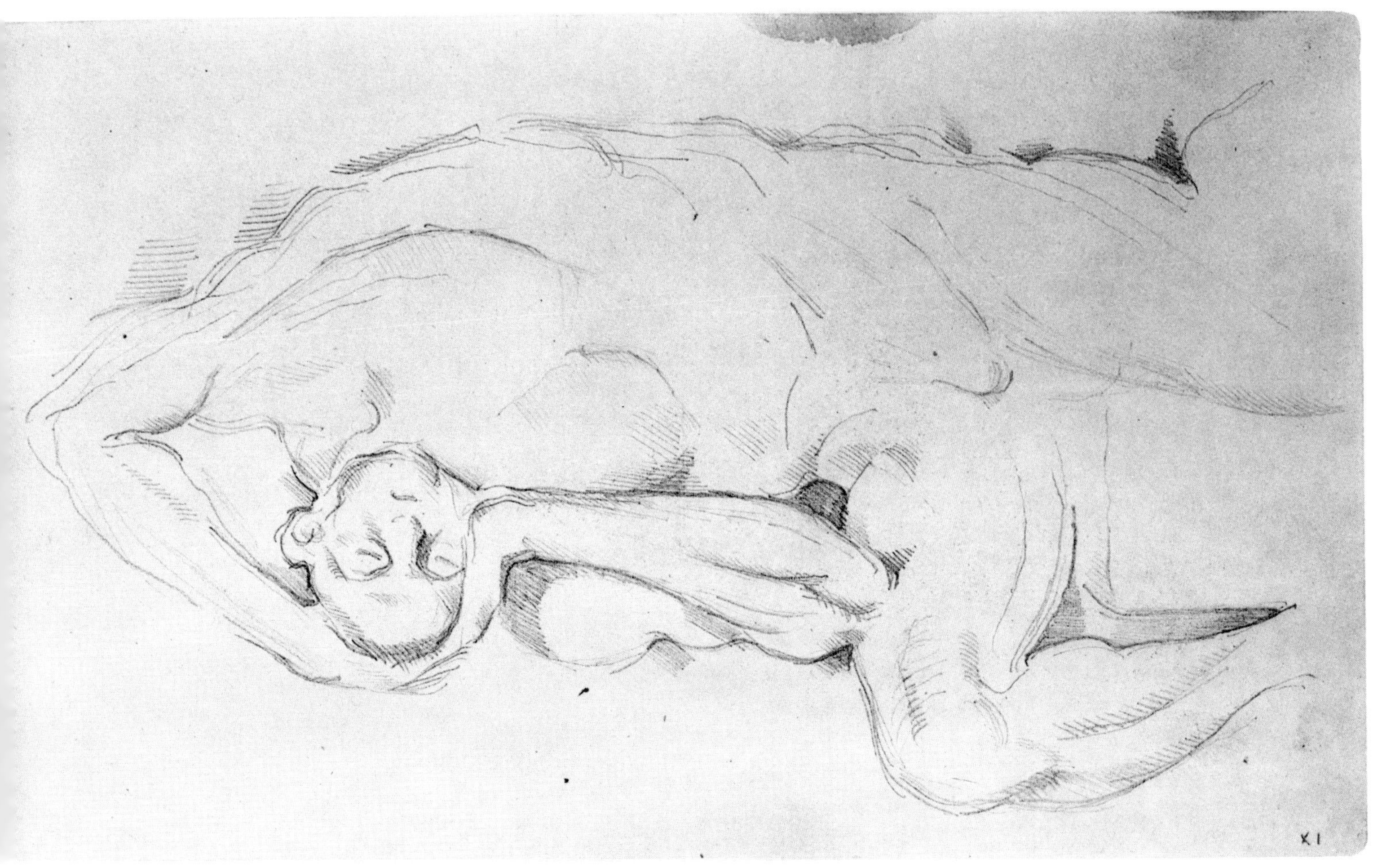
X I

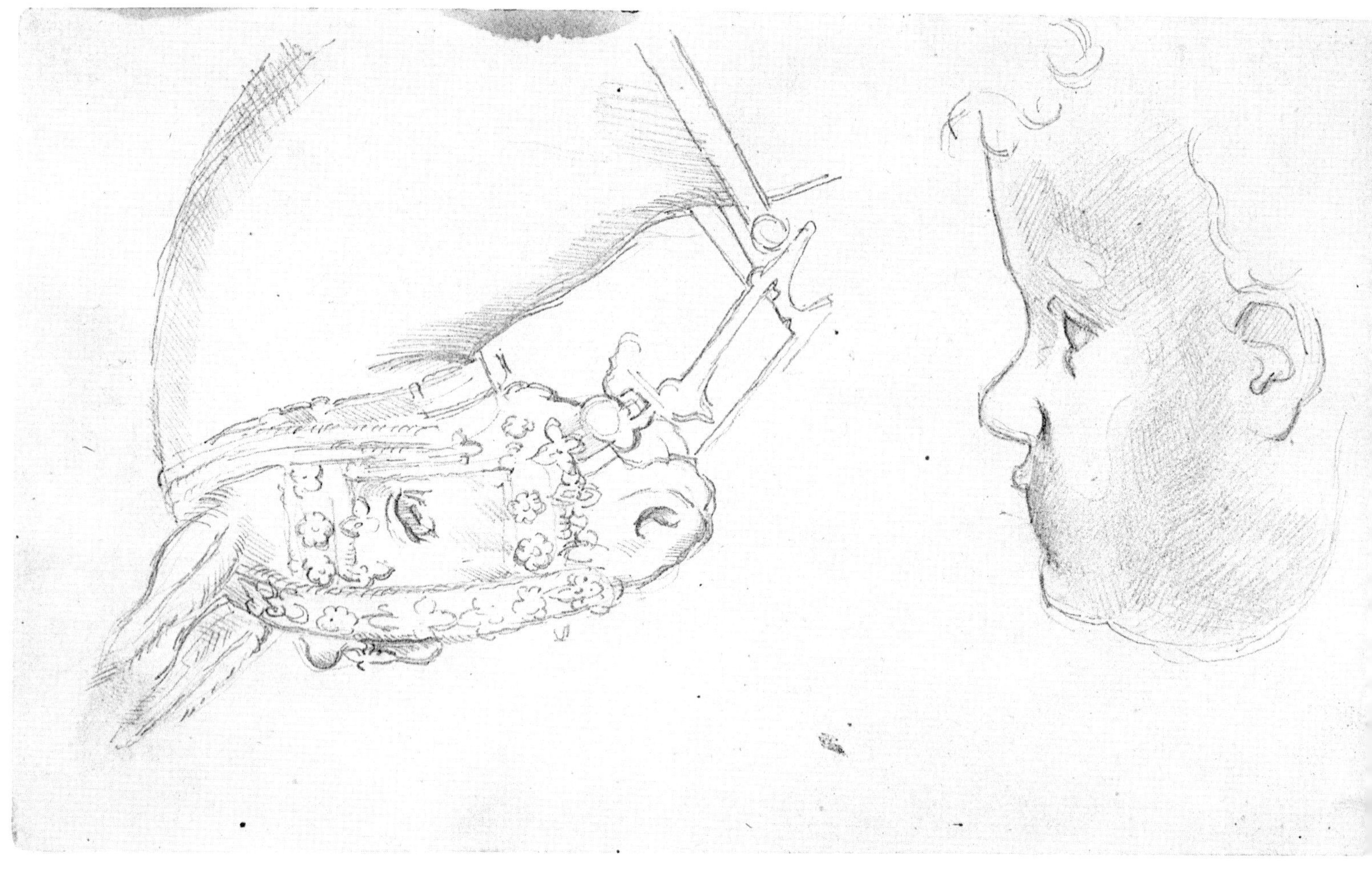

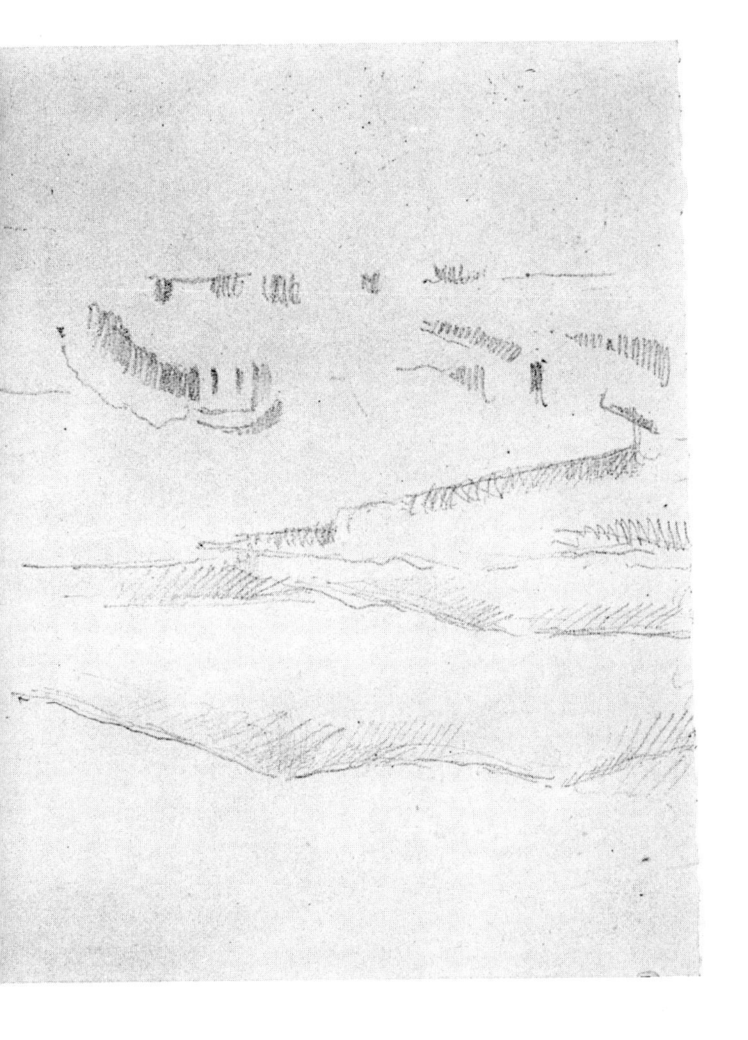

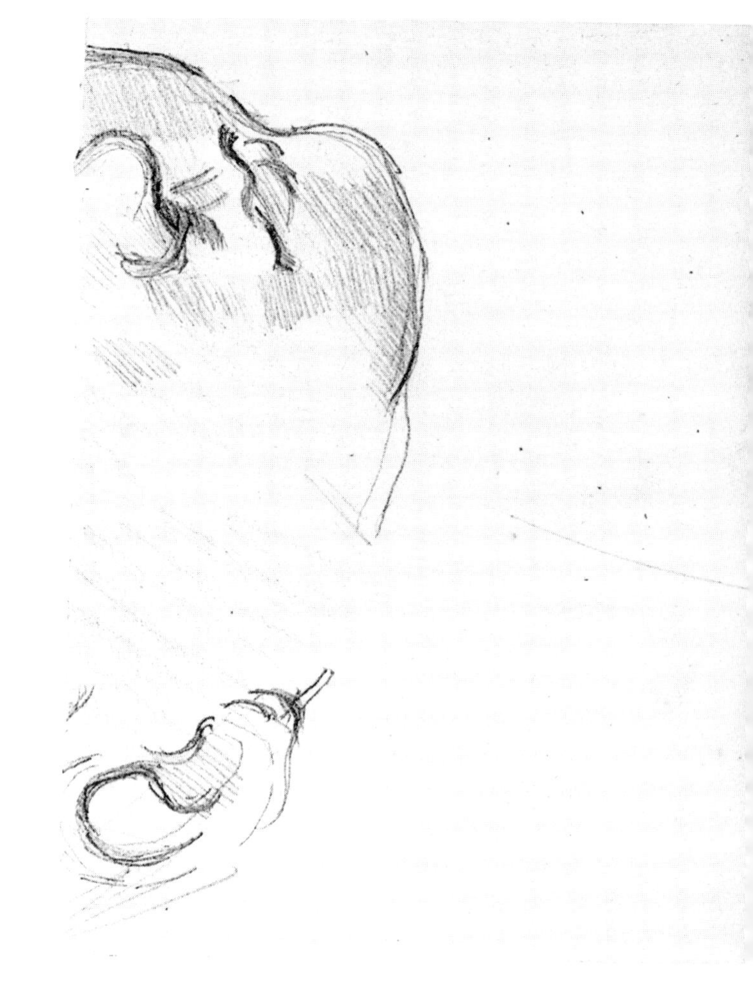

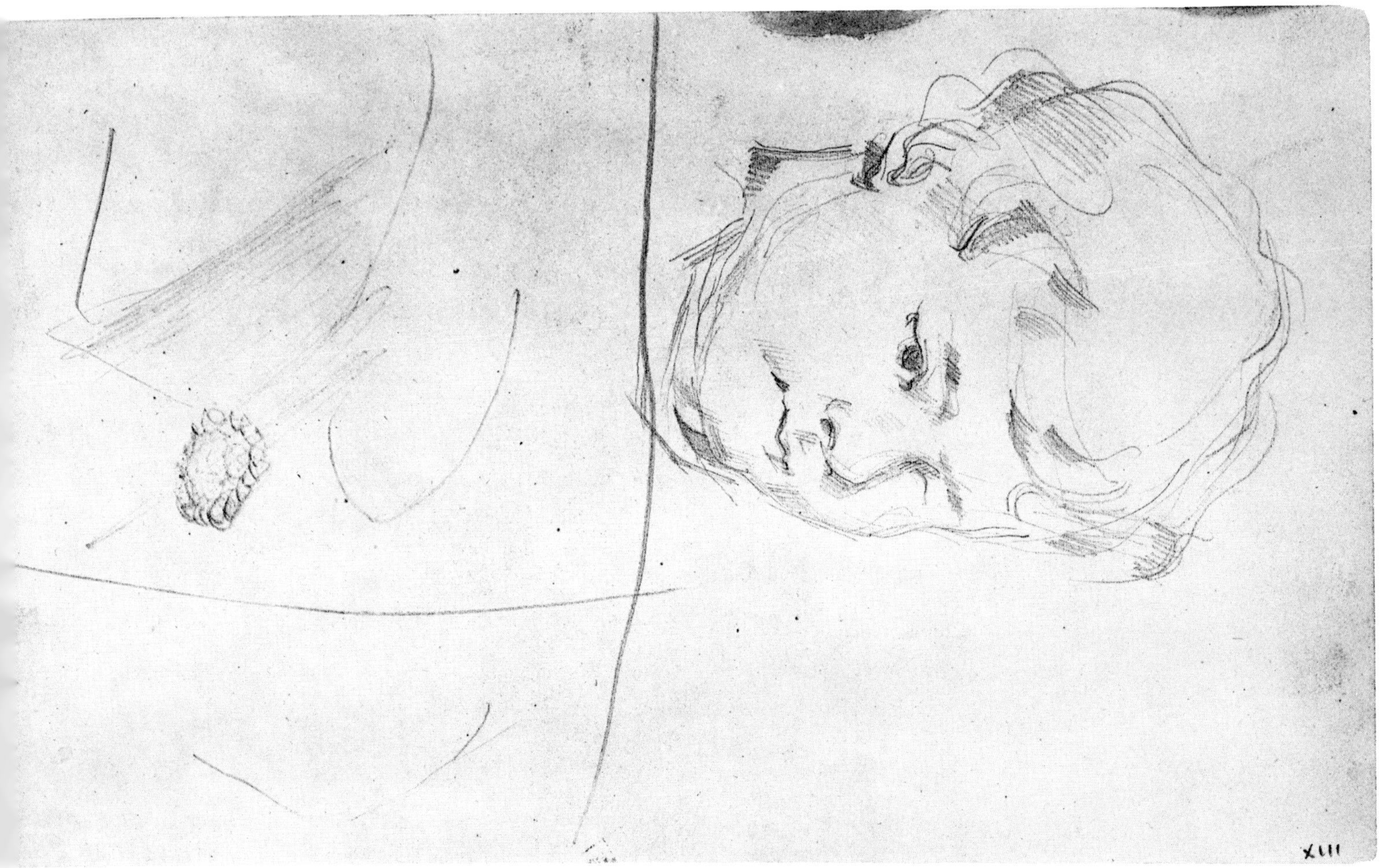
XIII

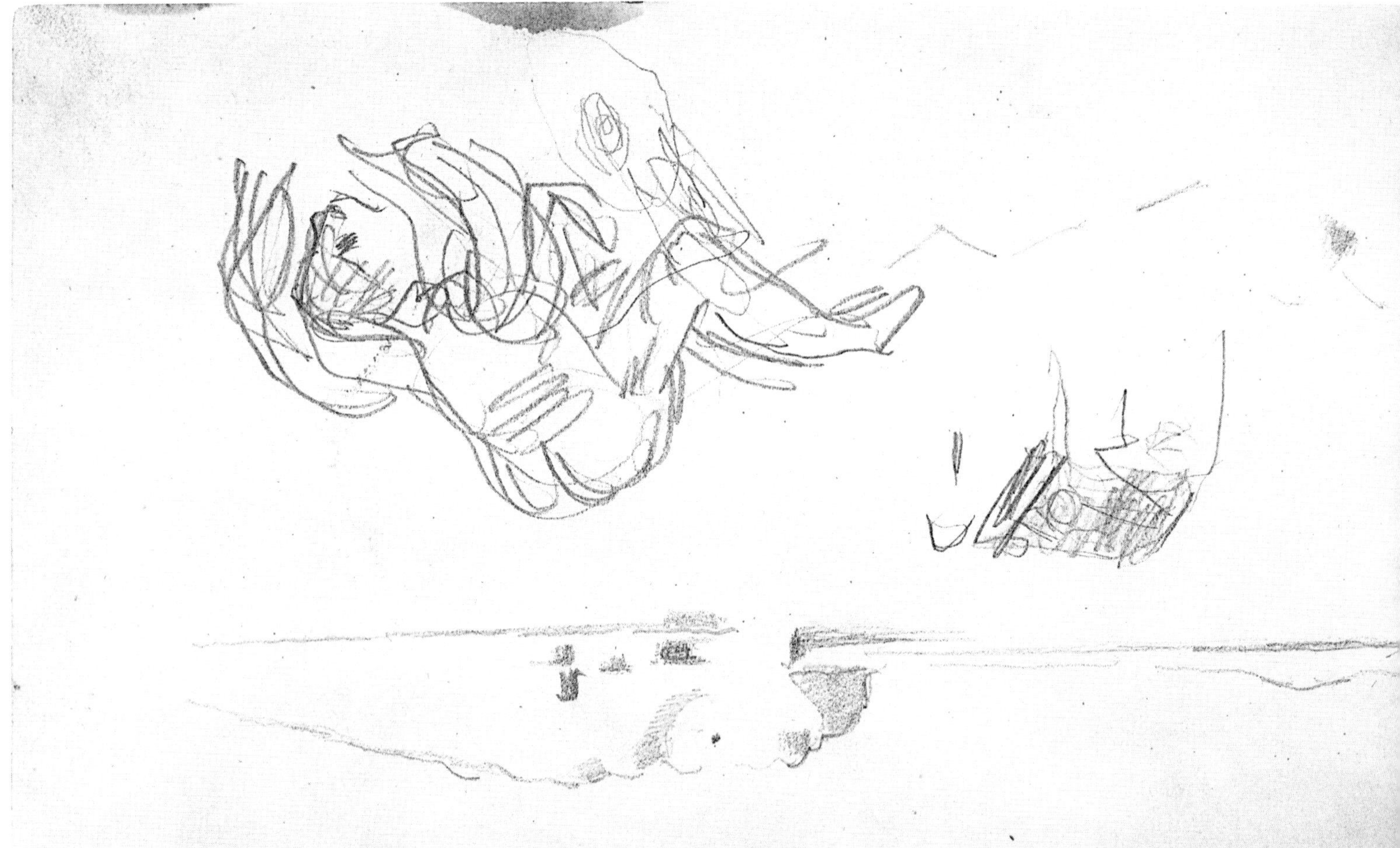

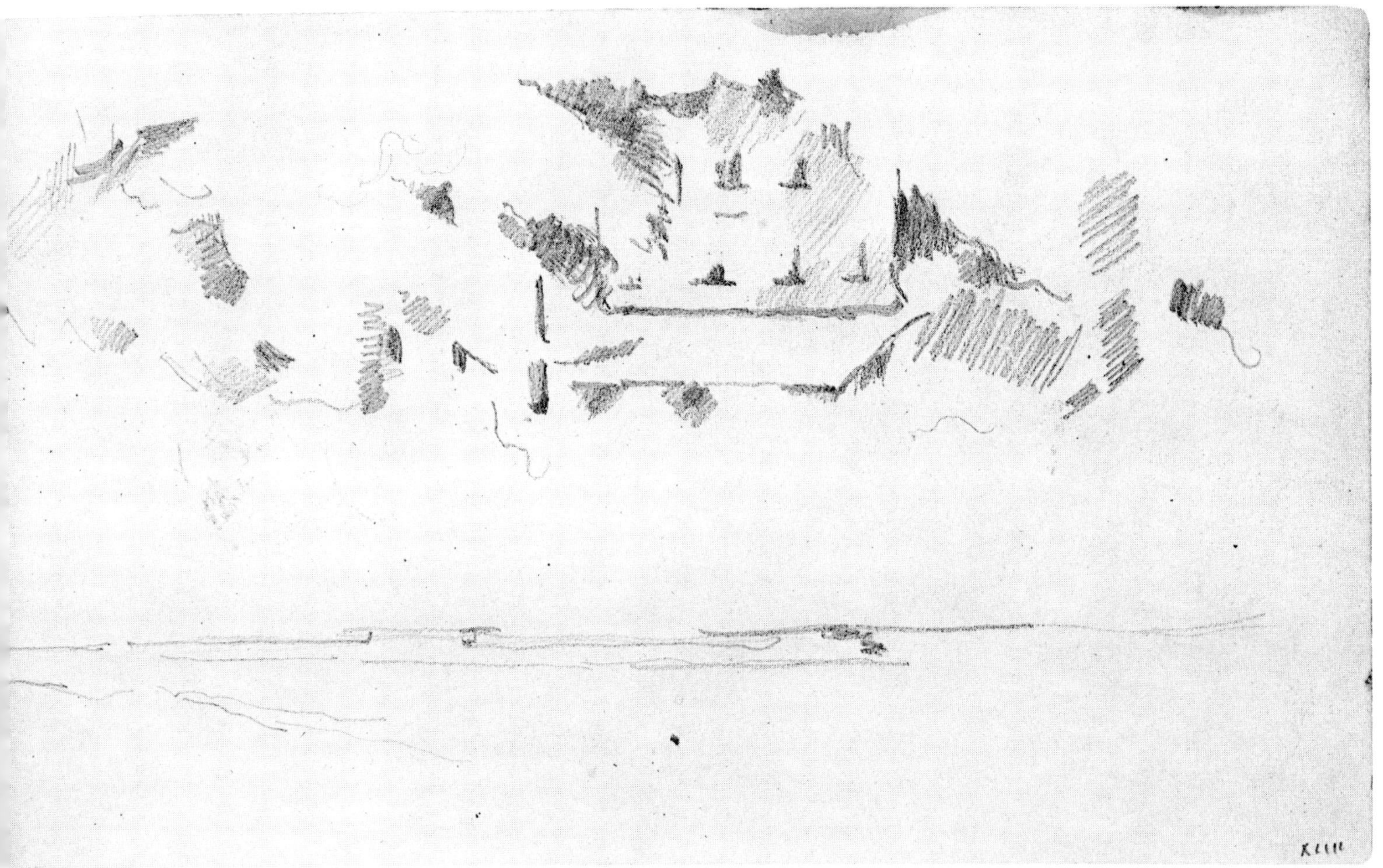

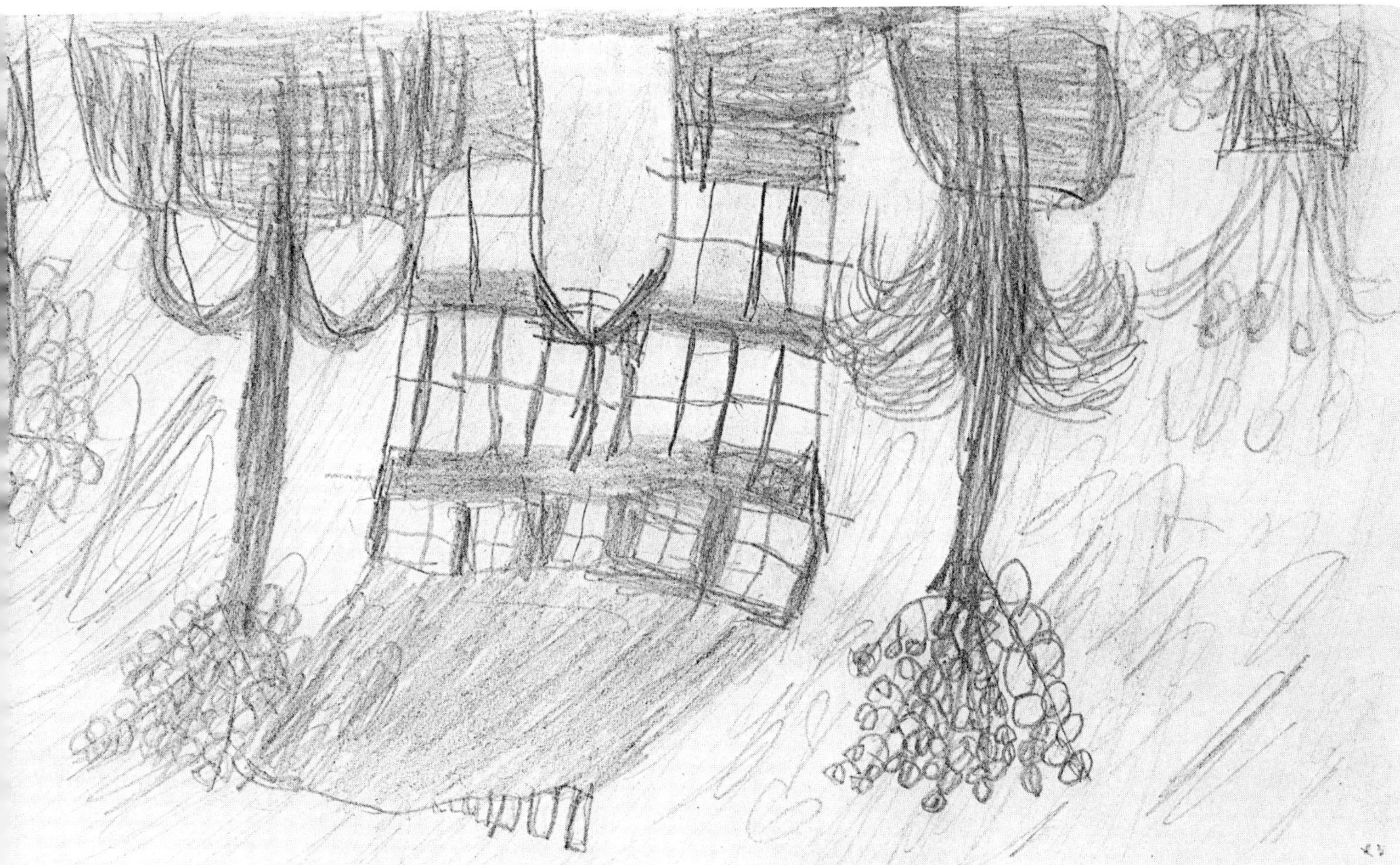

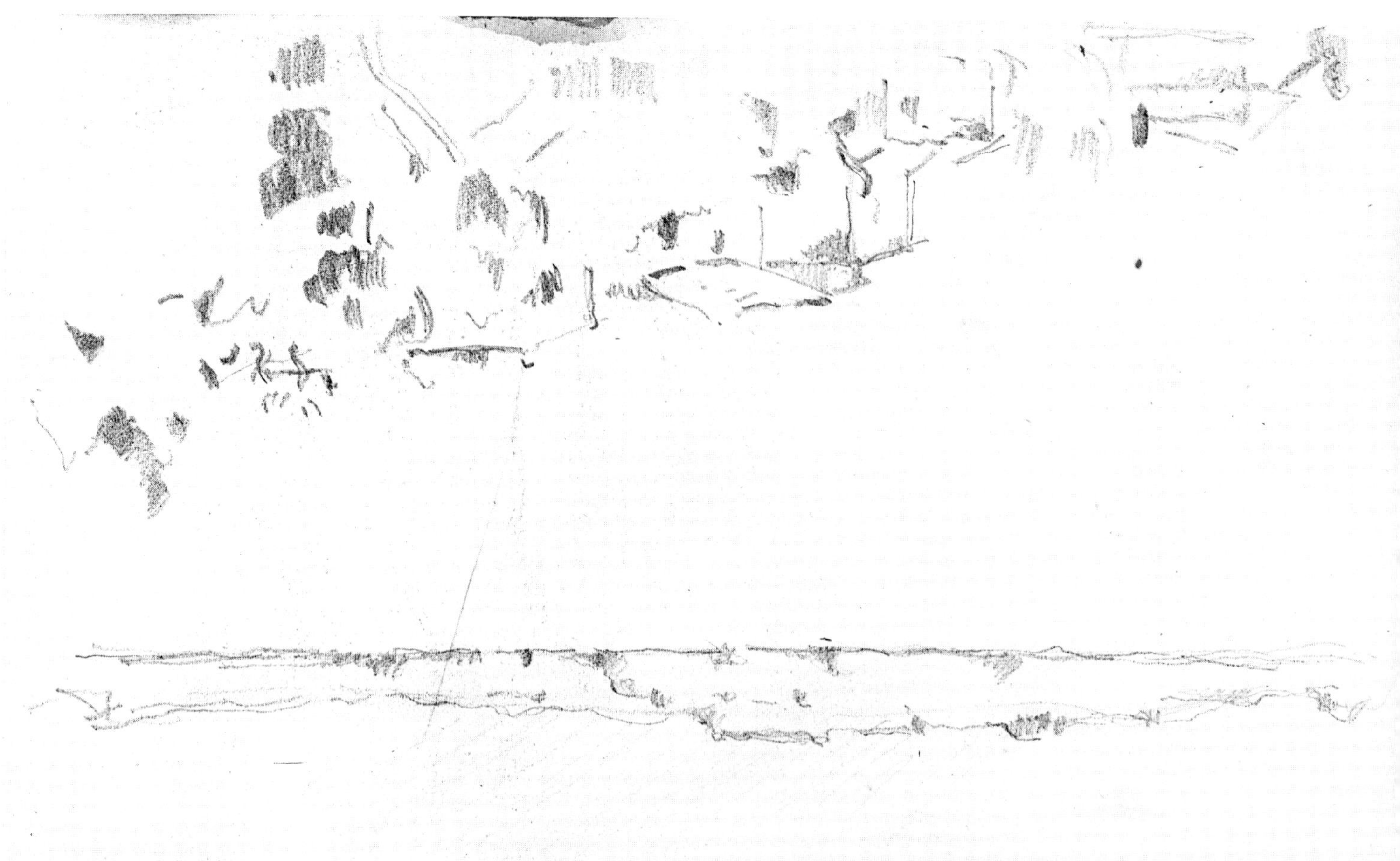

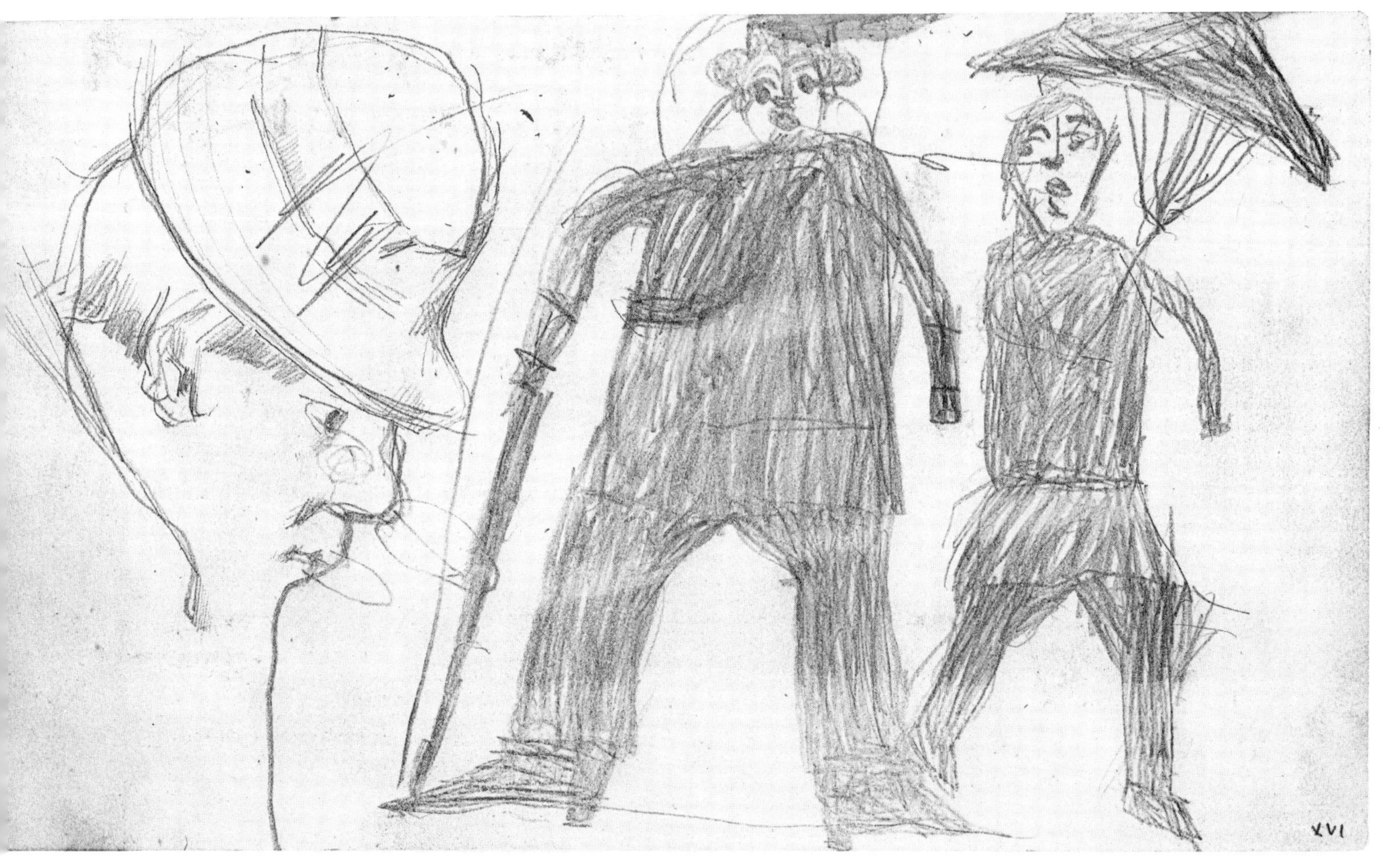

XVI

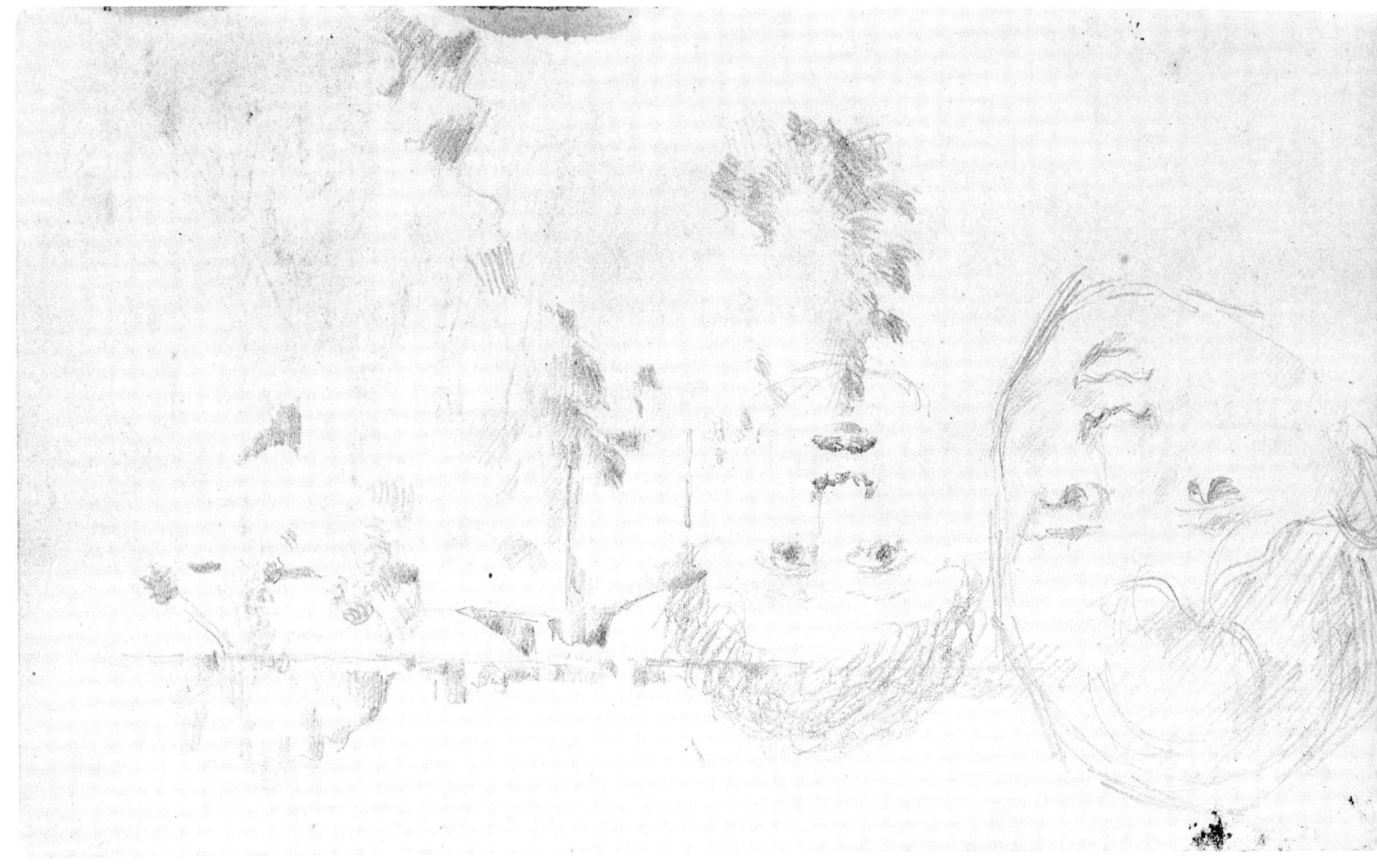

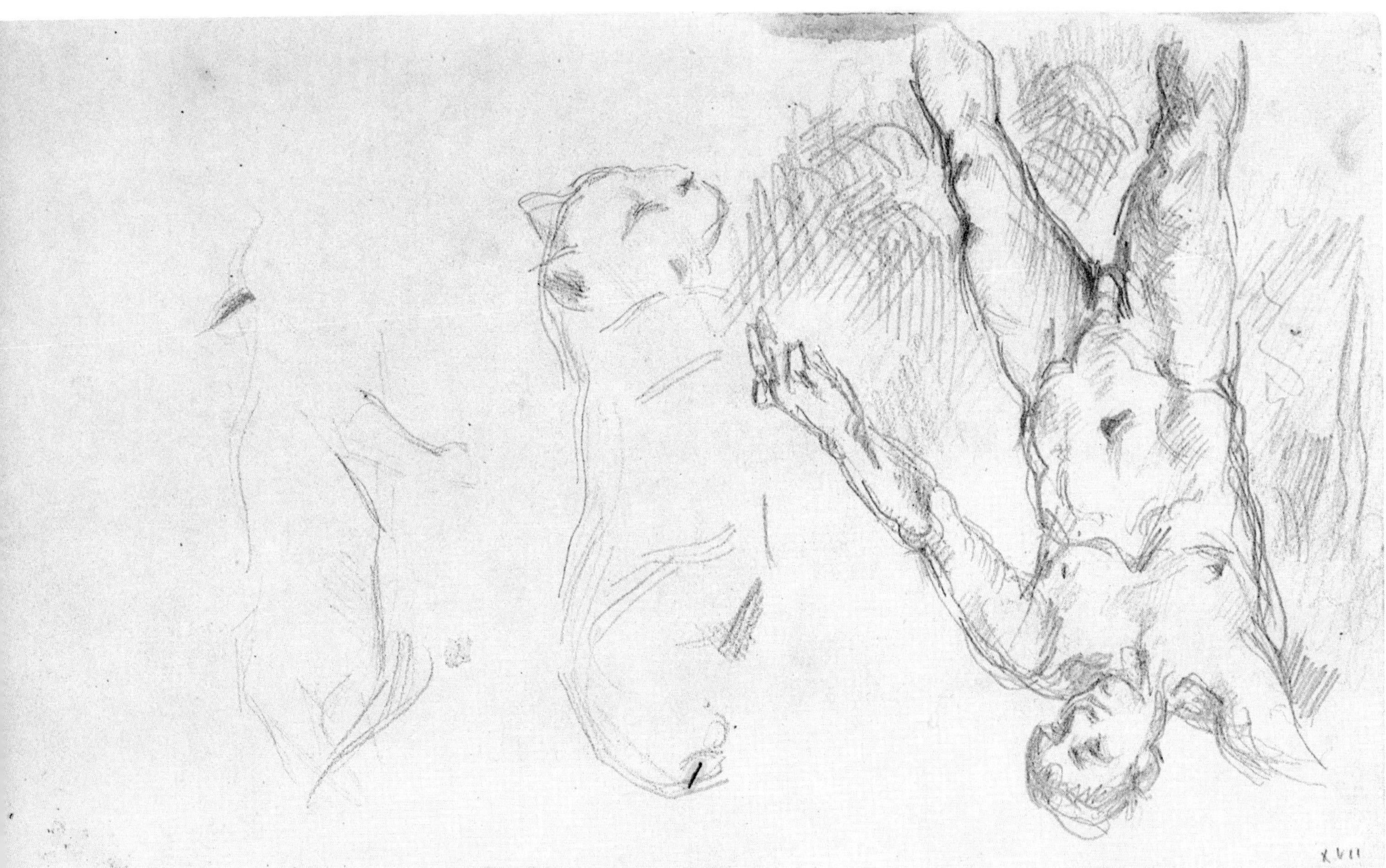
XVII

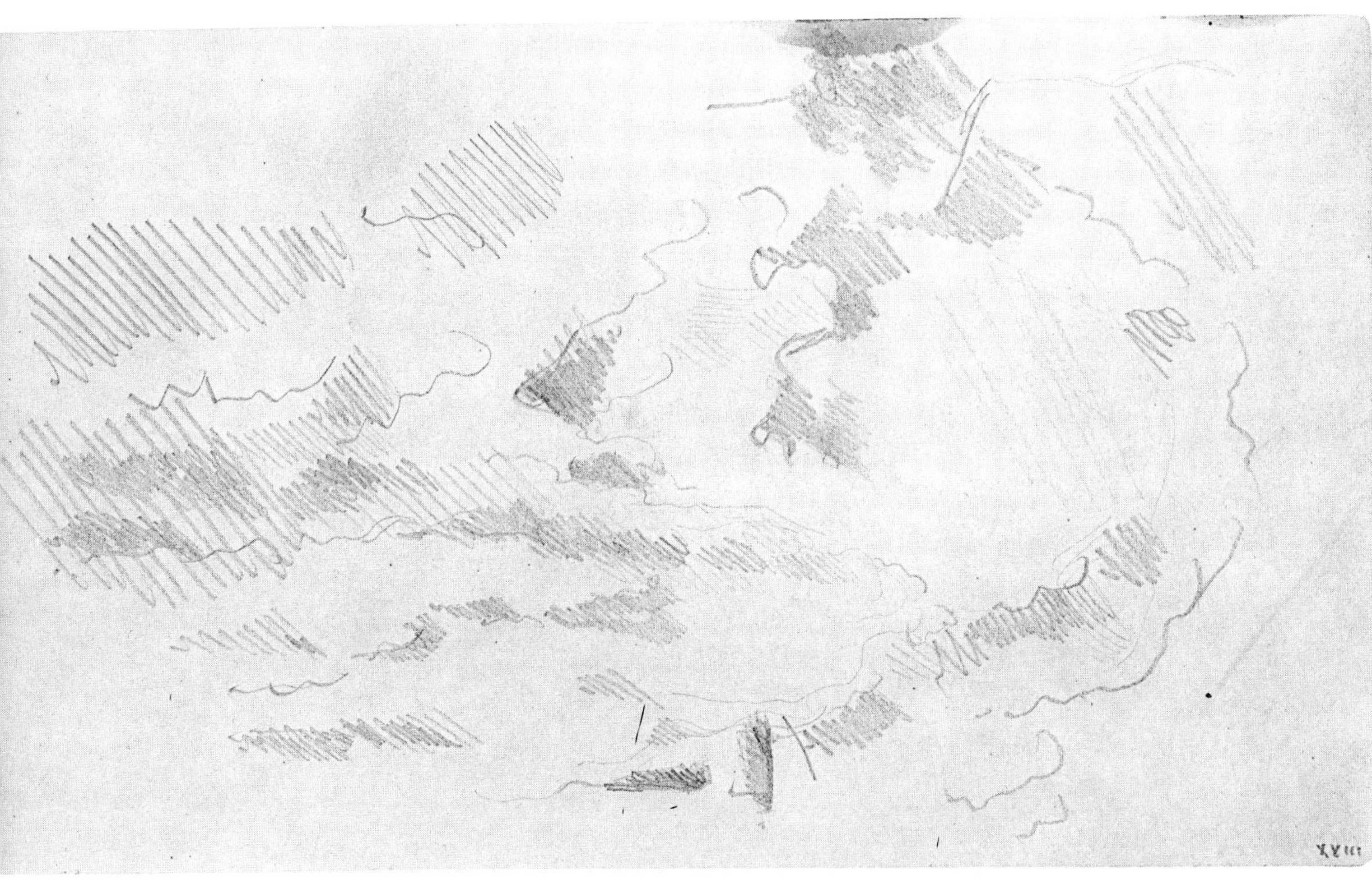
XVIII

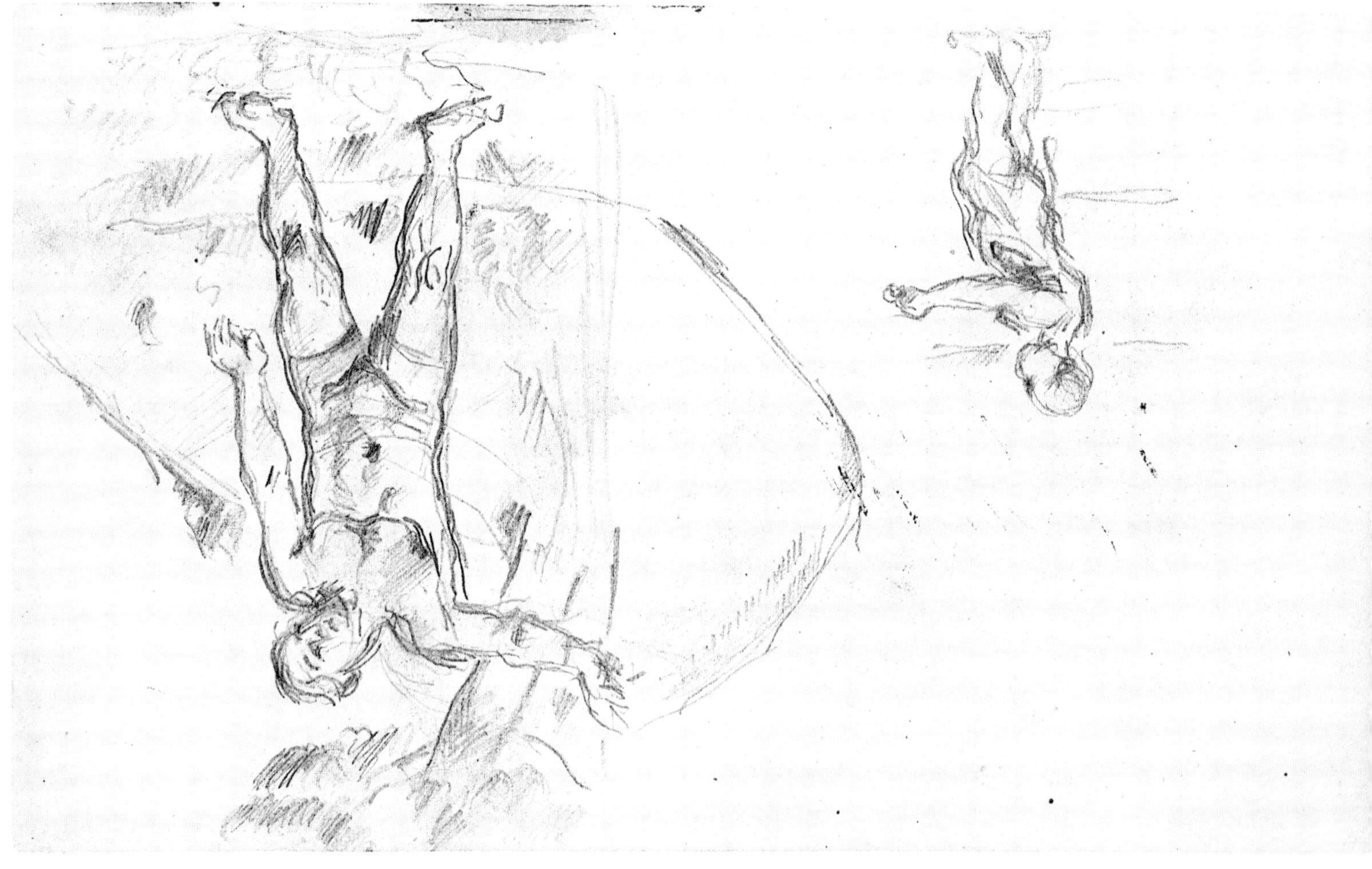

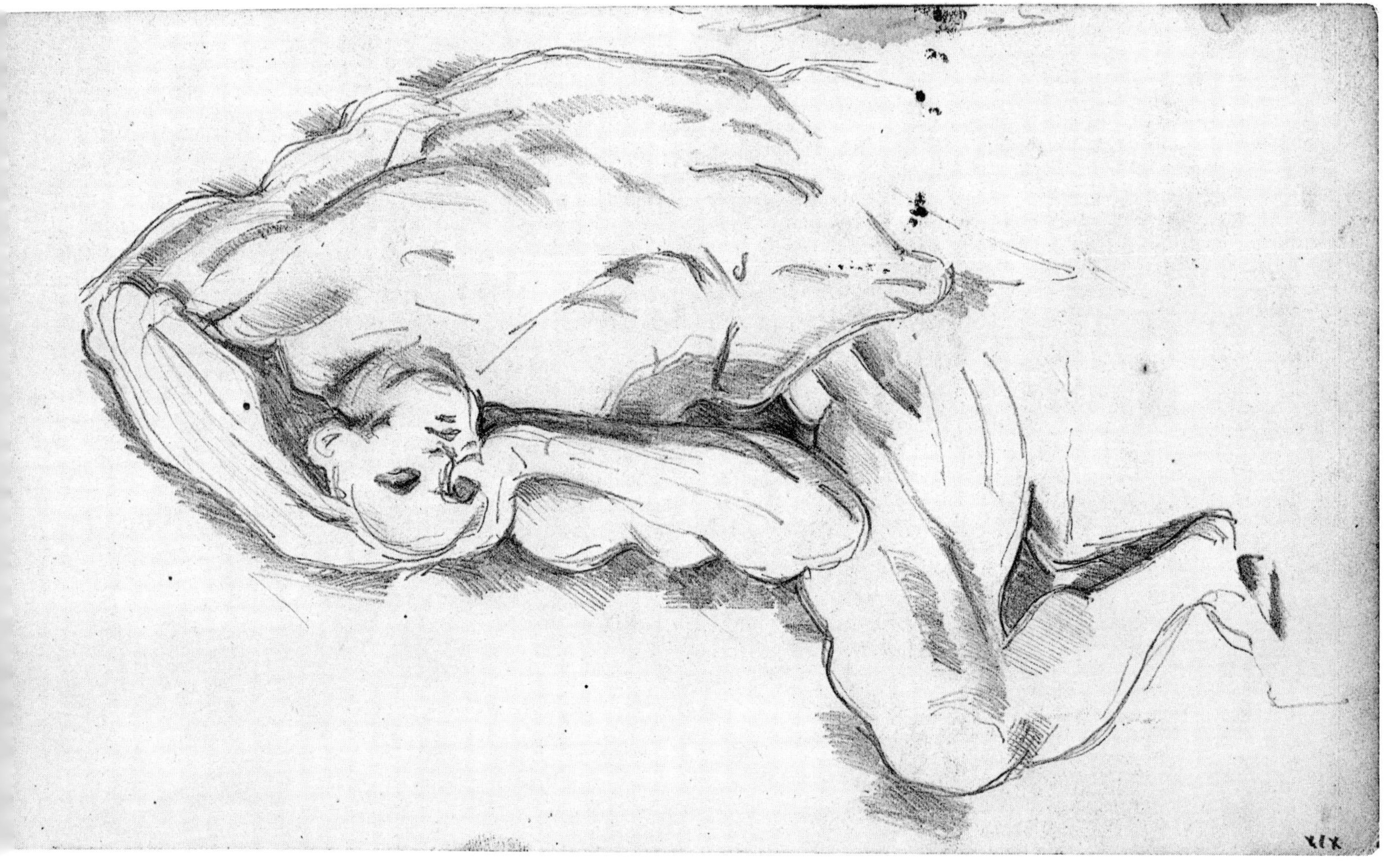

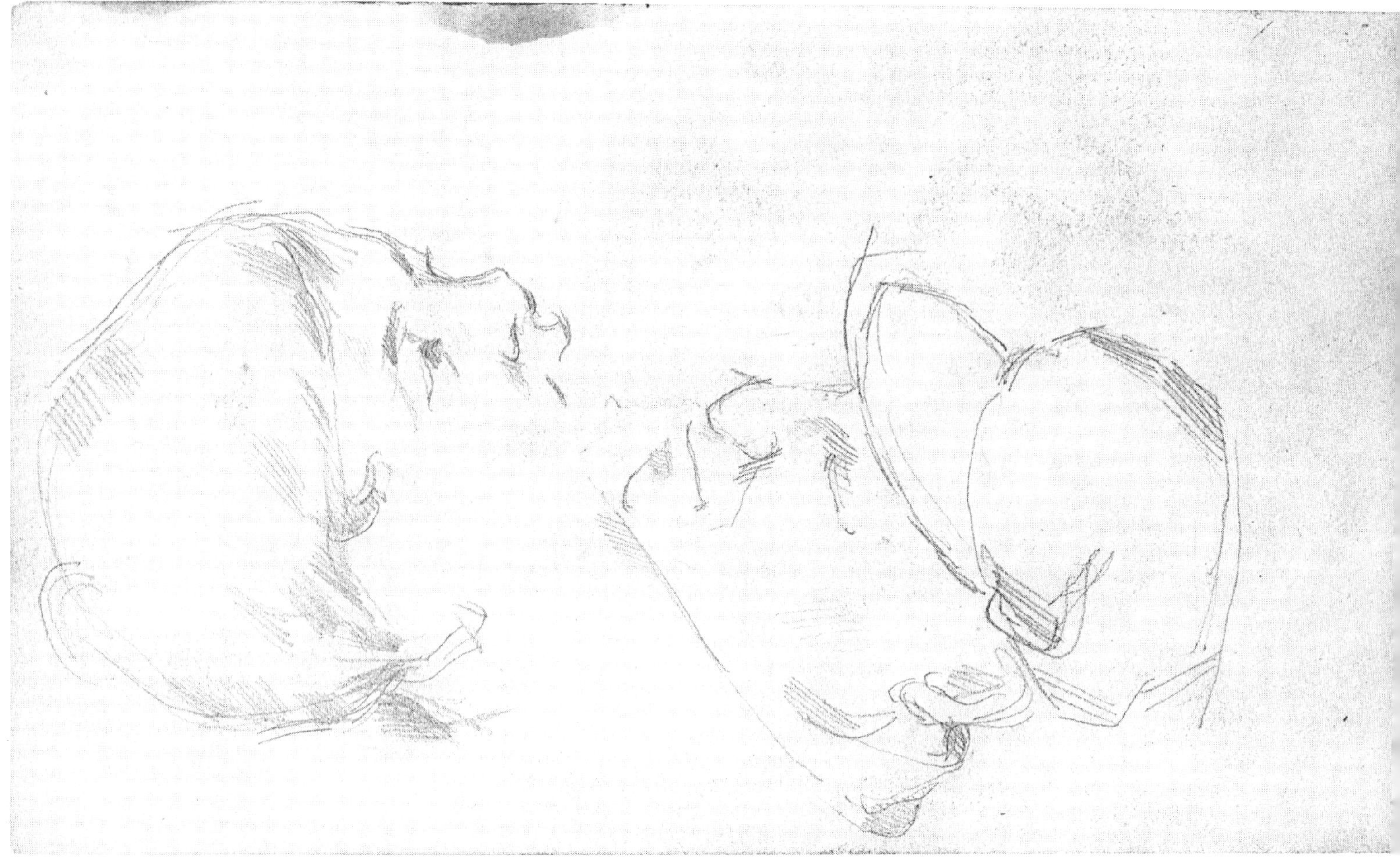

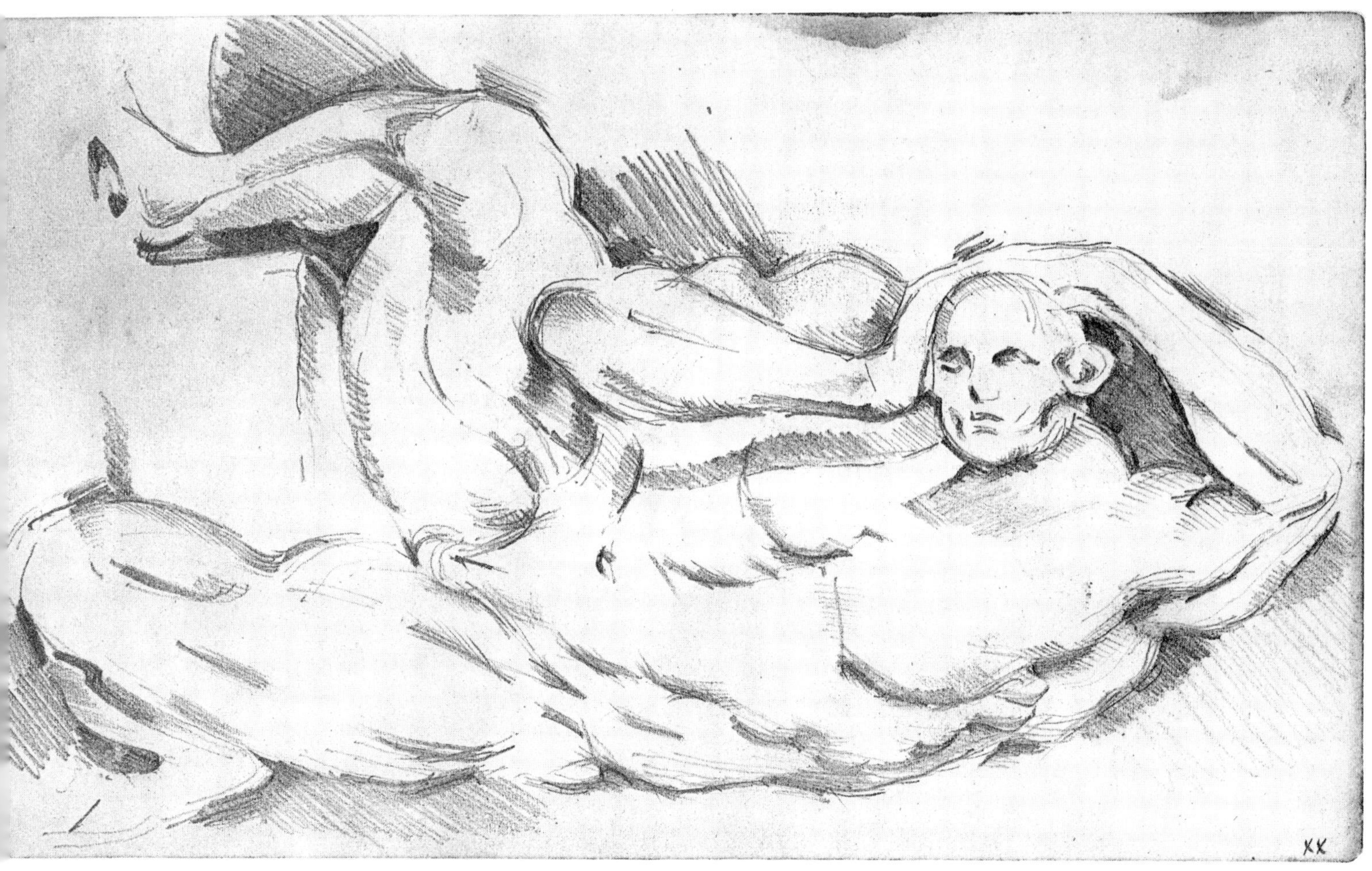
XX

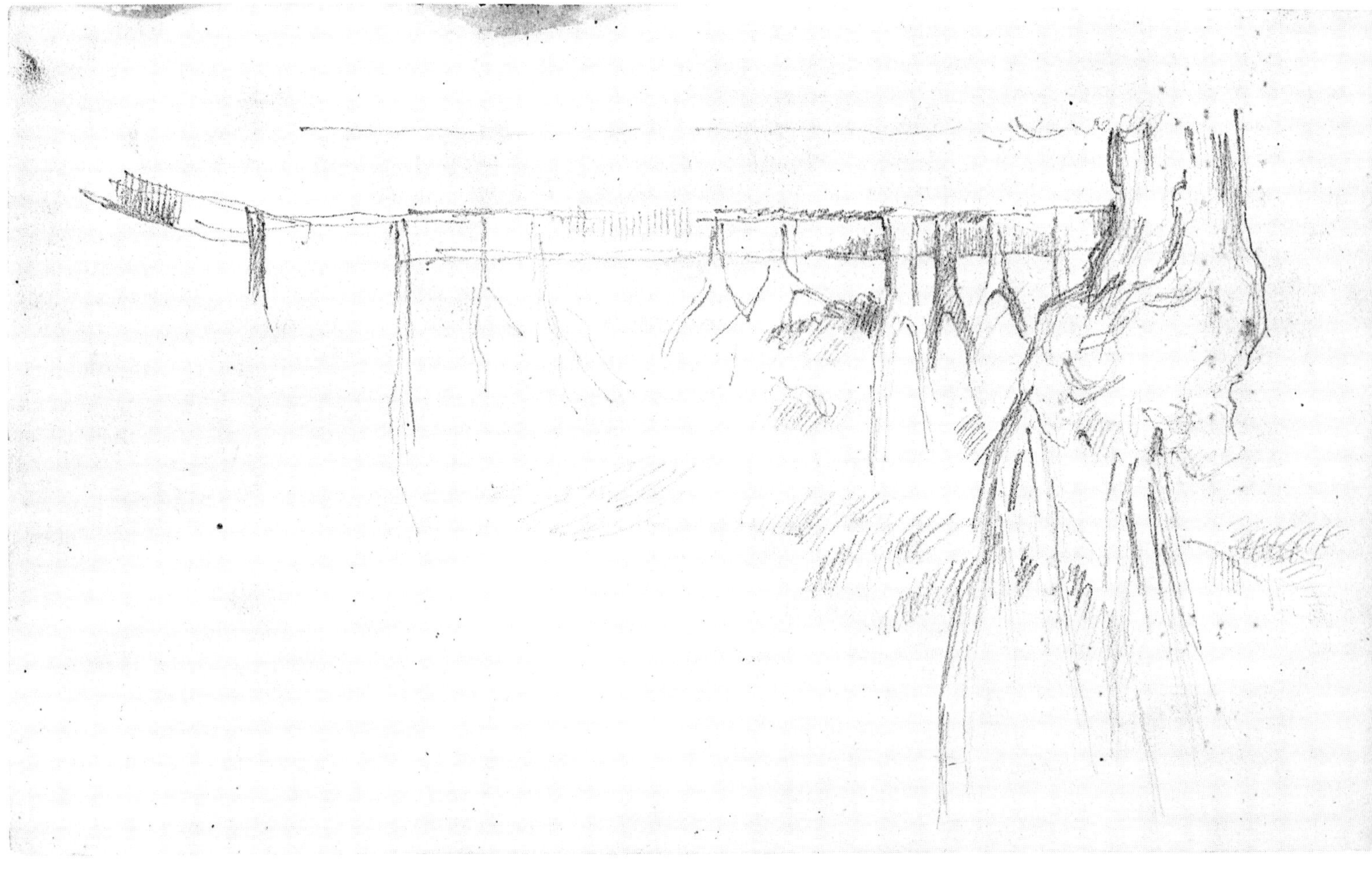

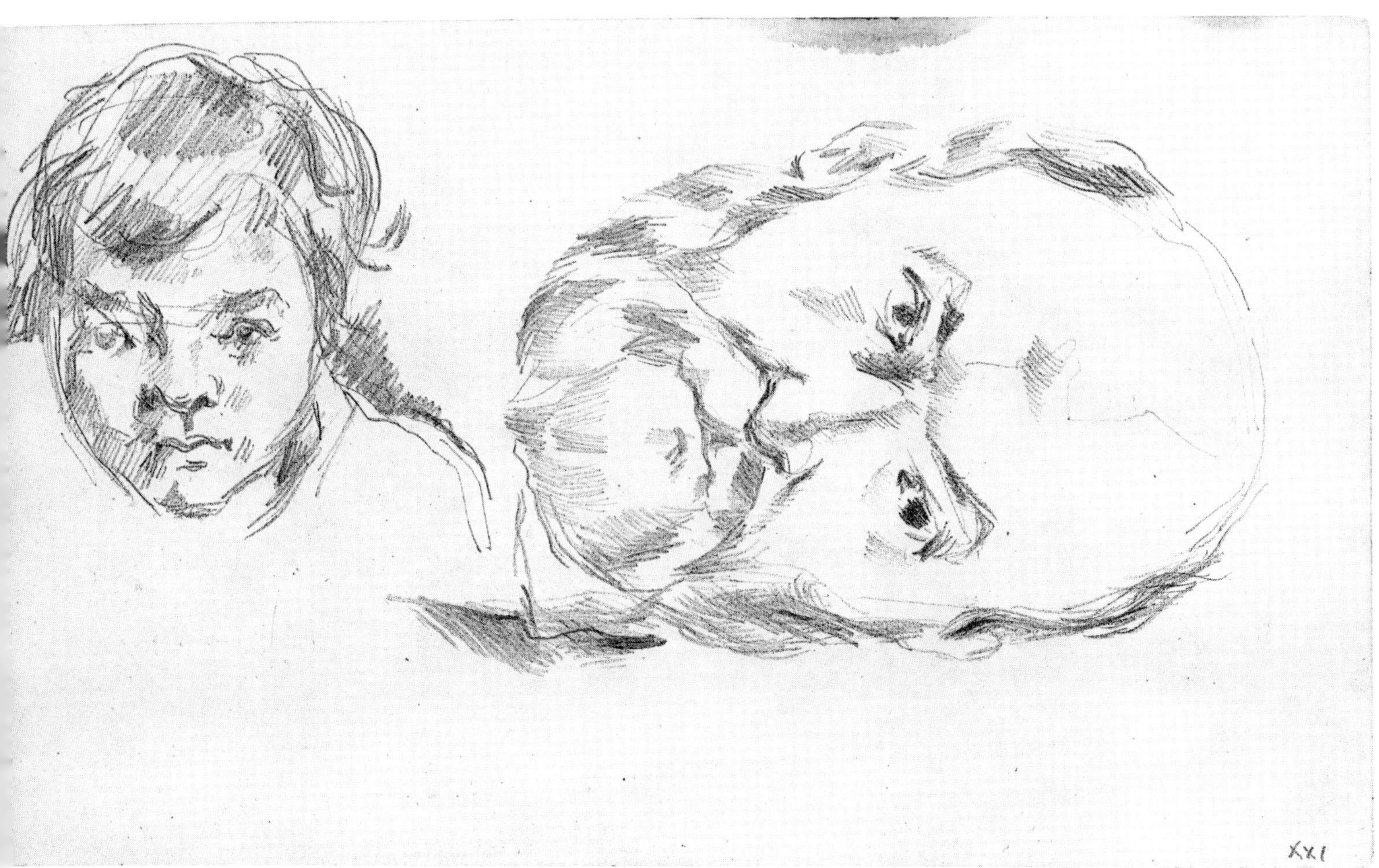

XXI

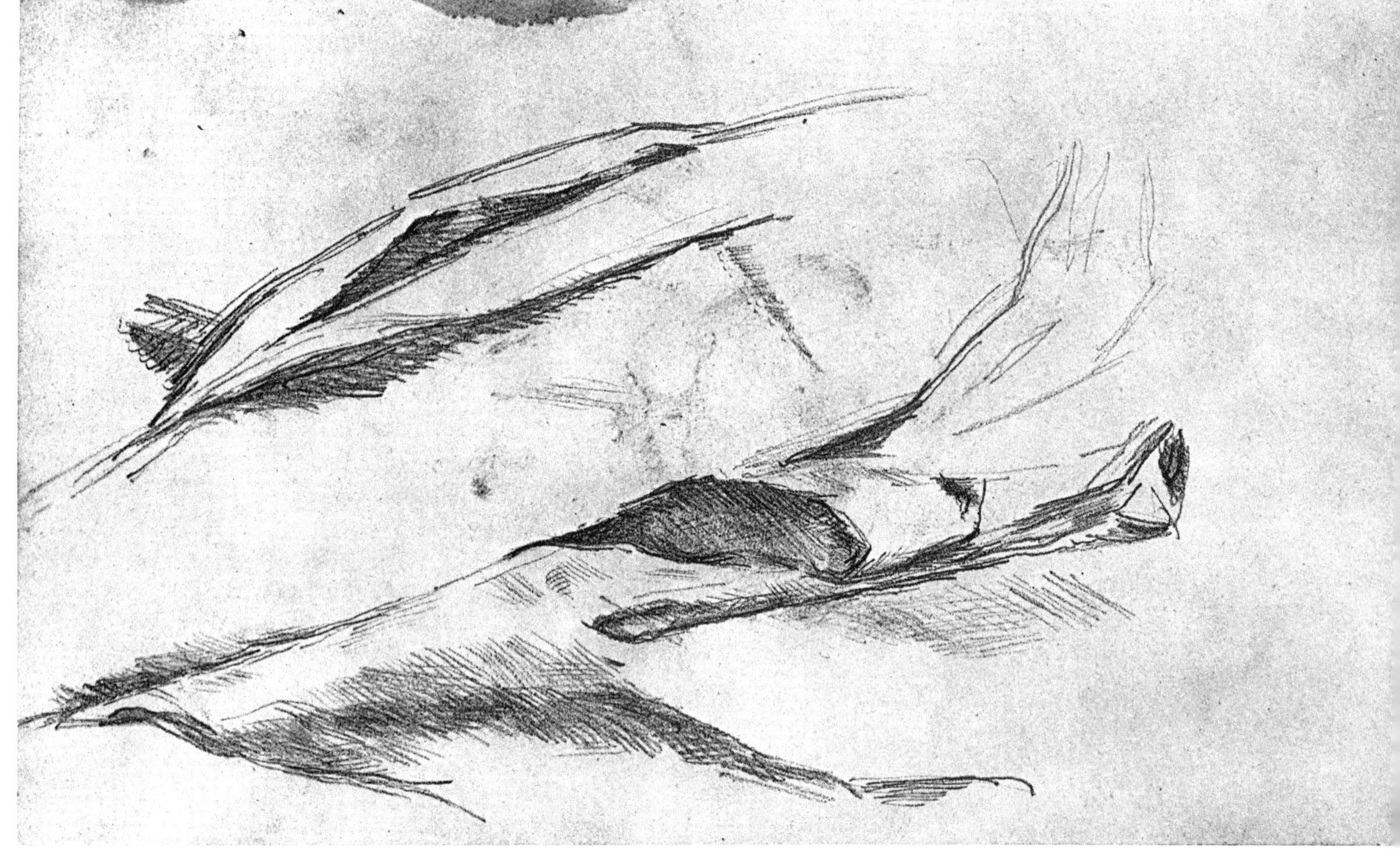

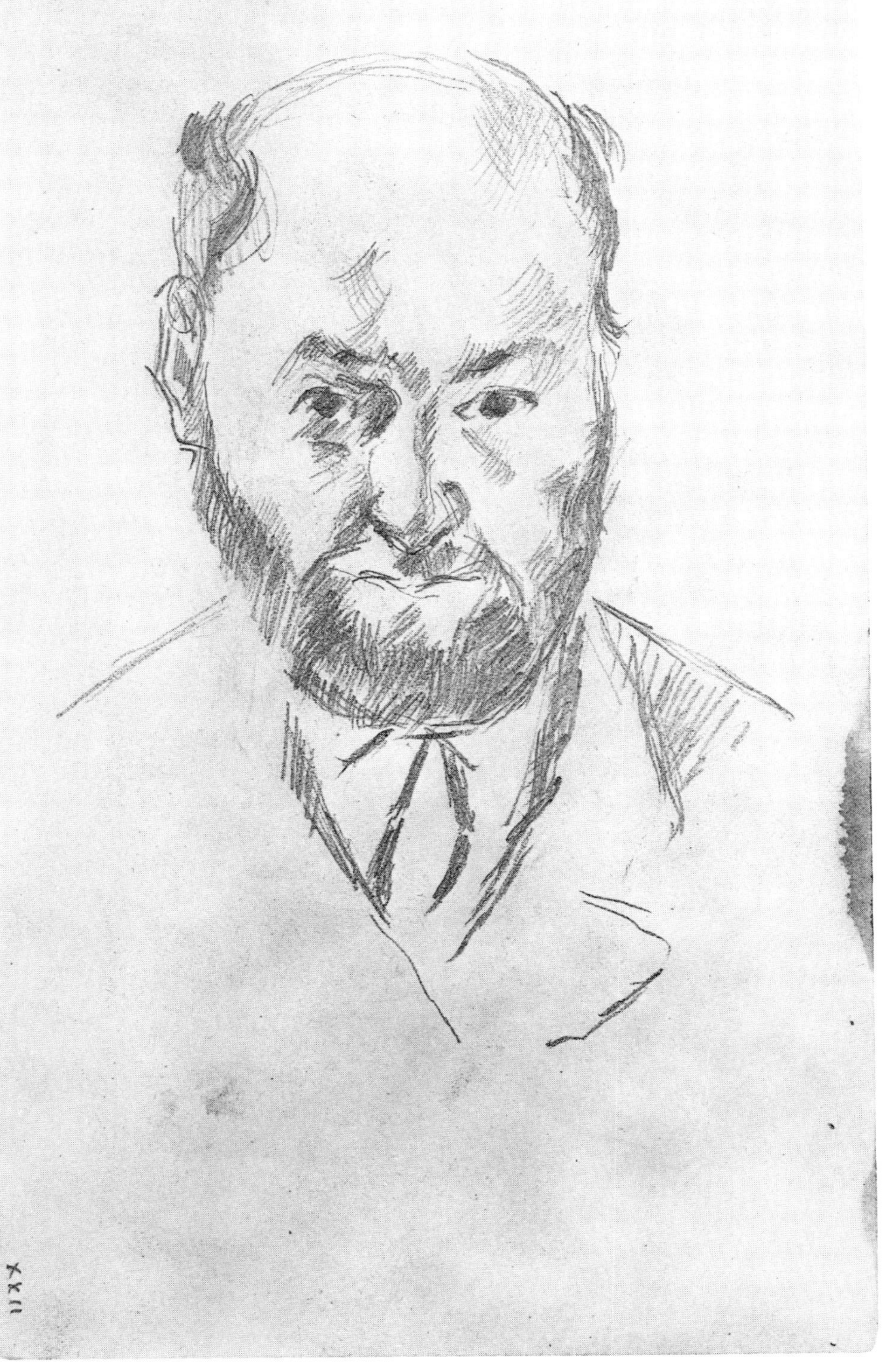
XXII

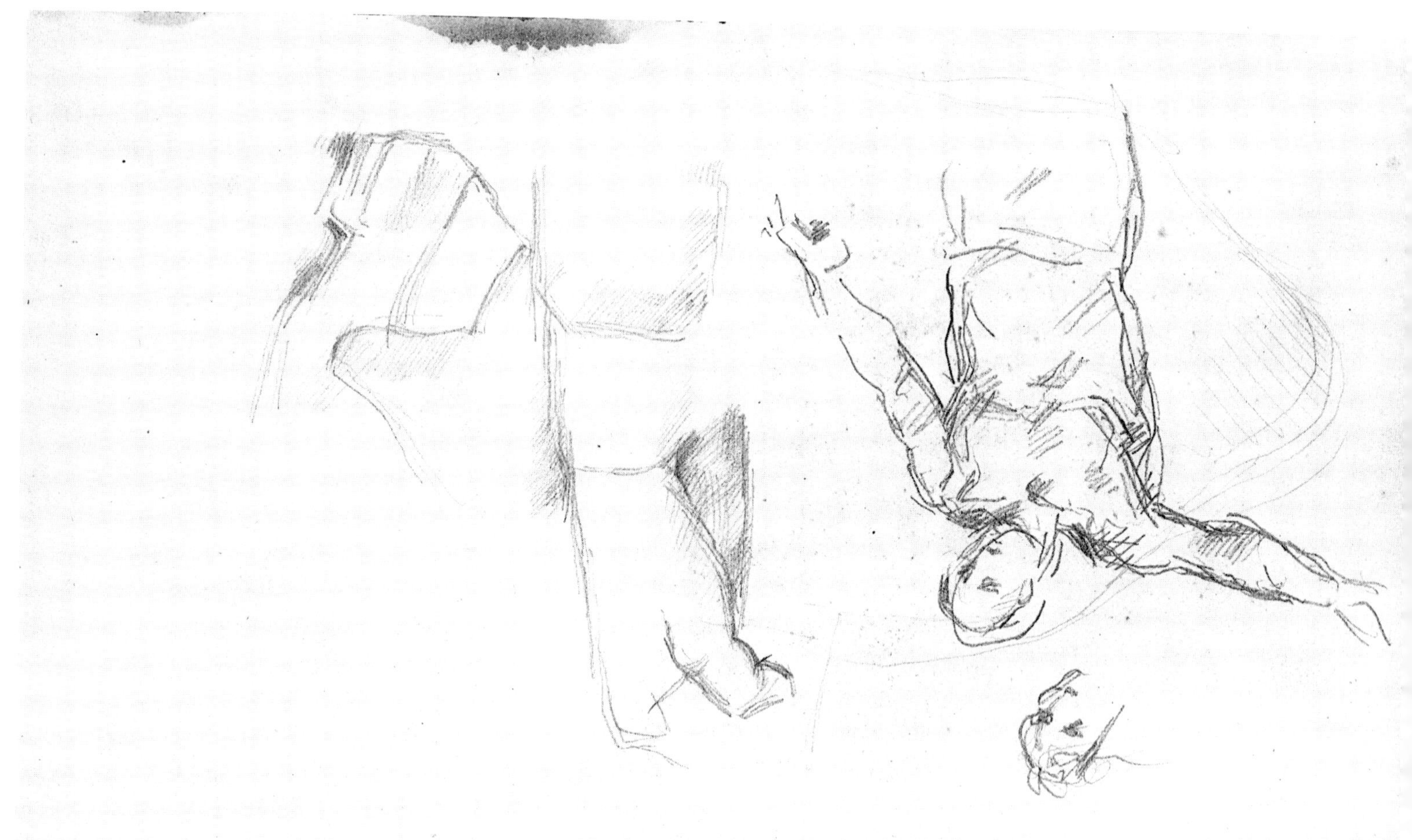

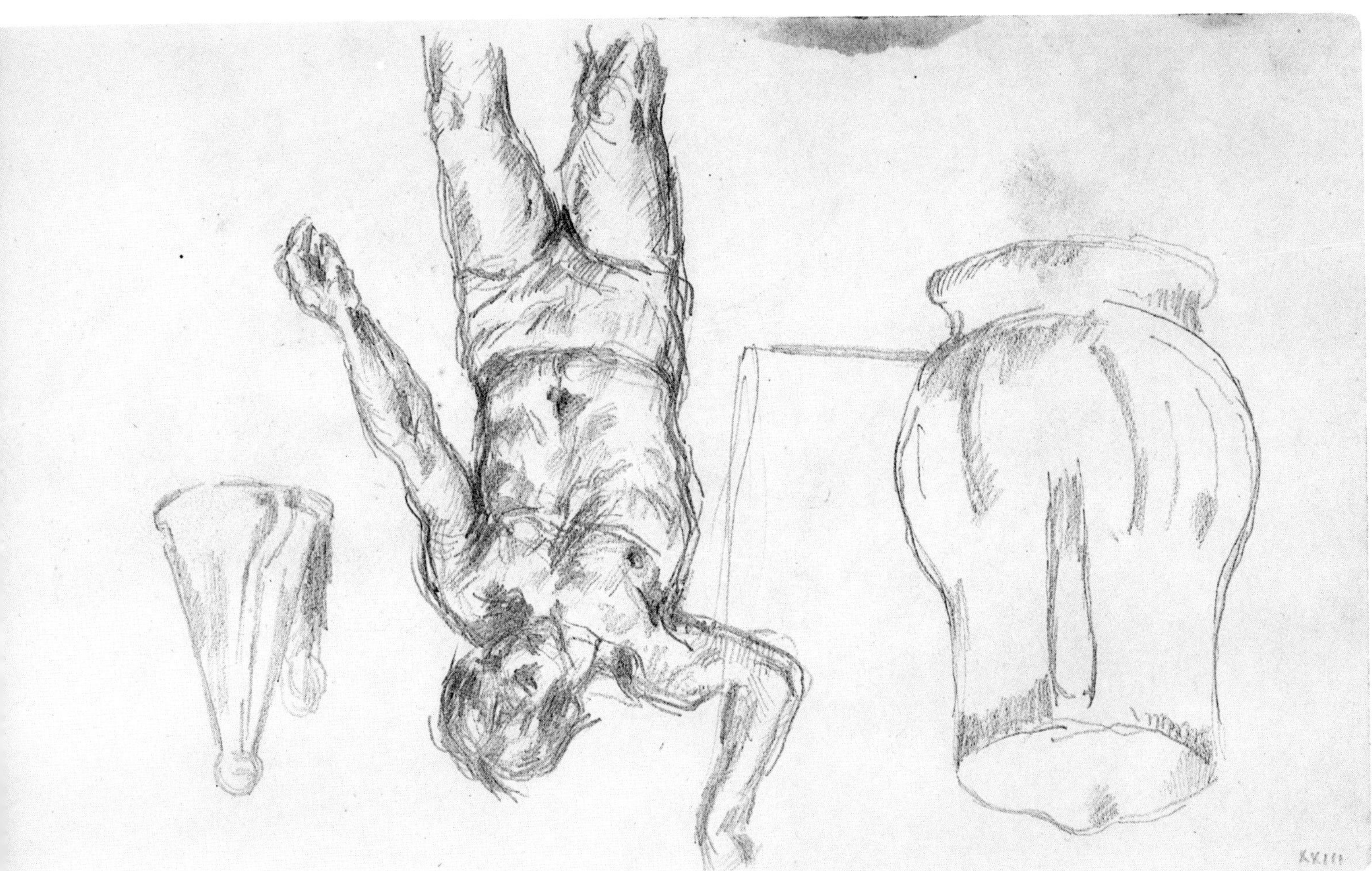
XVIII

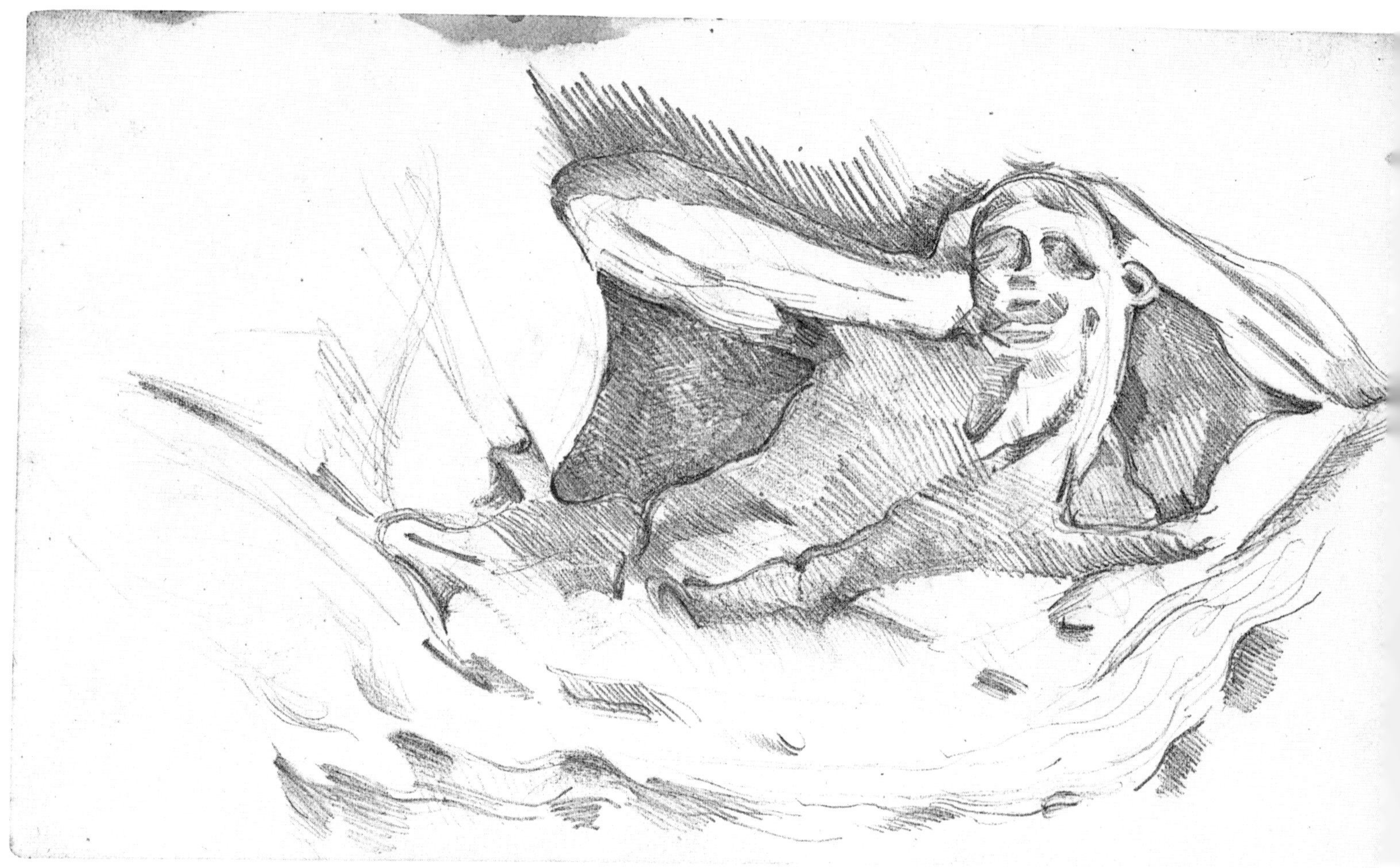

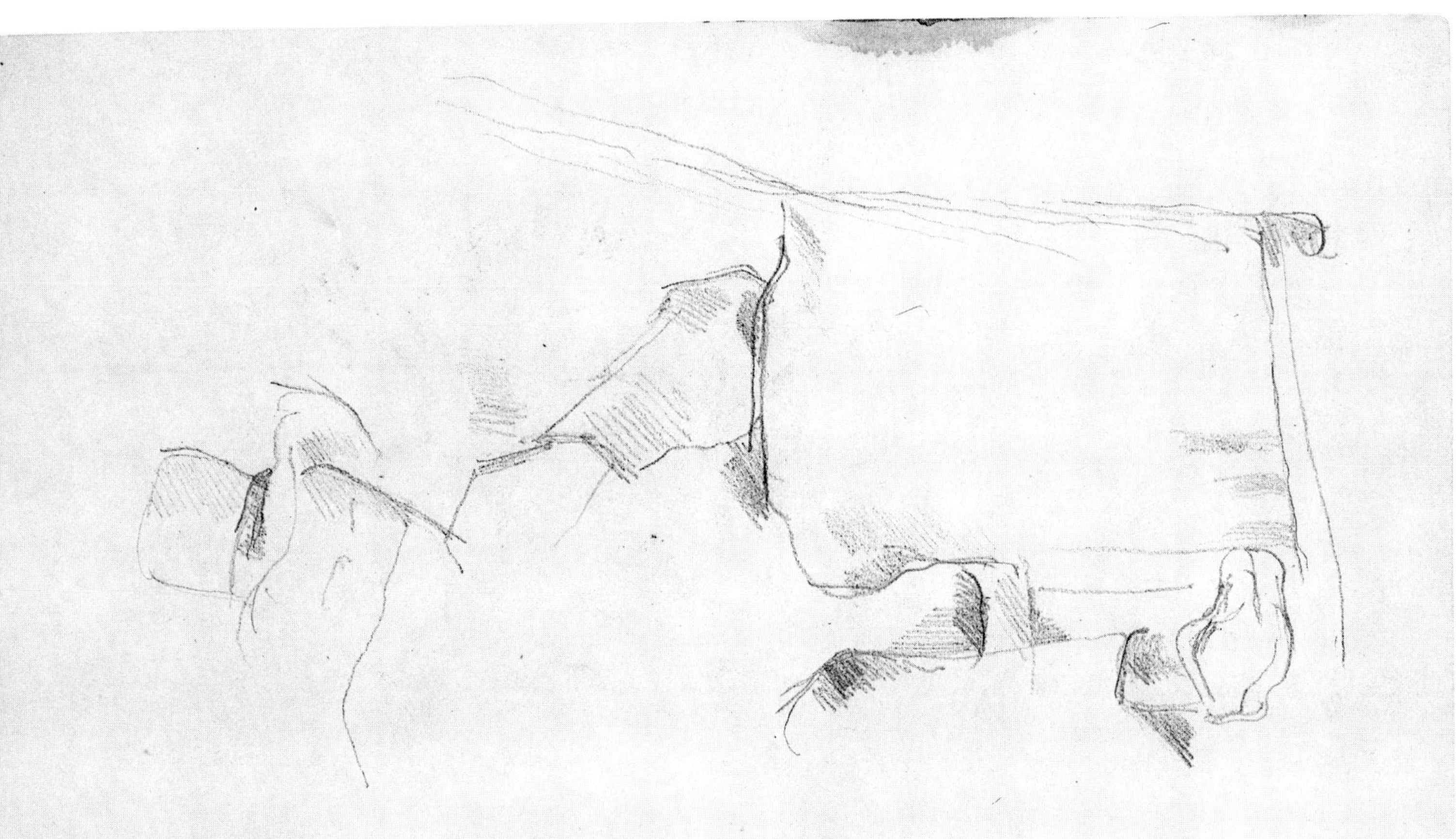

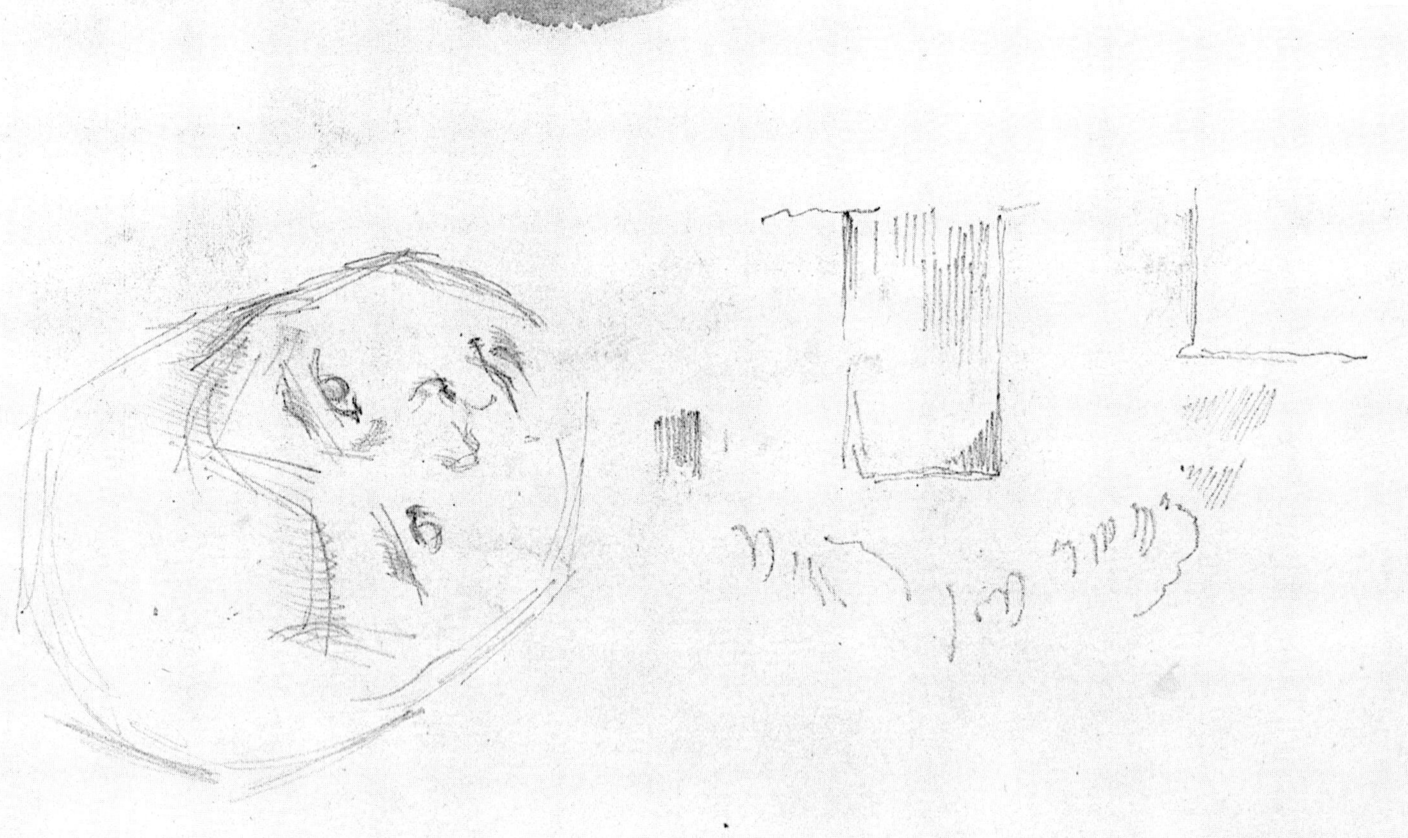

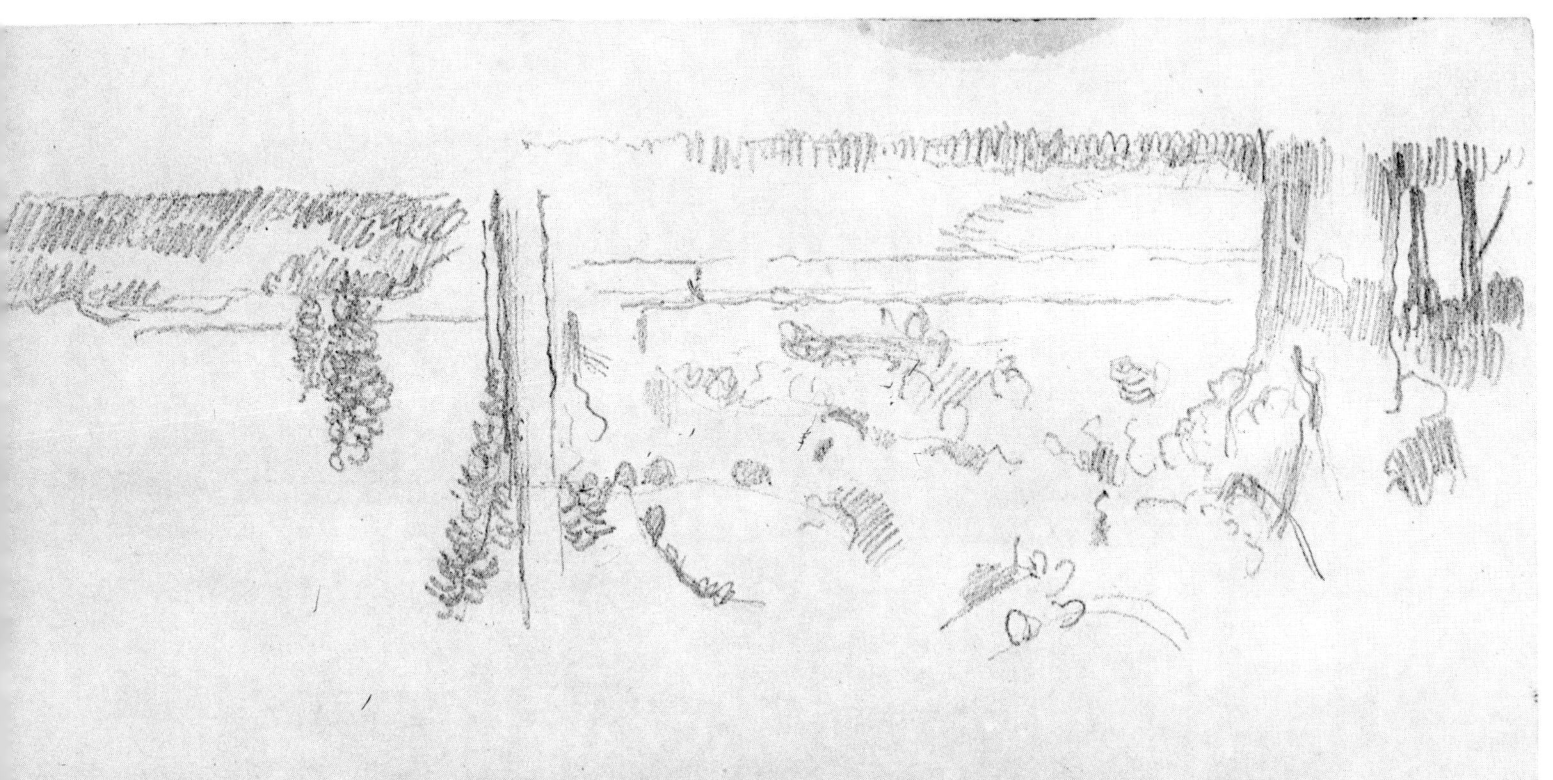

XXV

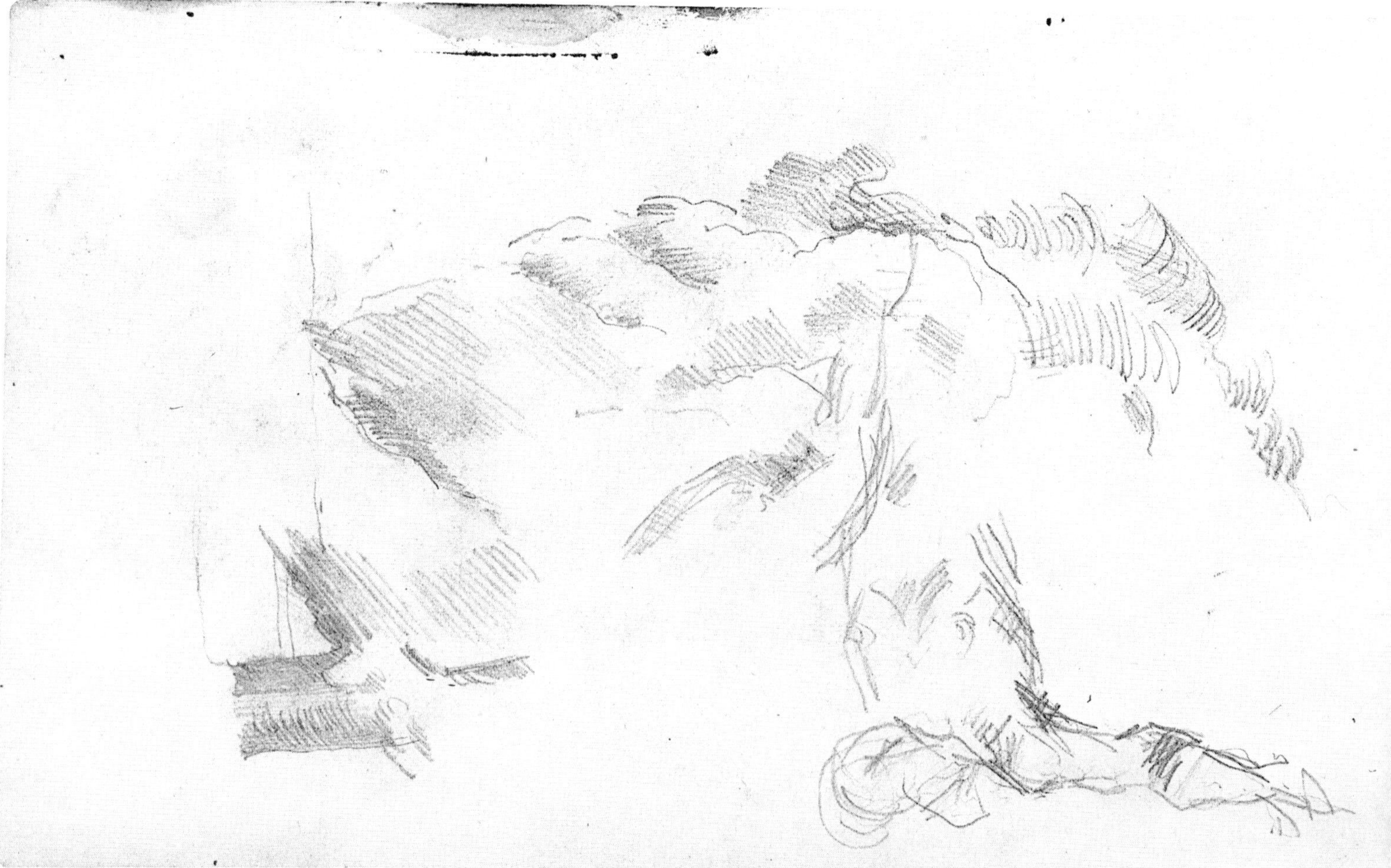

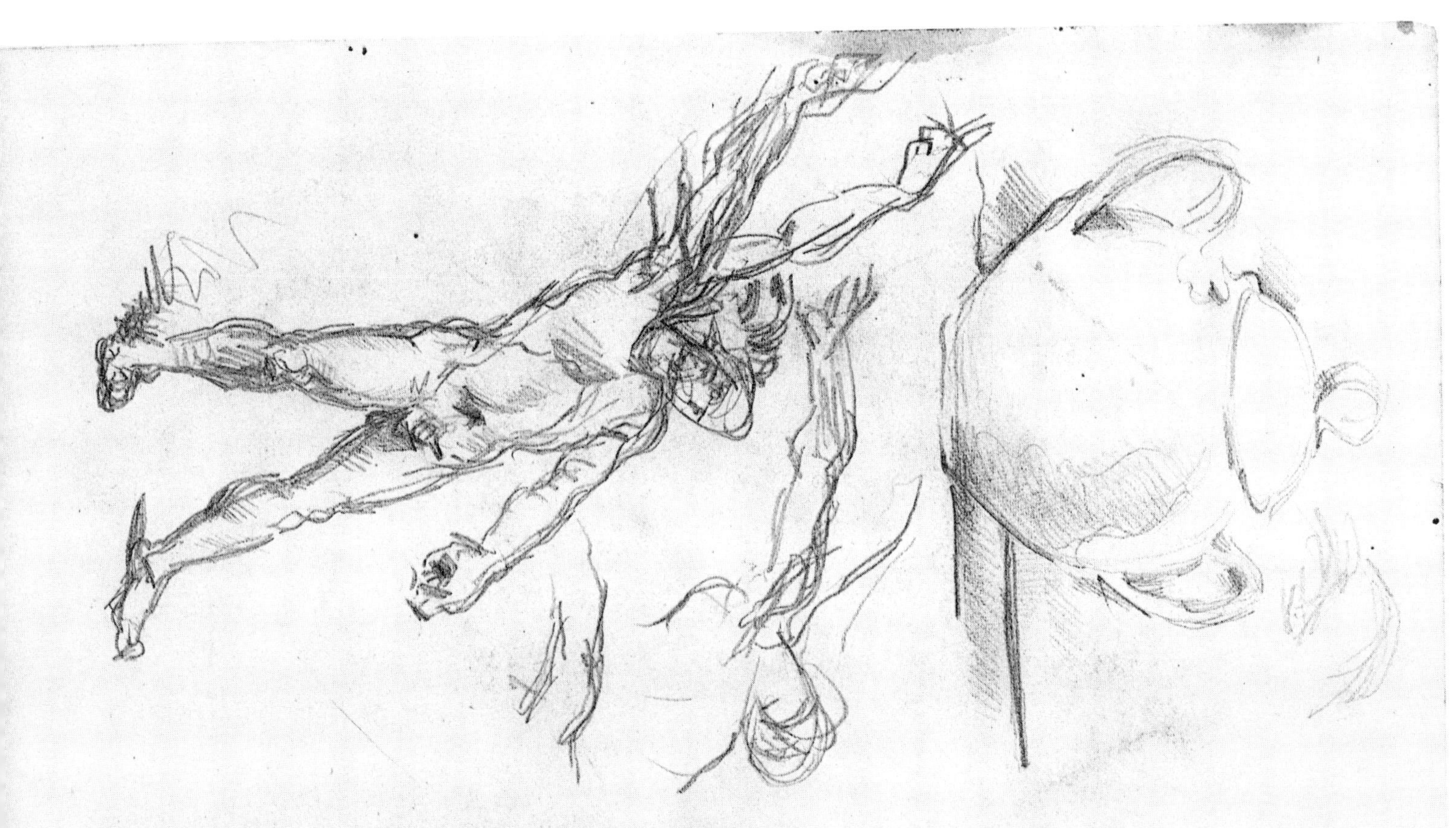

XXVI

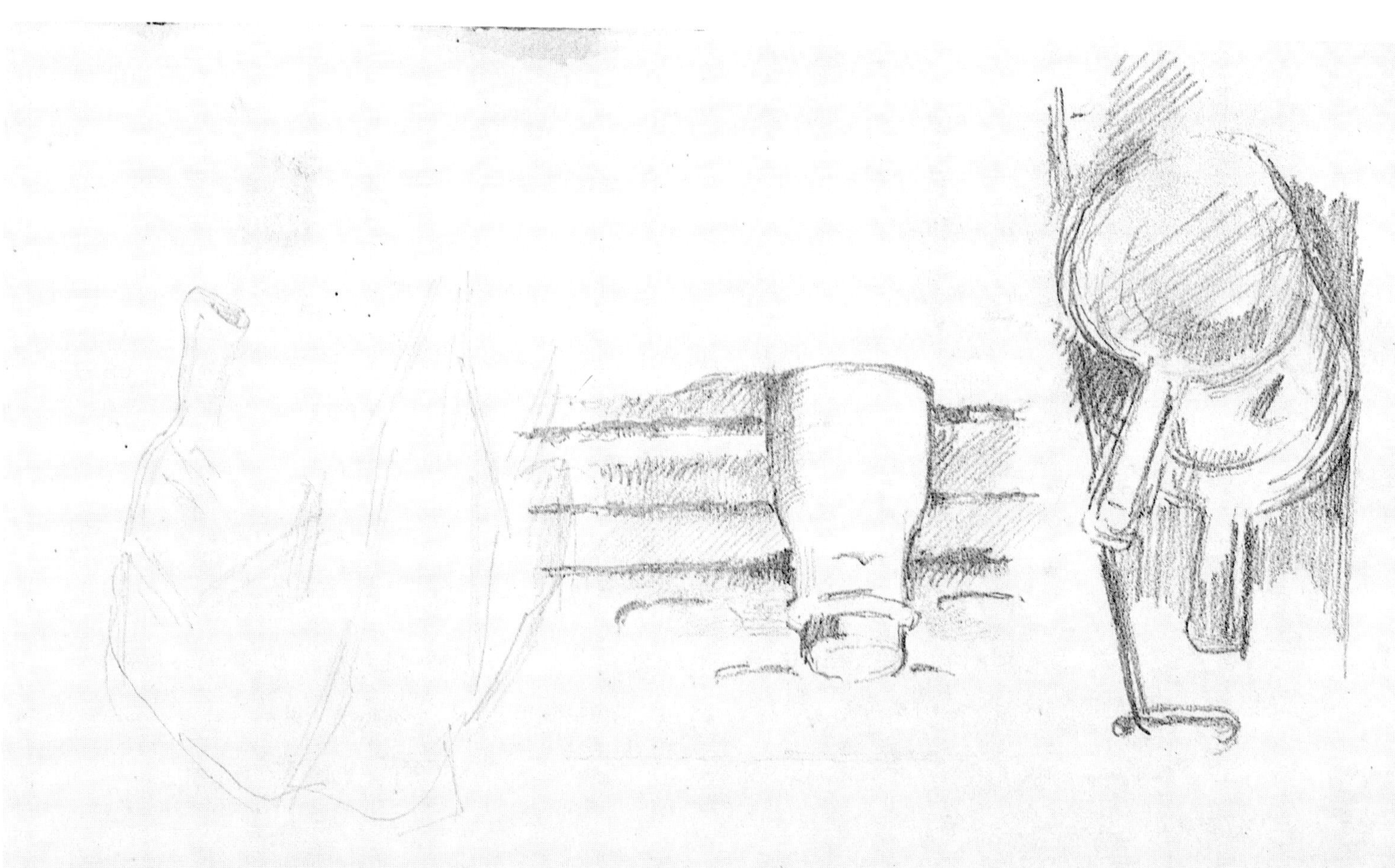

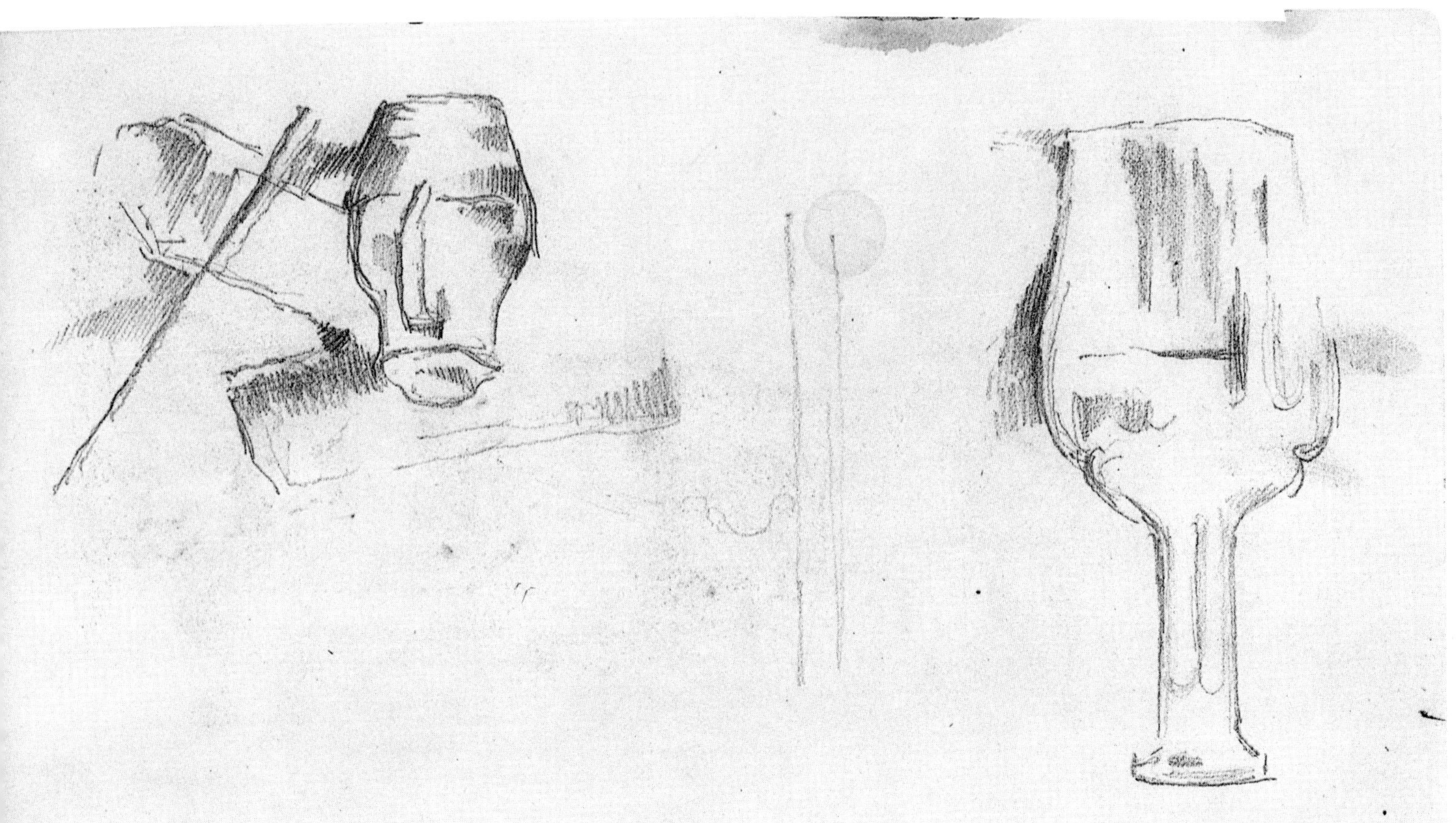

XXVII

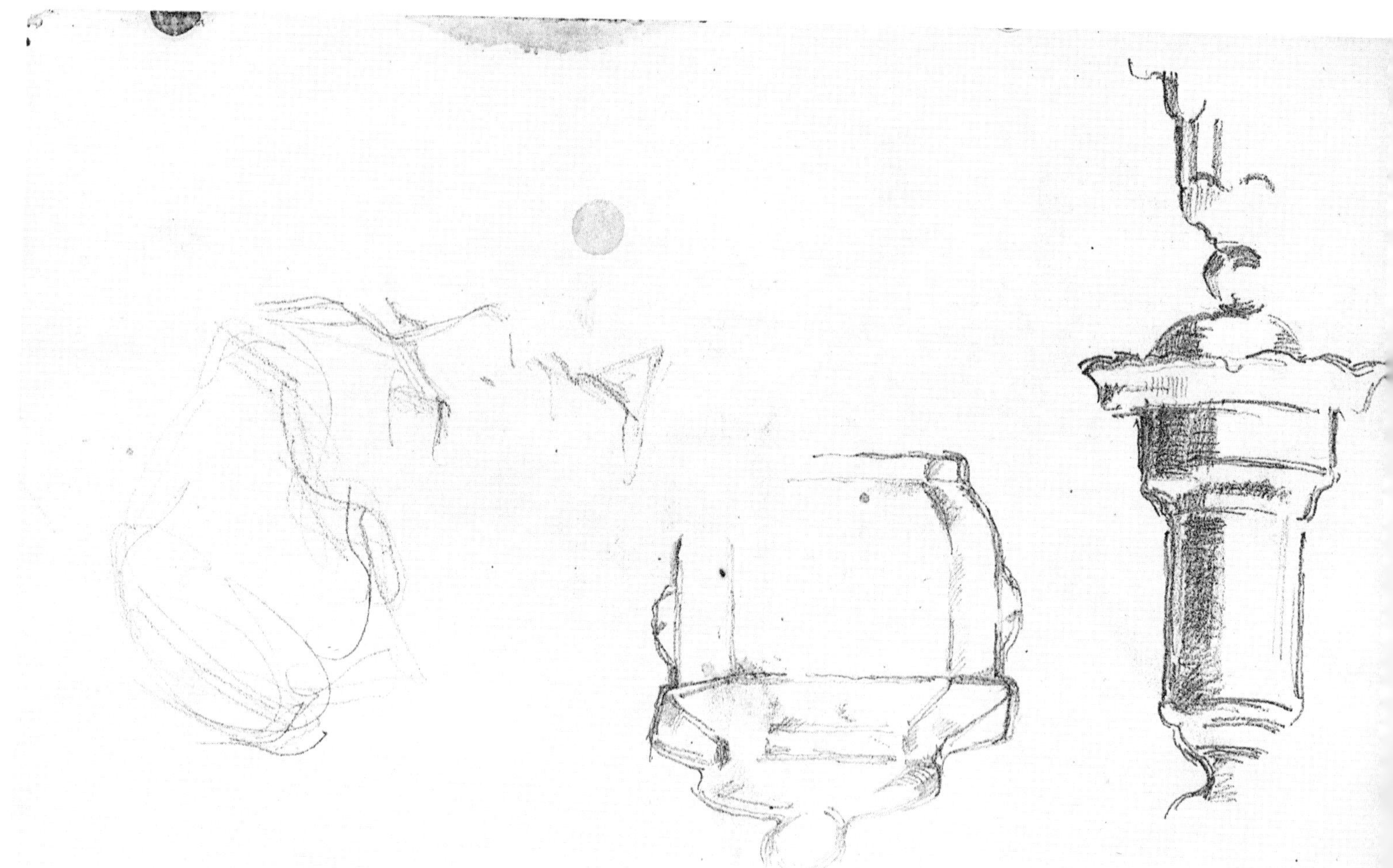

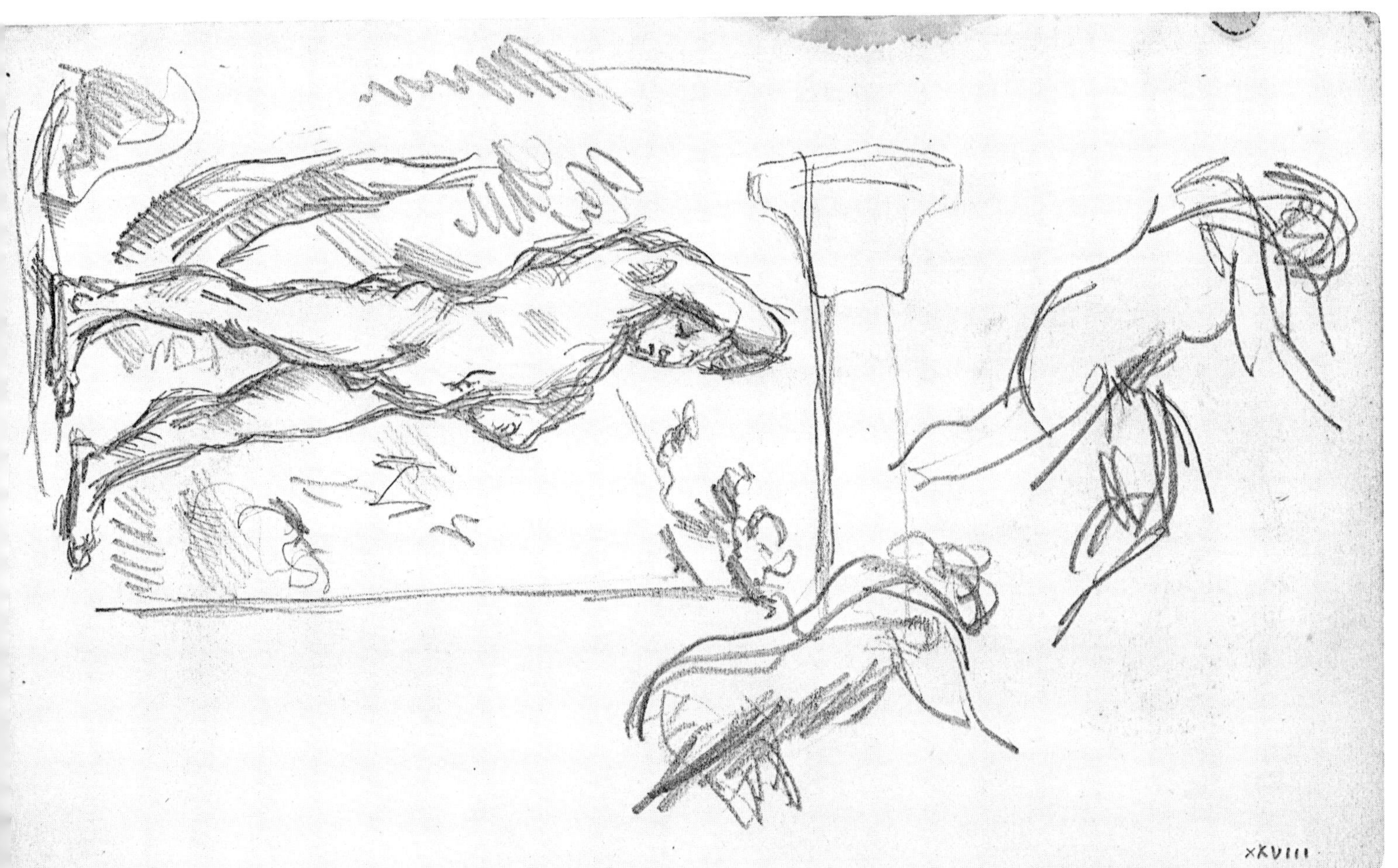

XVIII

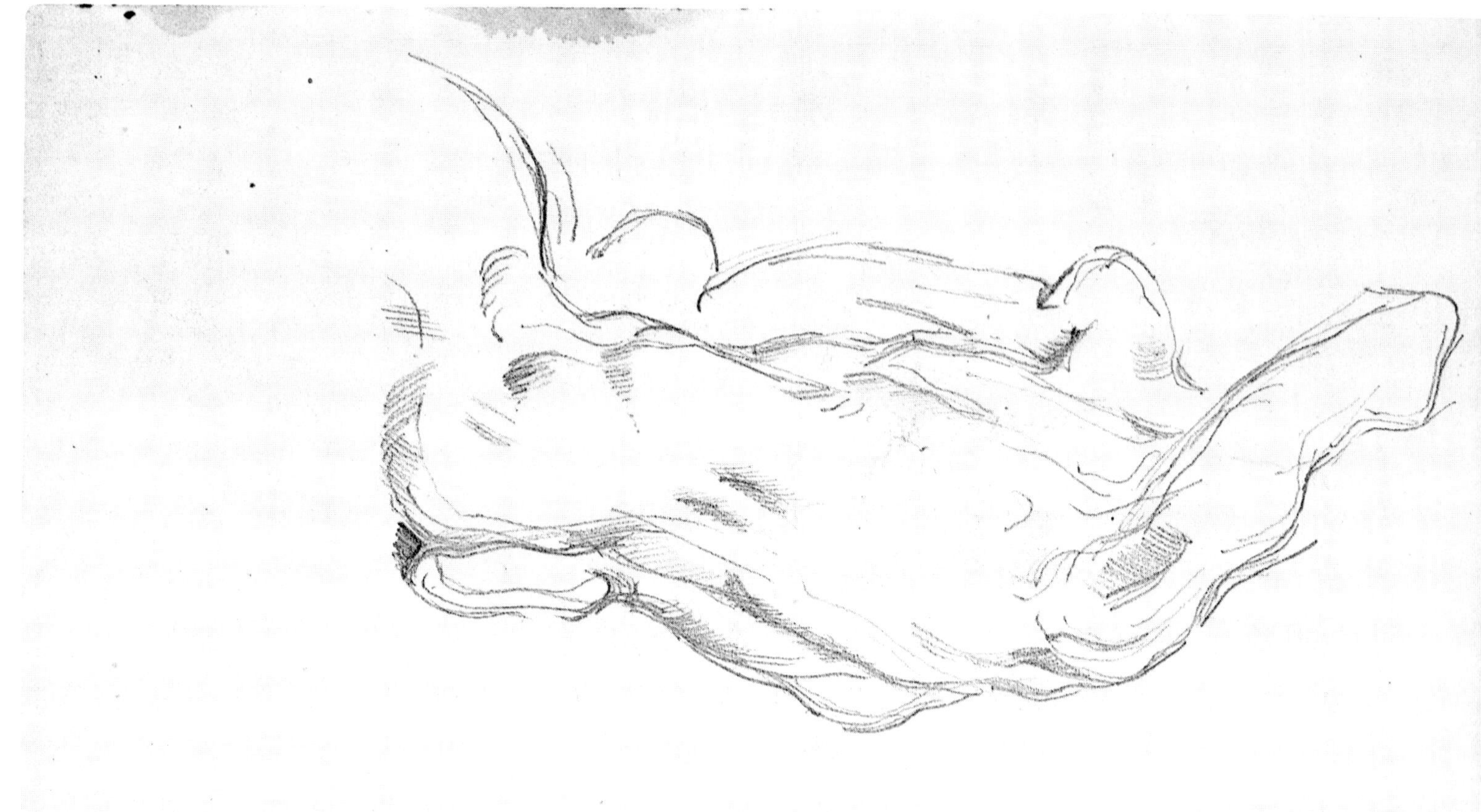

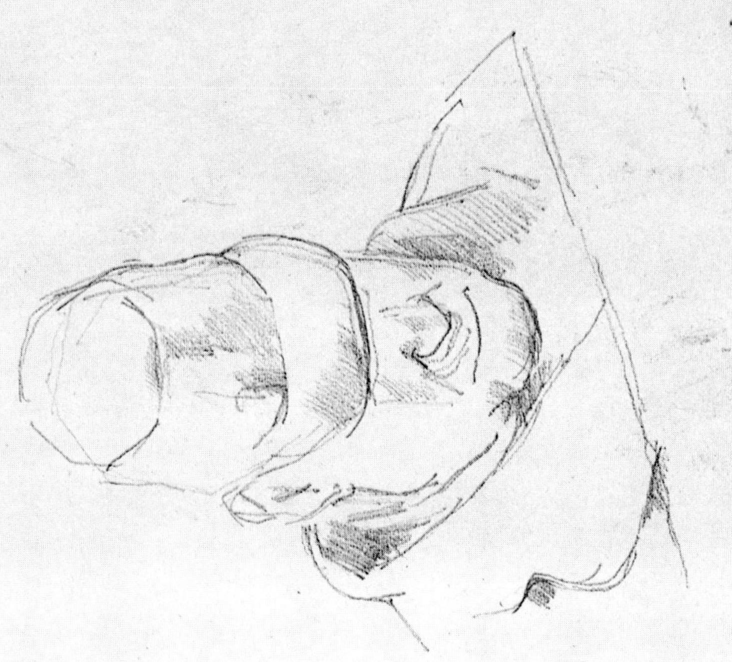

XXIX

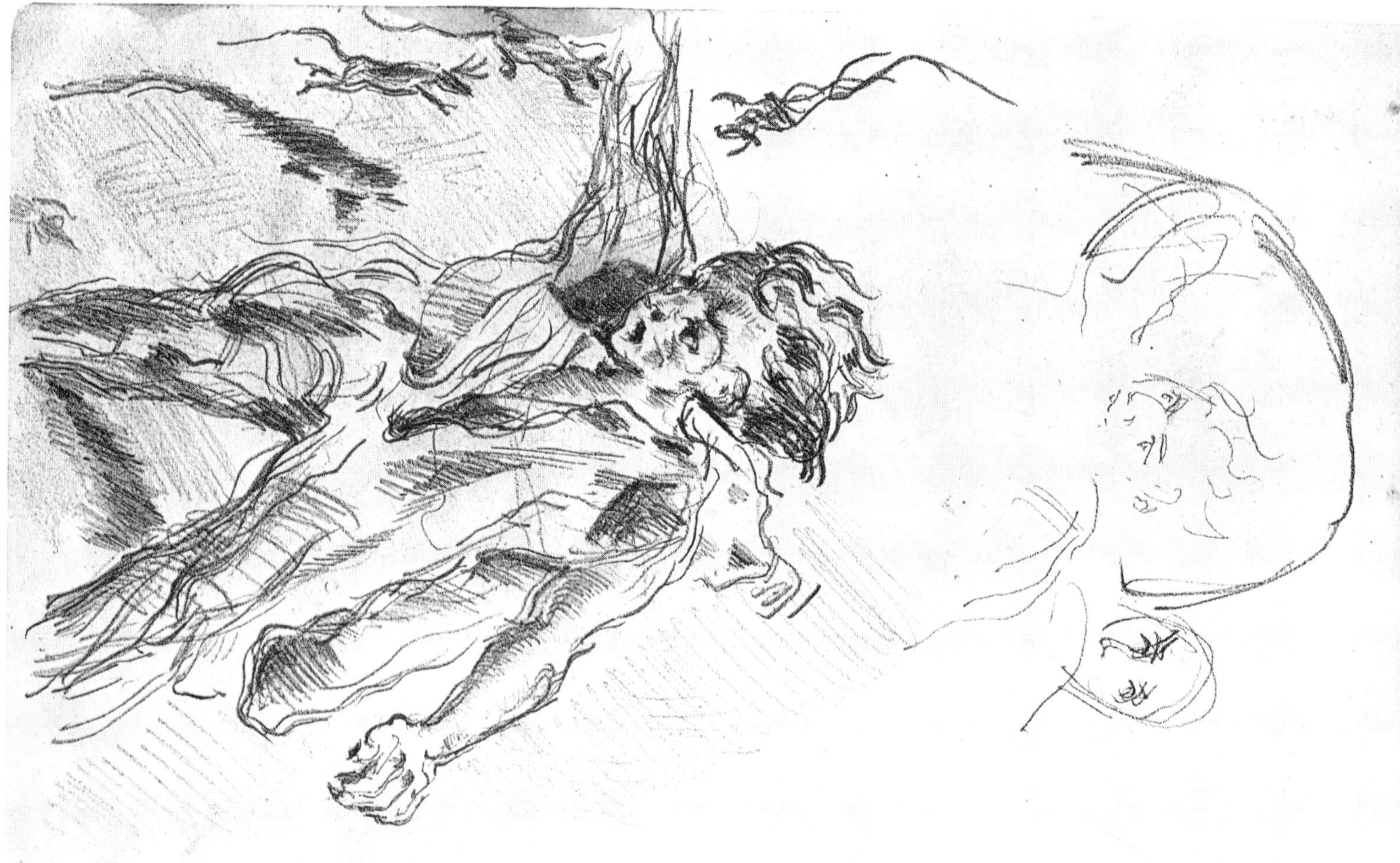

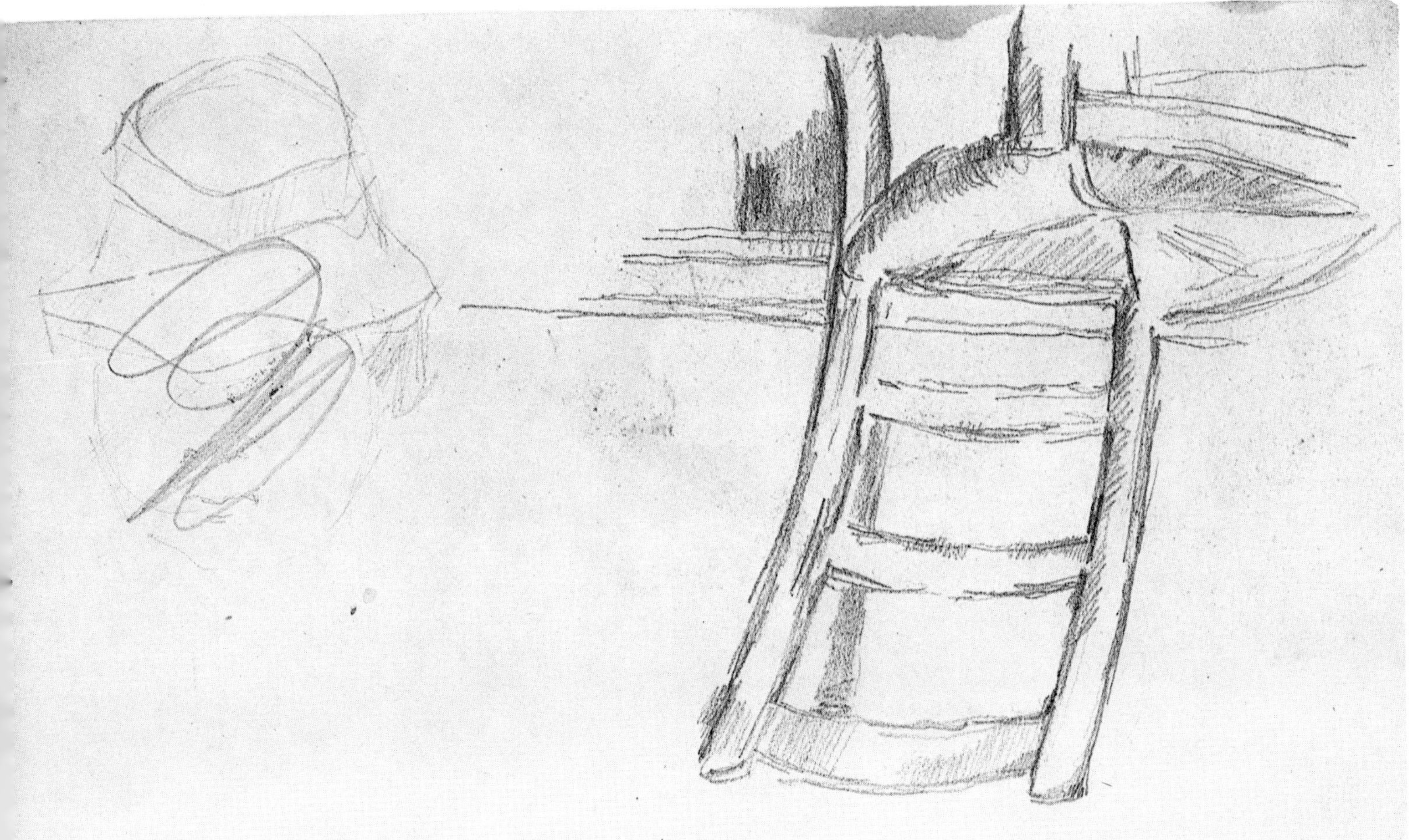

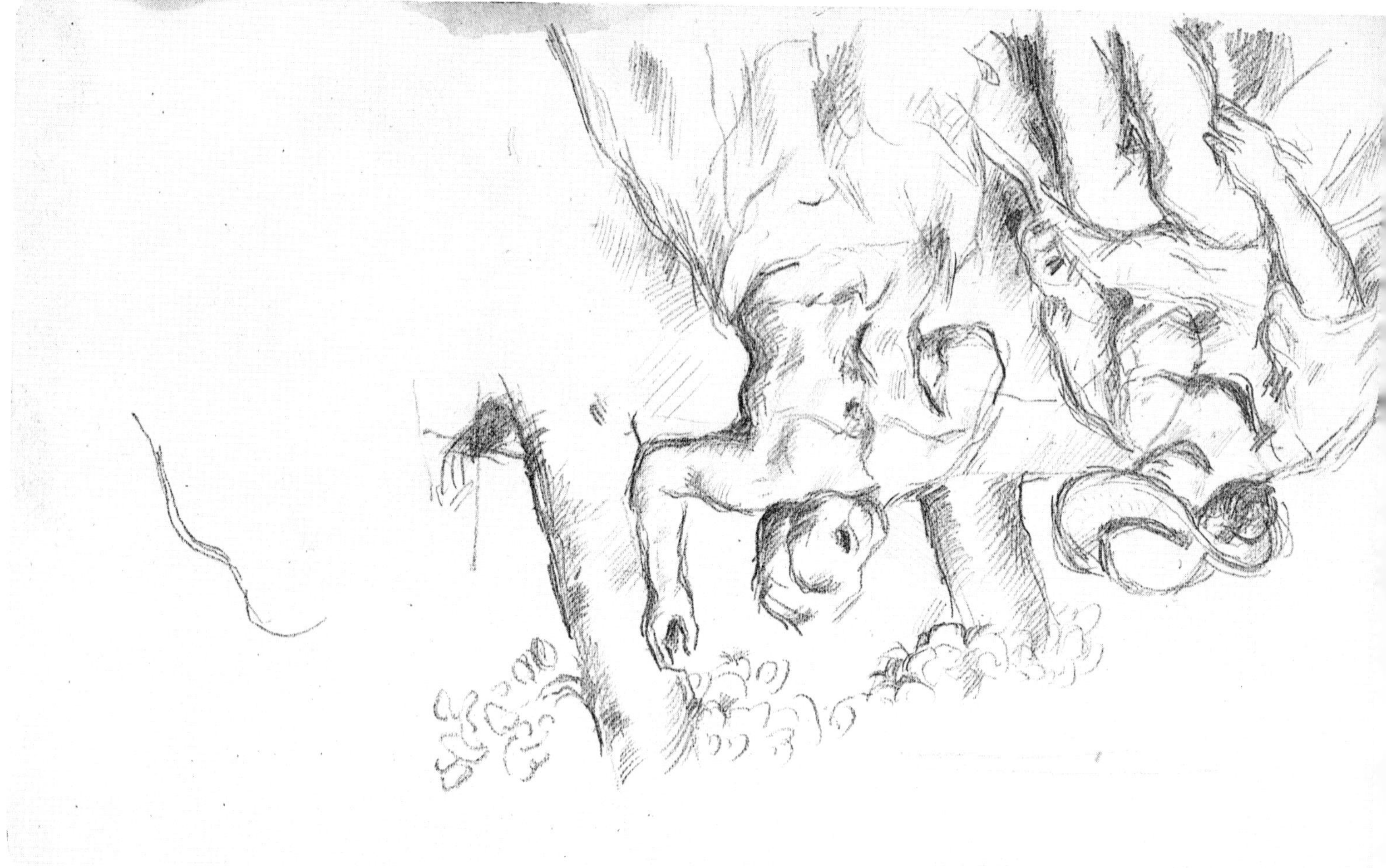

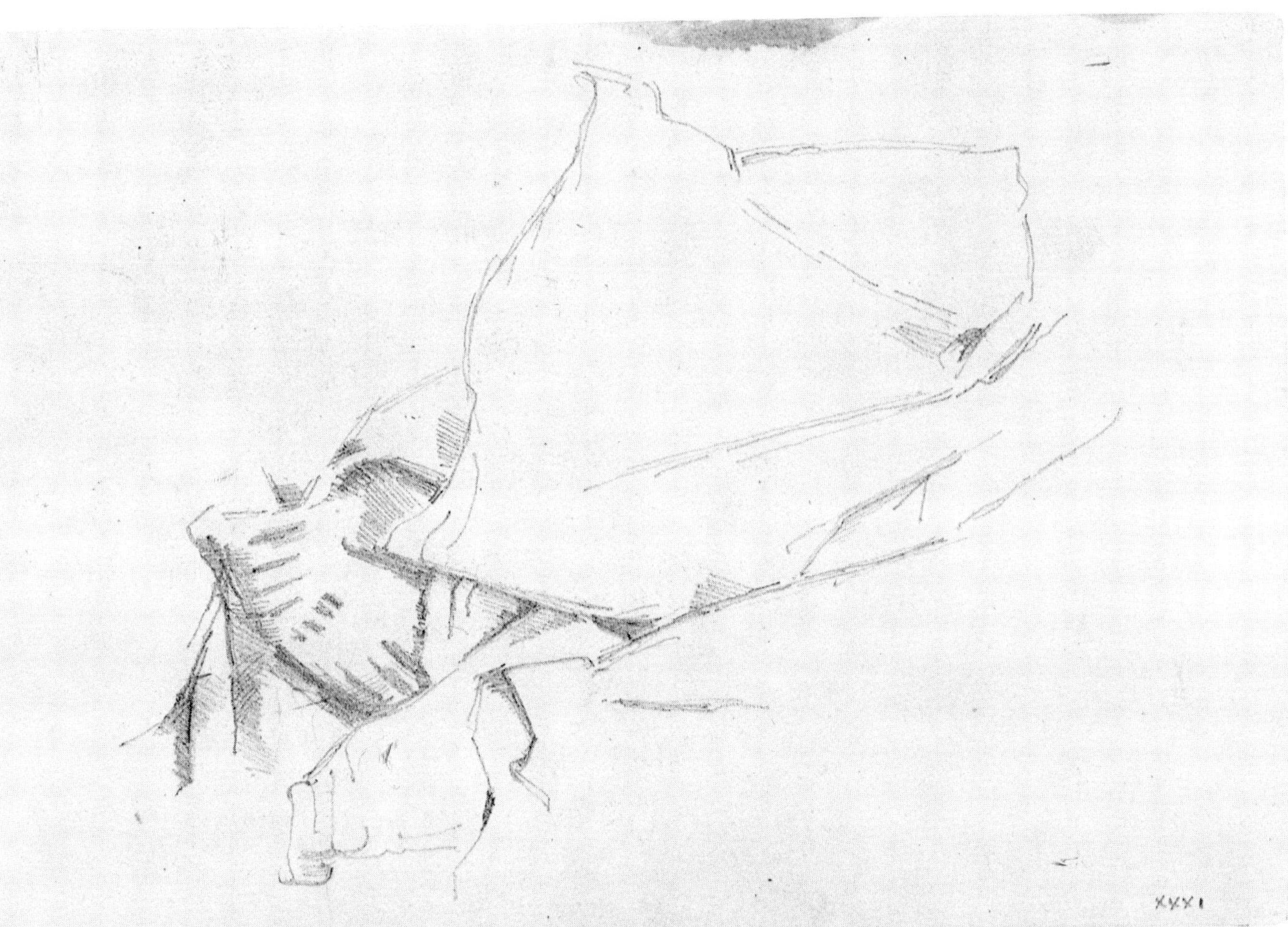
XXXI

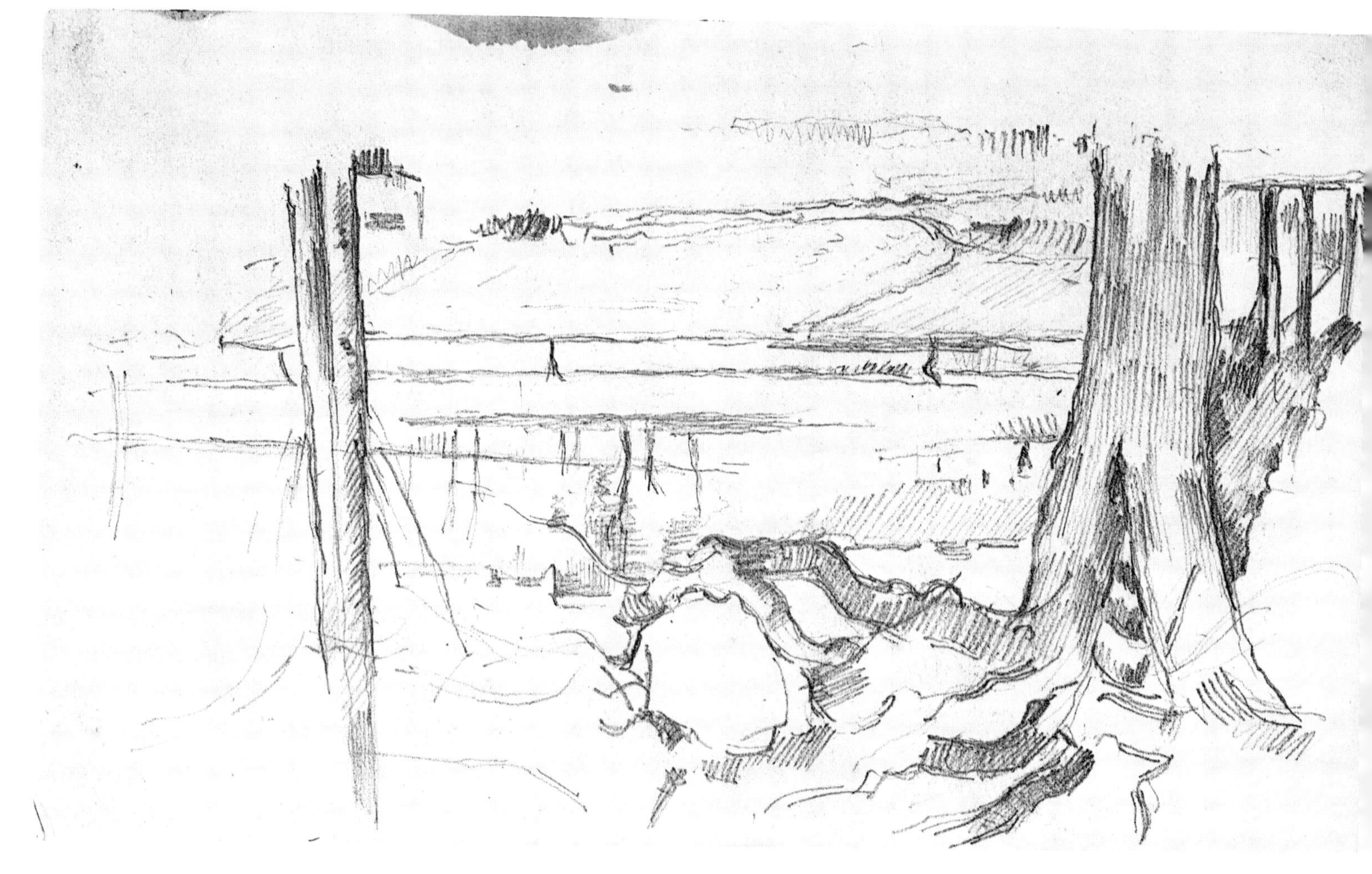

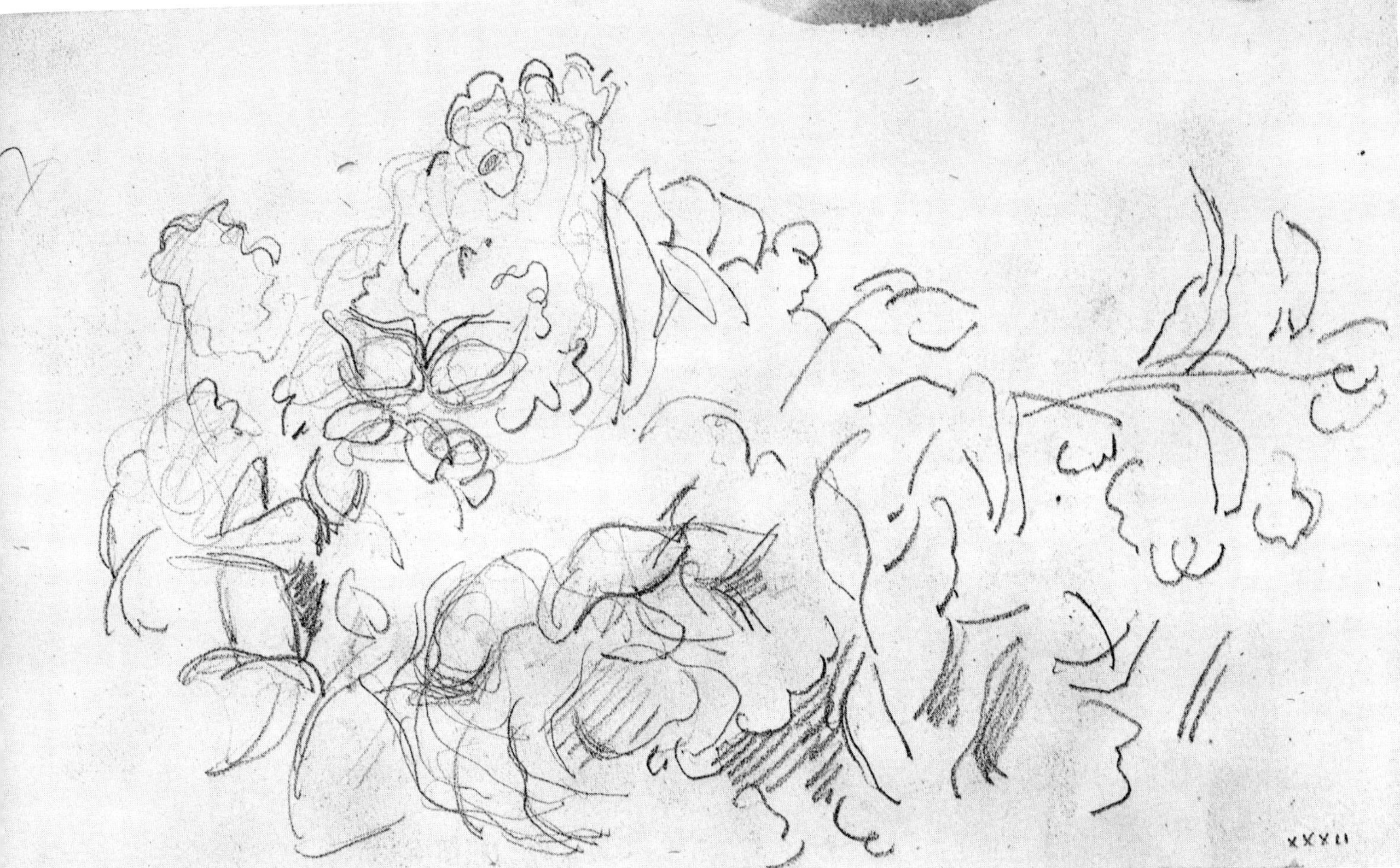
XXXII

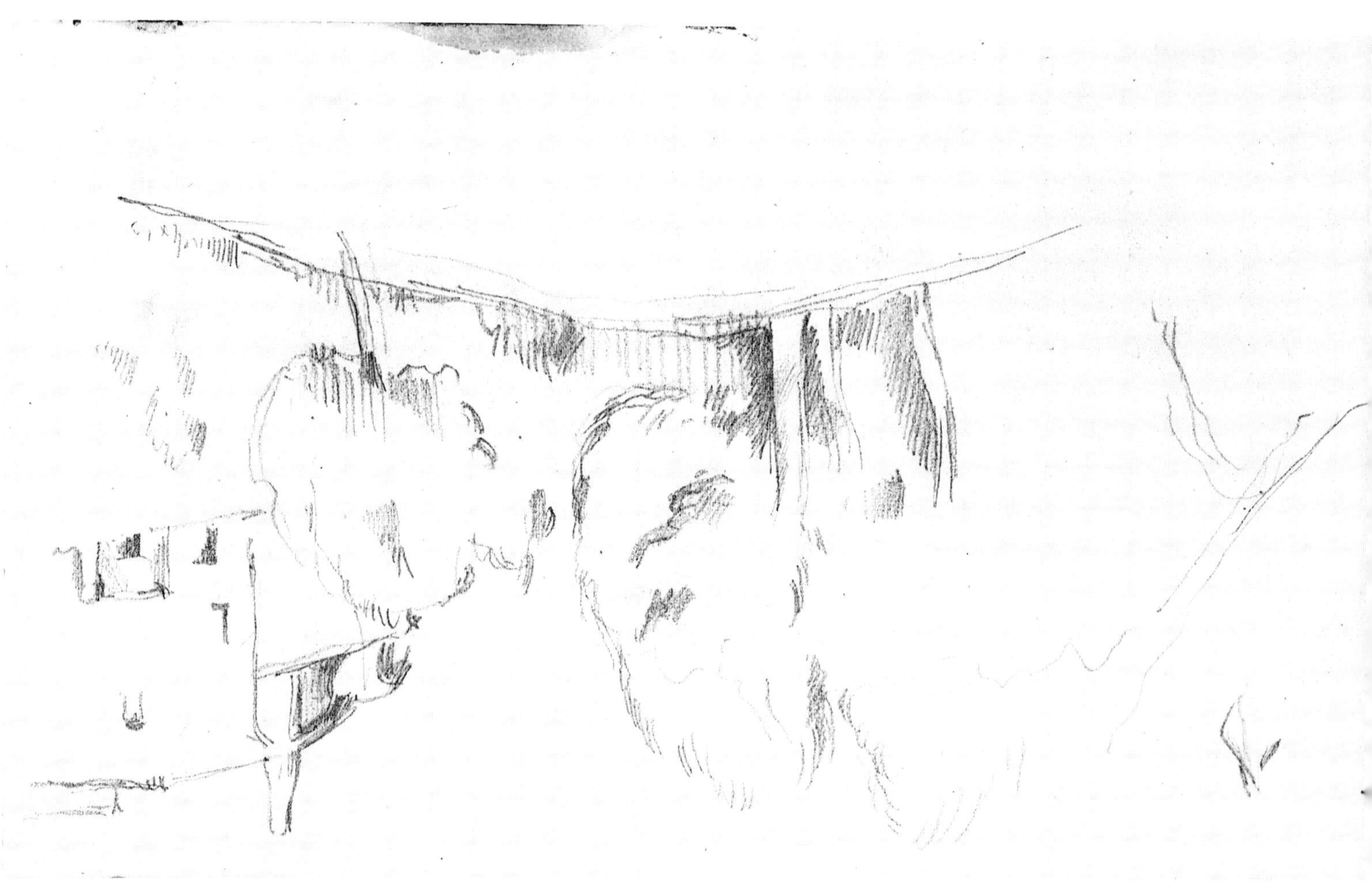

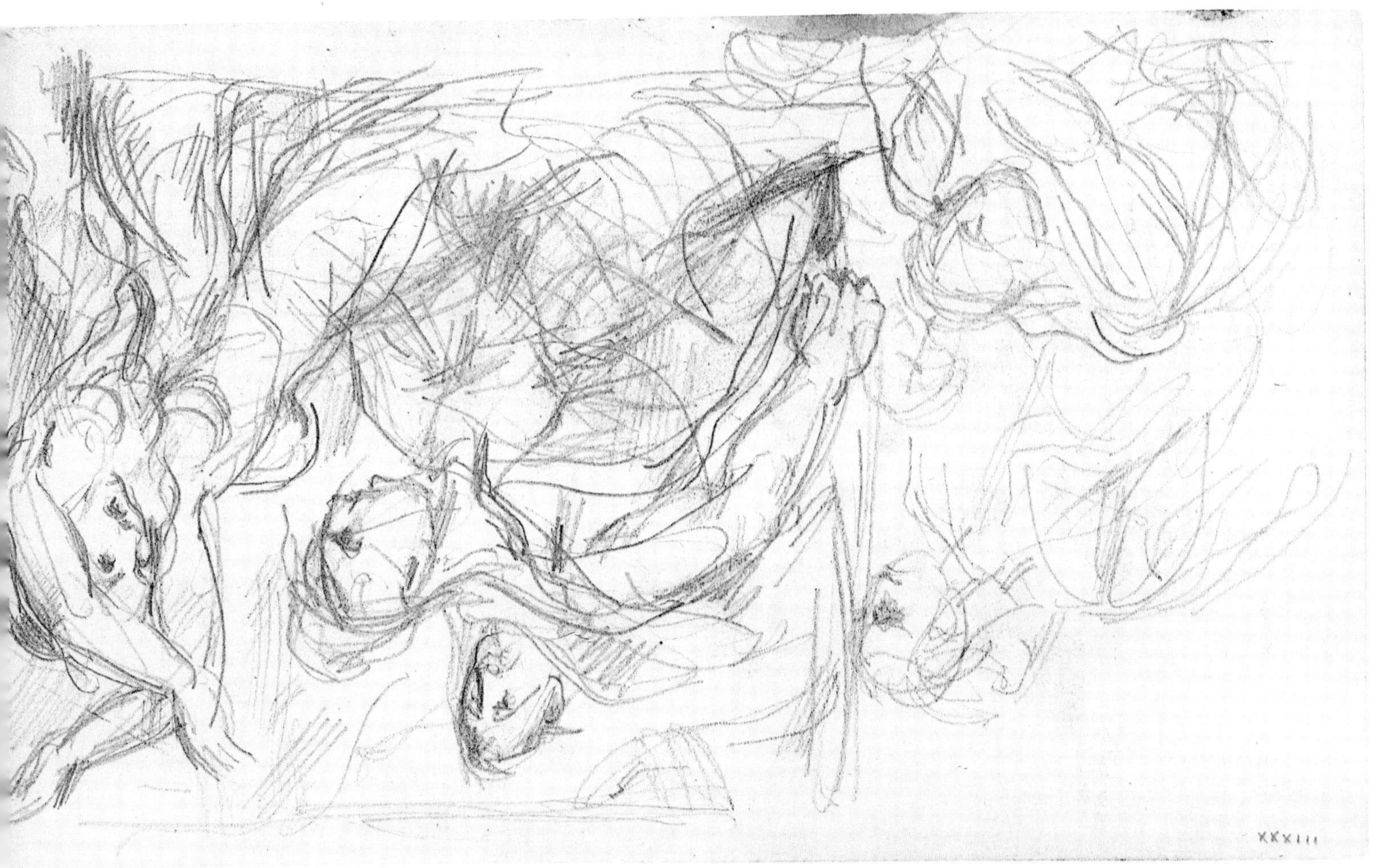

XXXIII

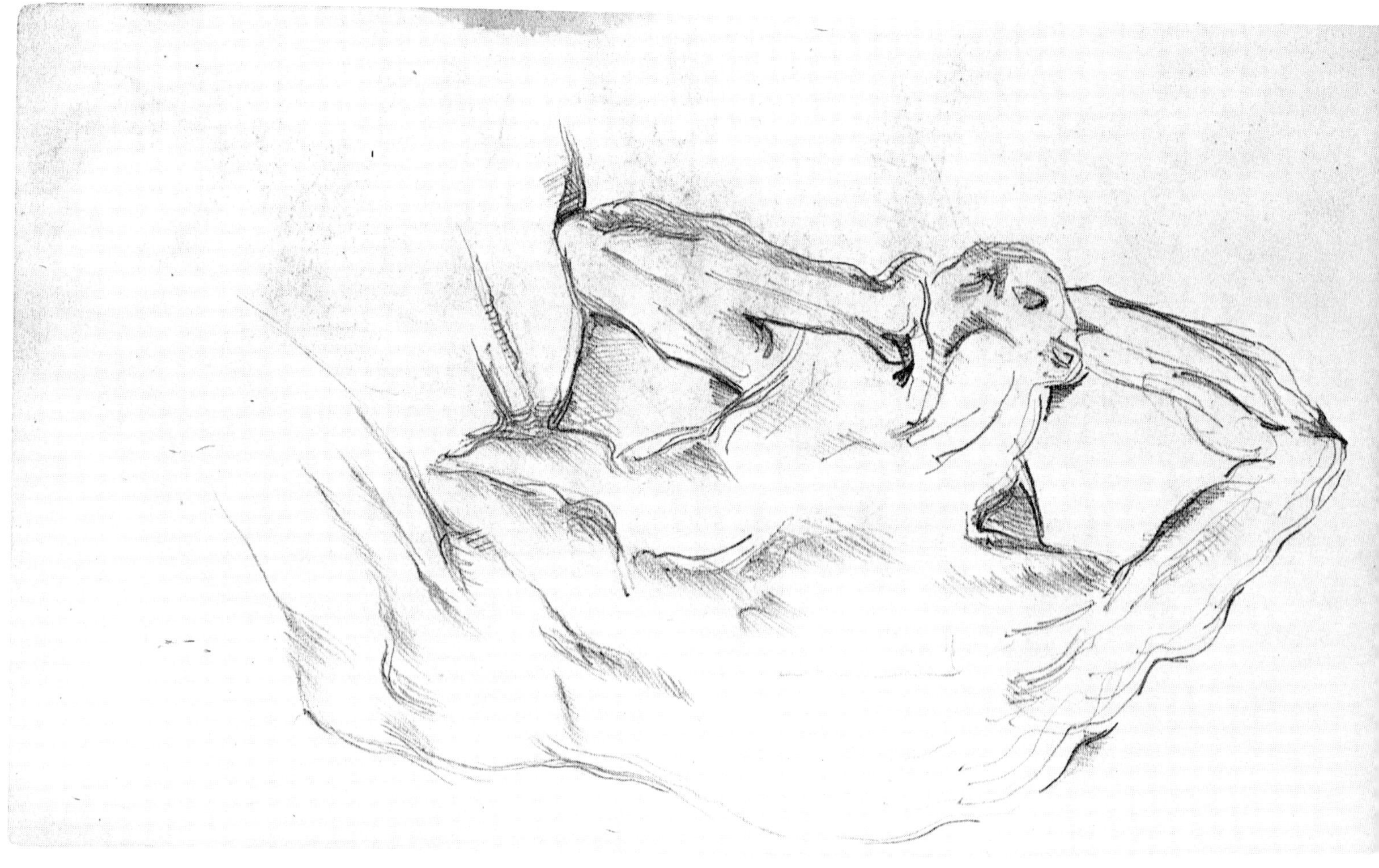

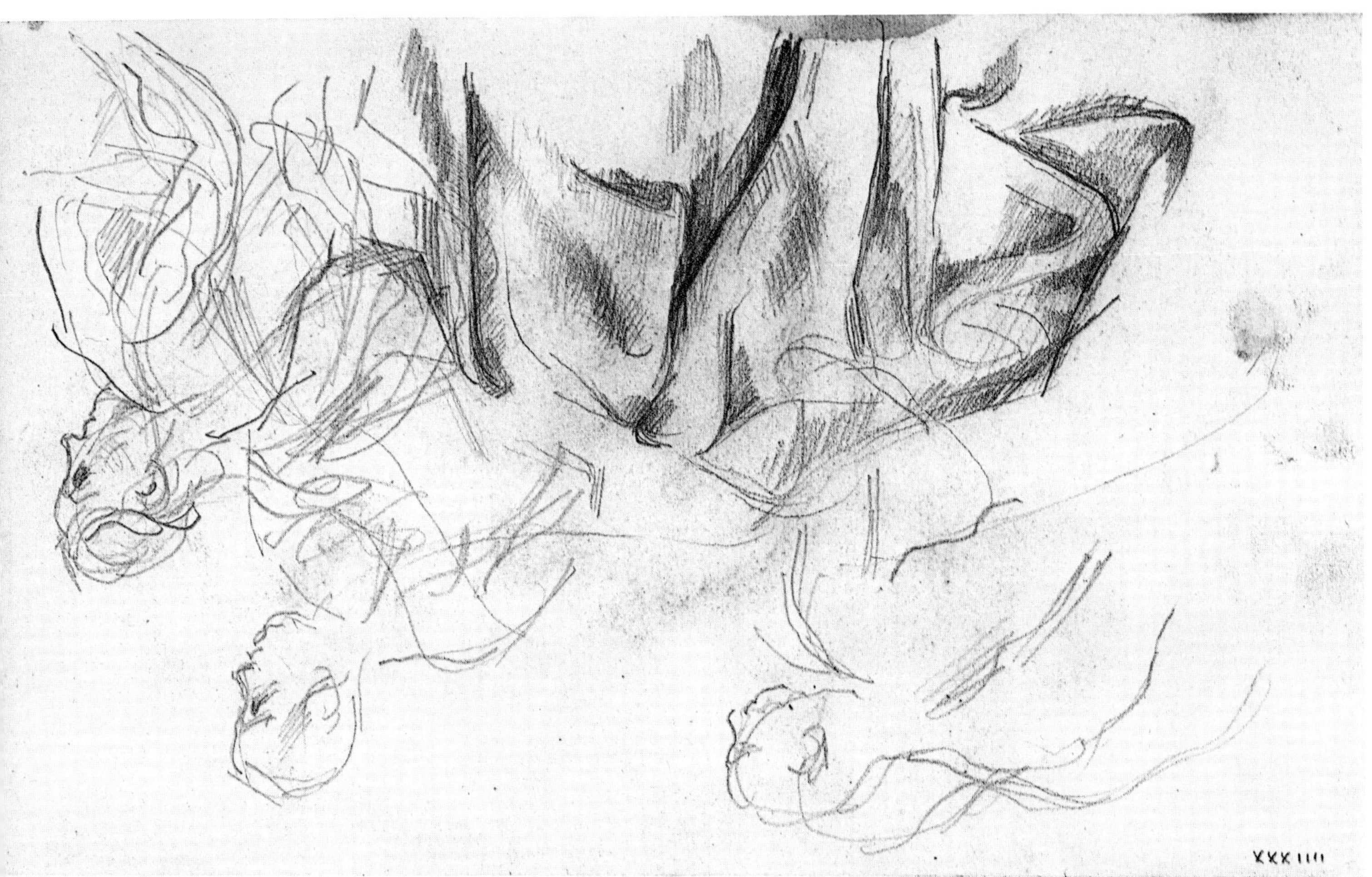

XXXIIII

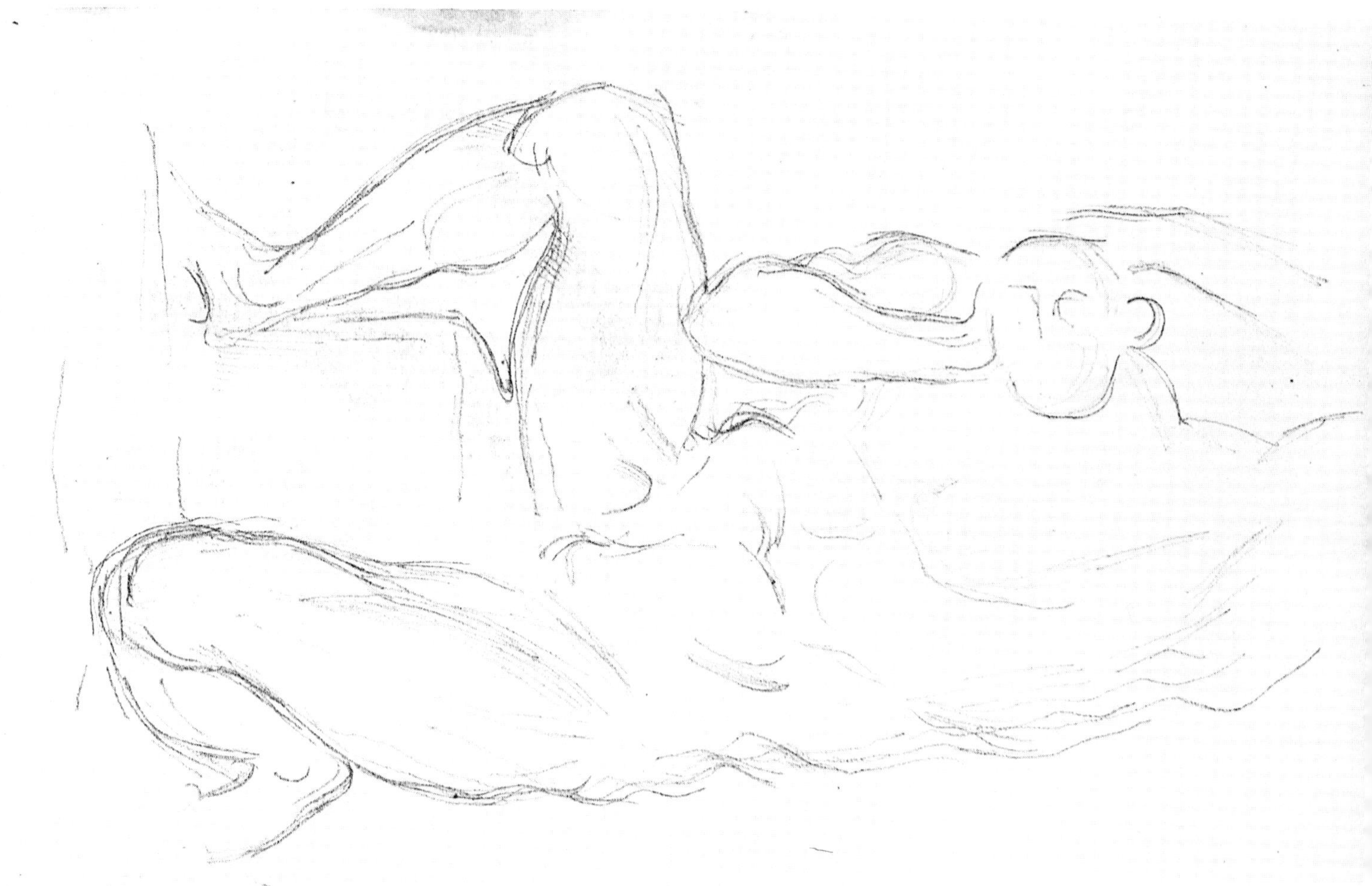

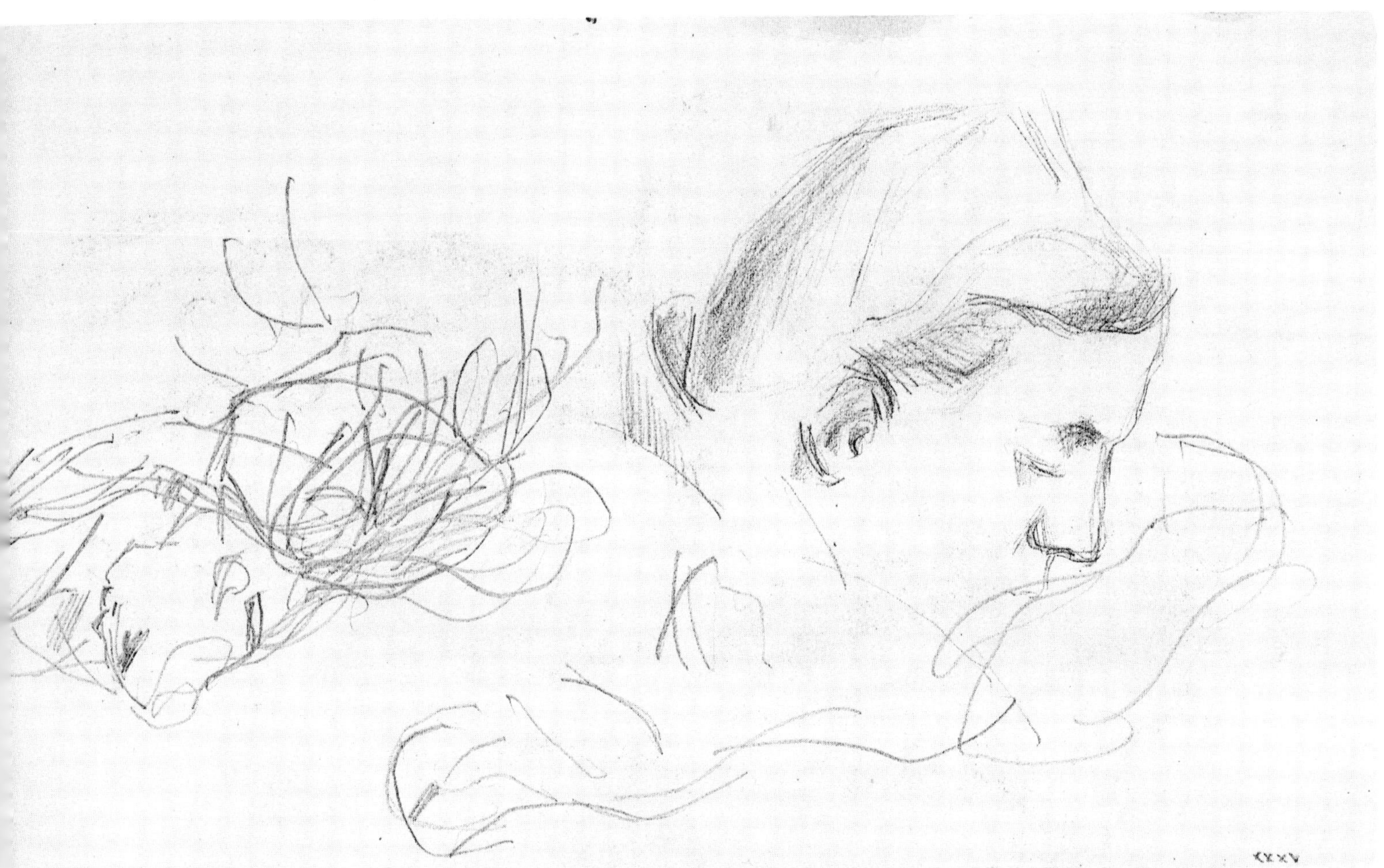

XXXV

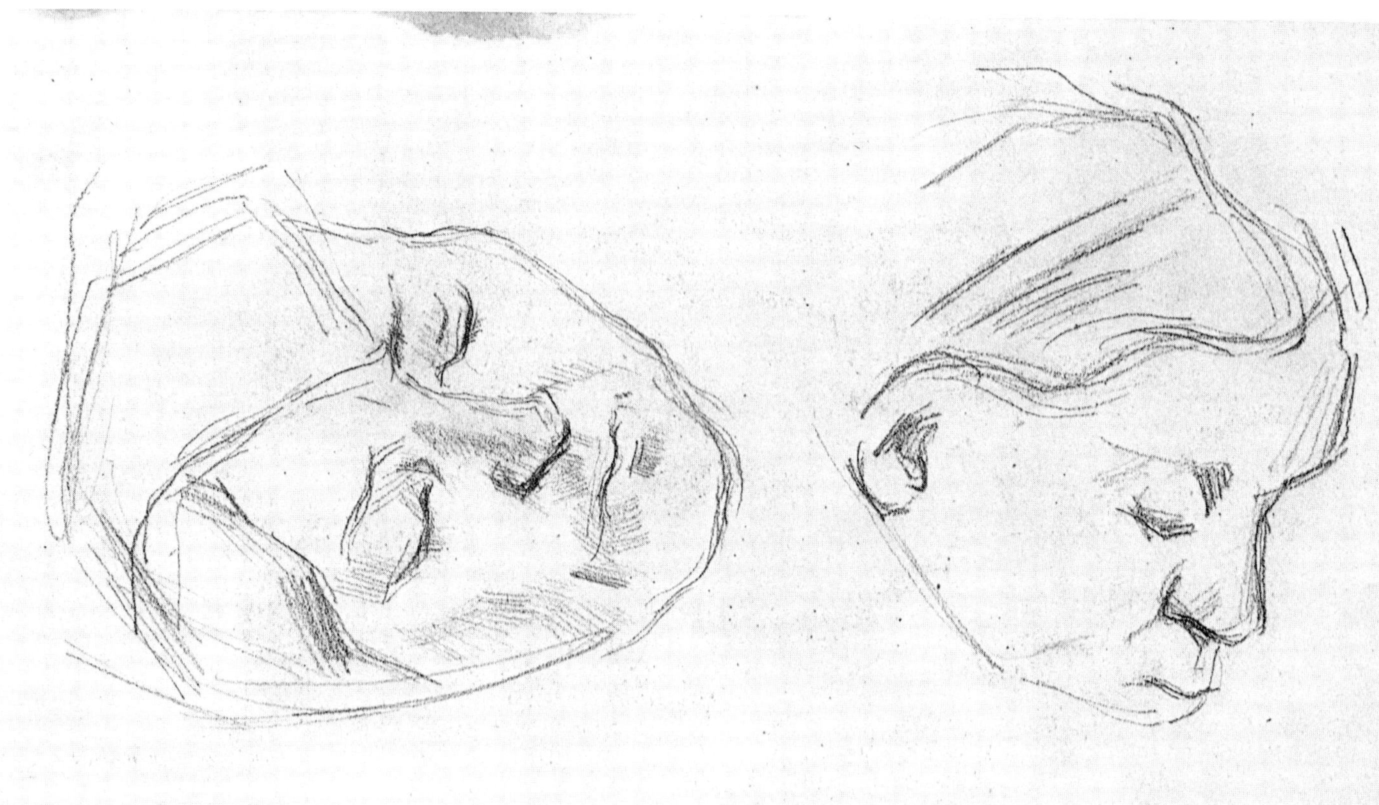

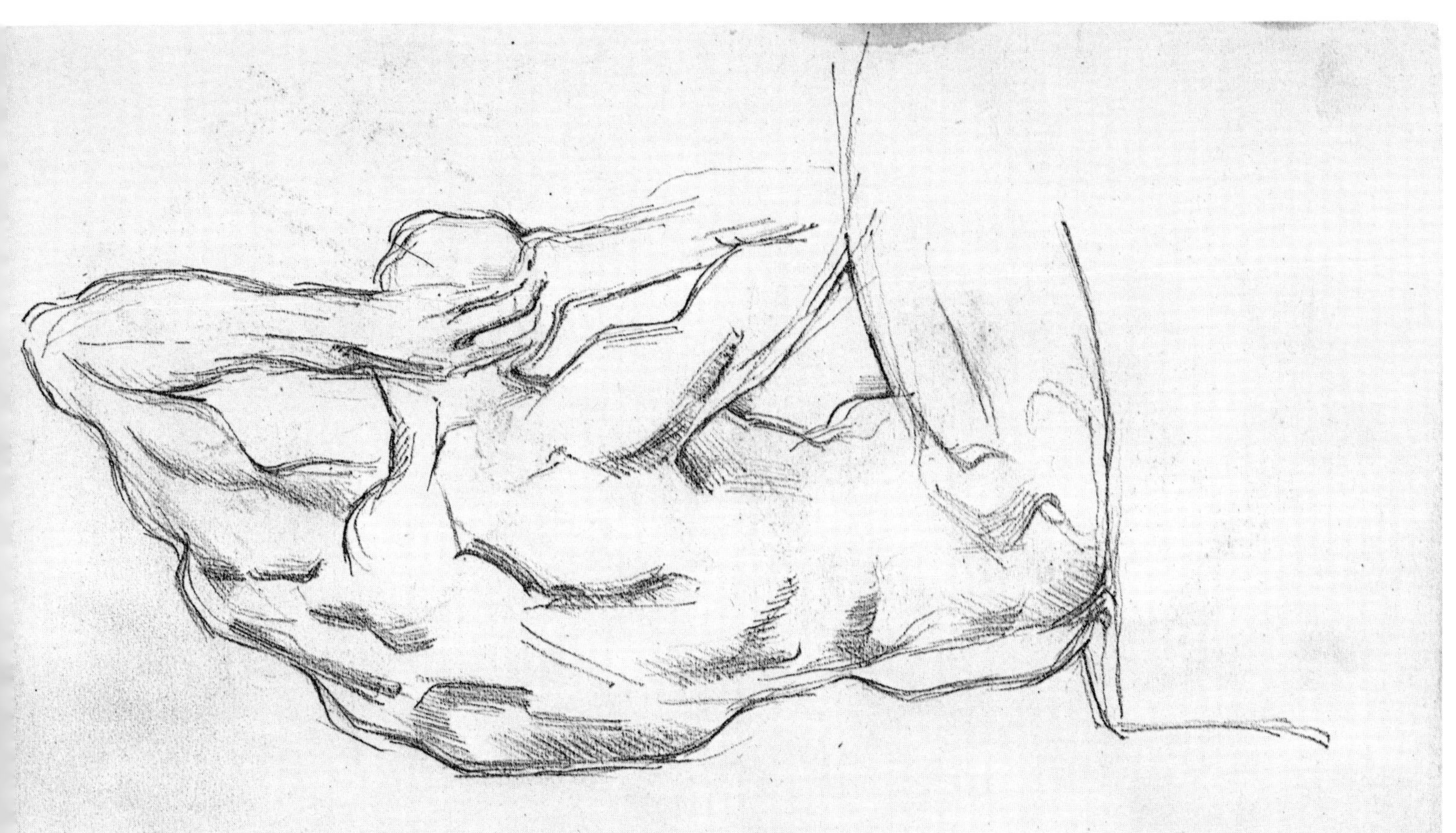

XXXVI

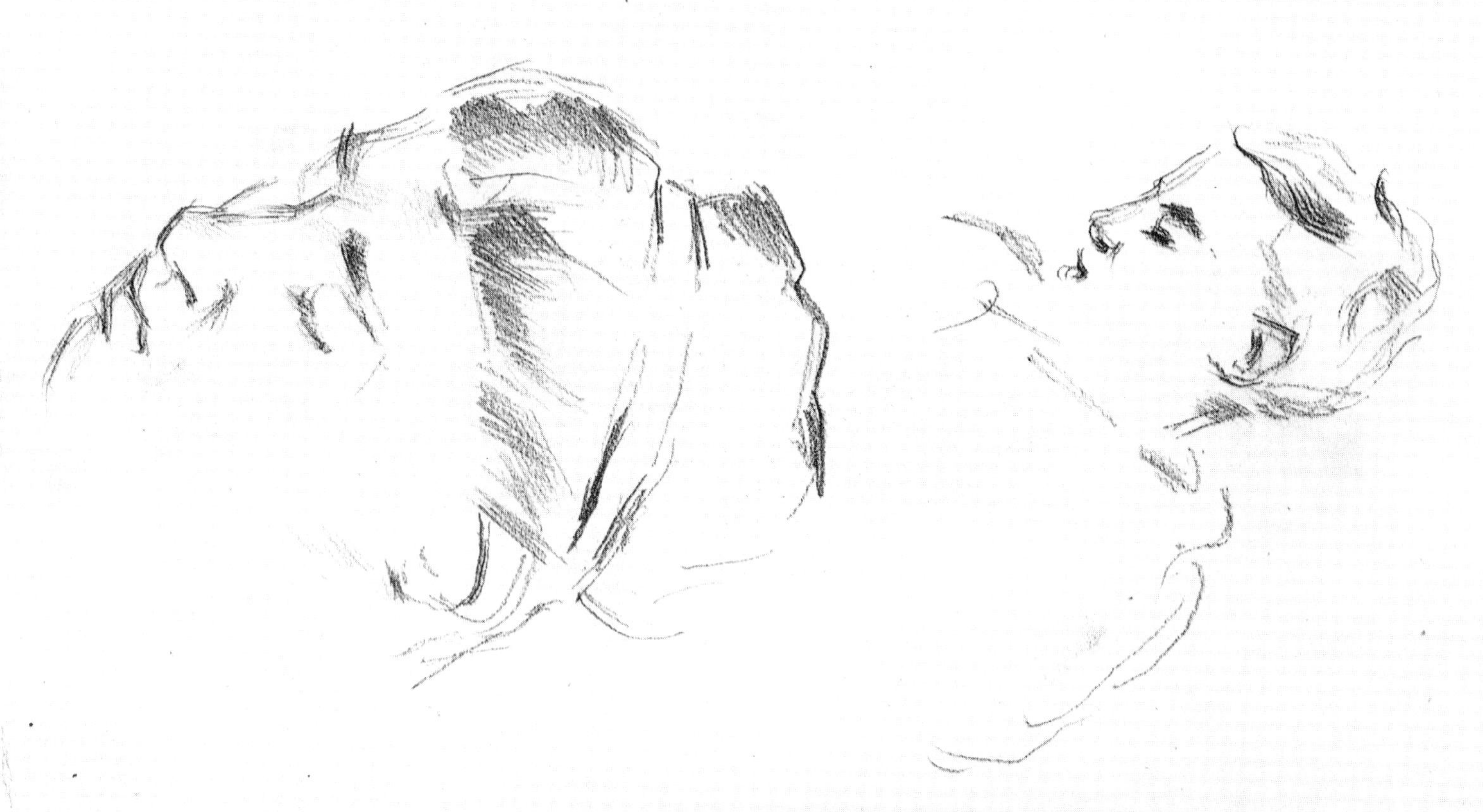

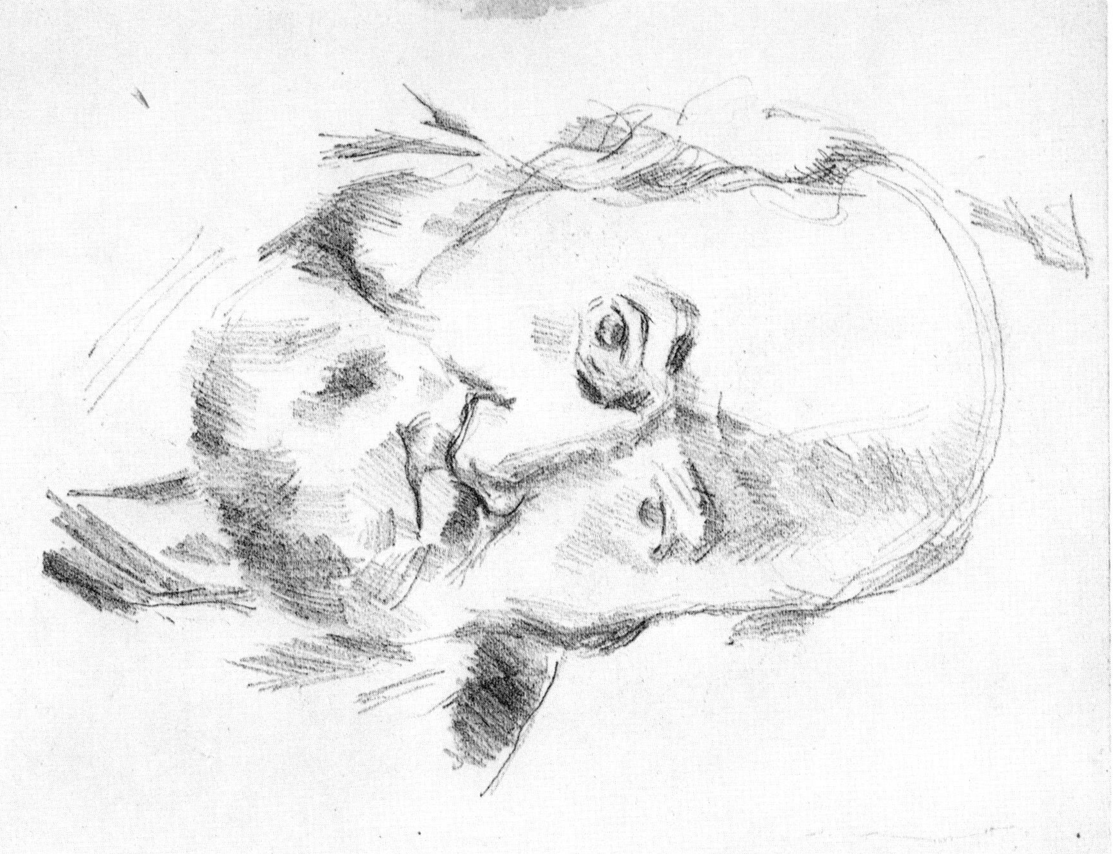

XXXVII

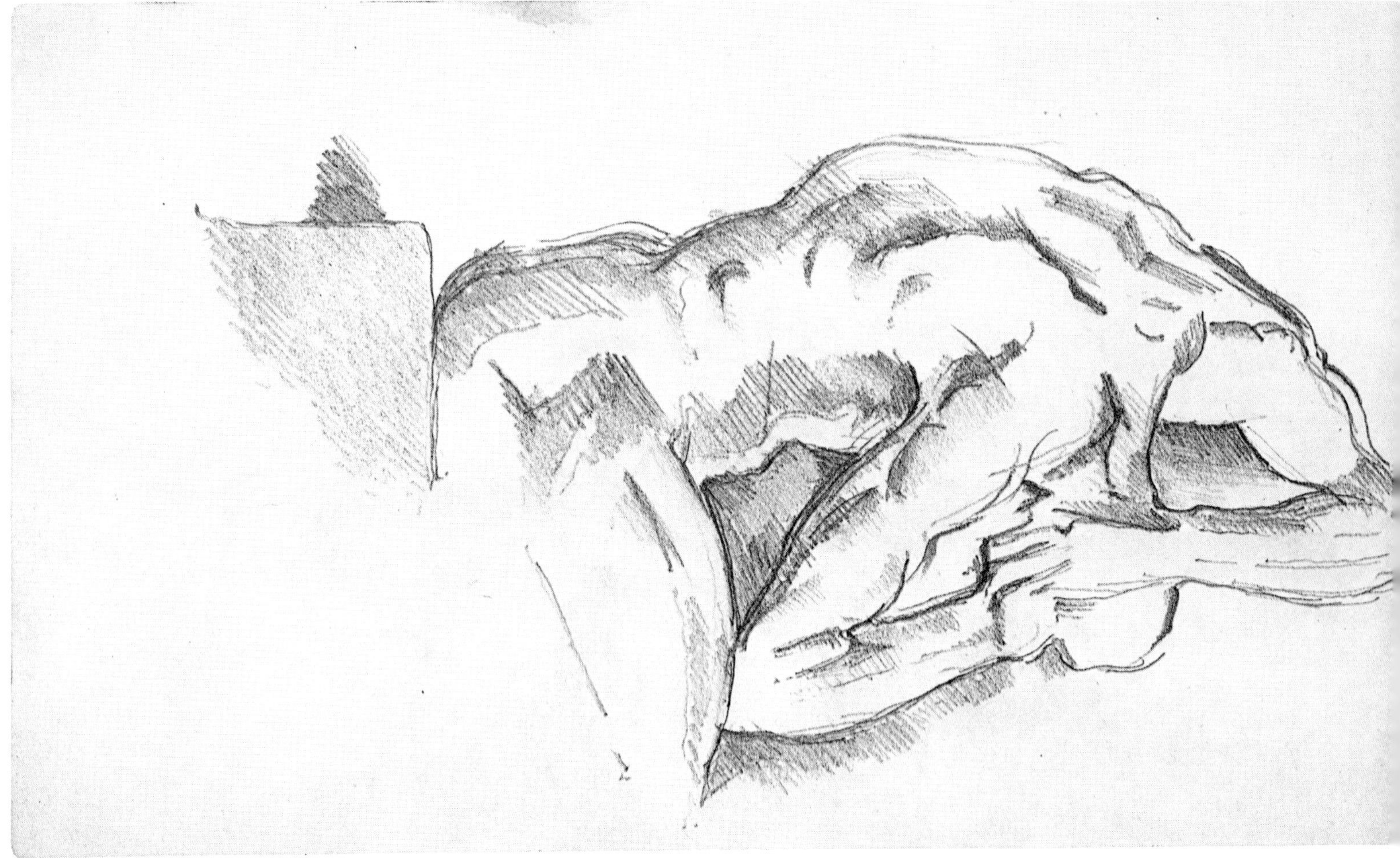

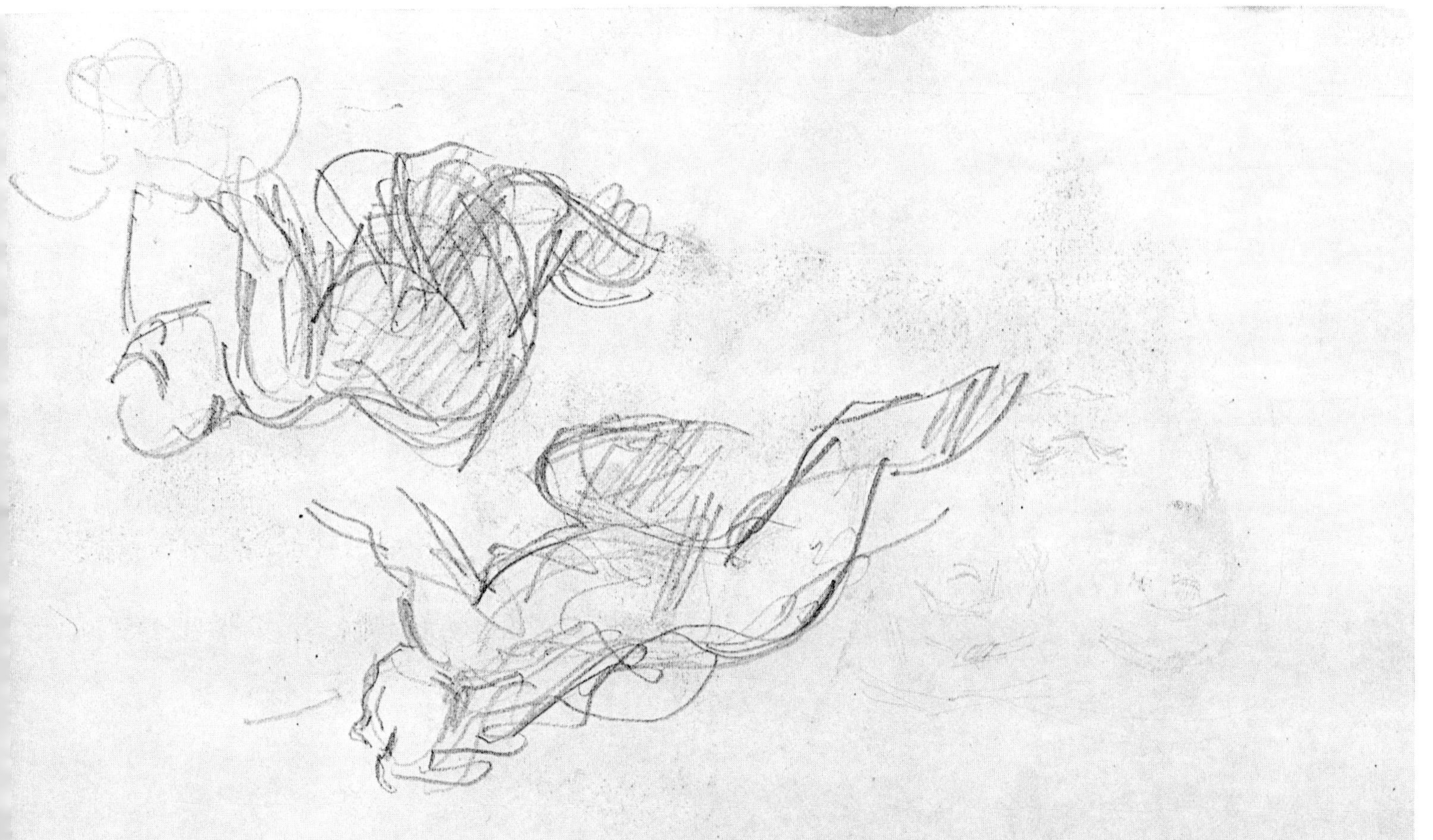

XXVIII

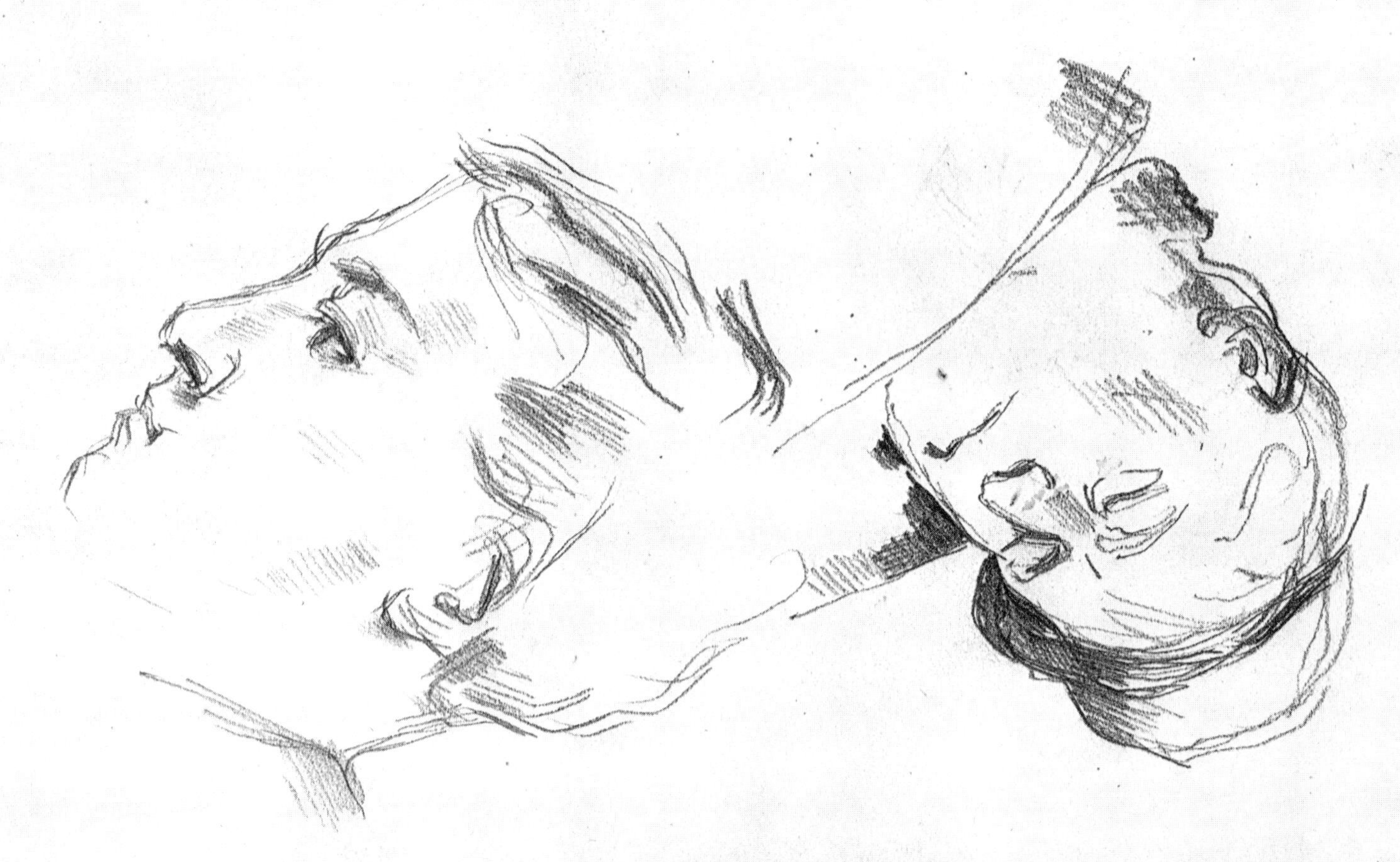

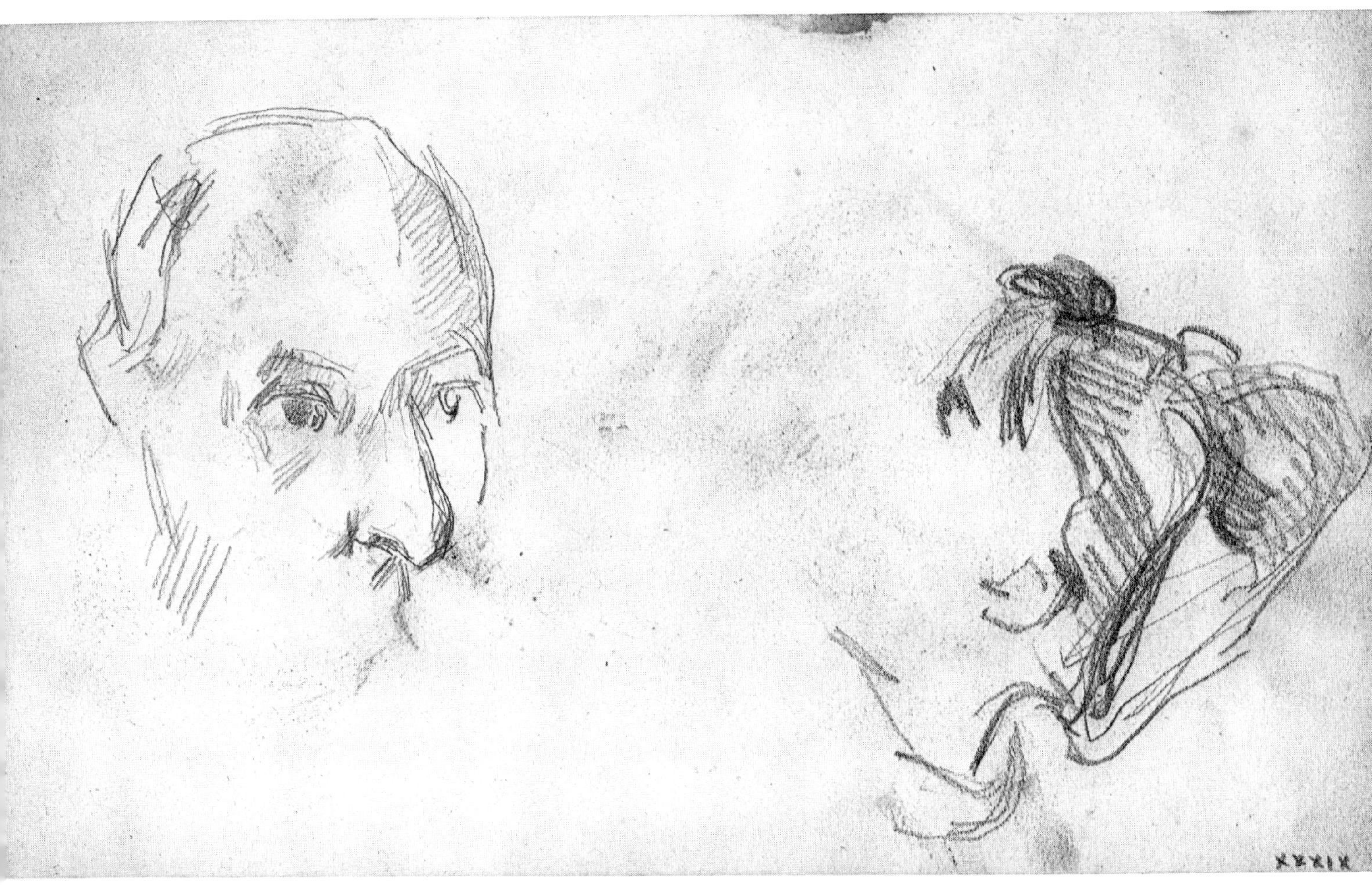
XXXIX

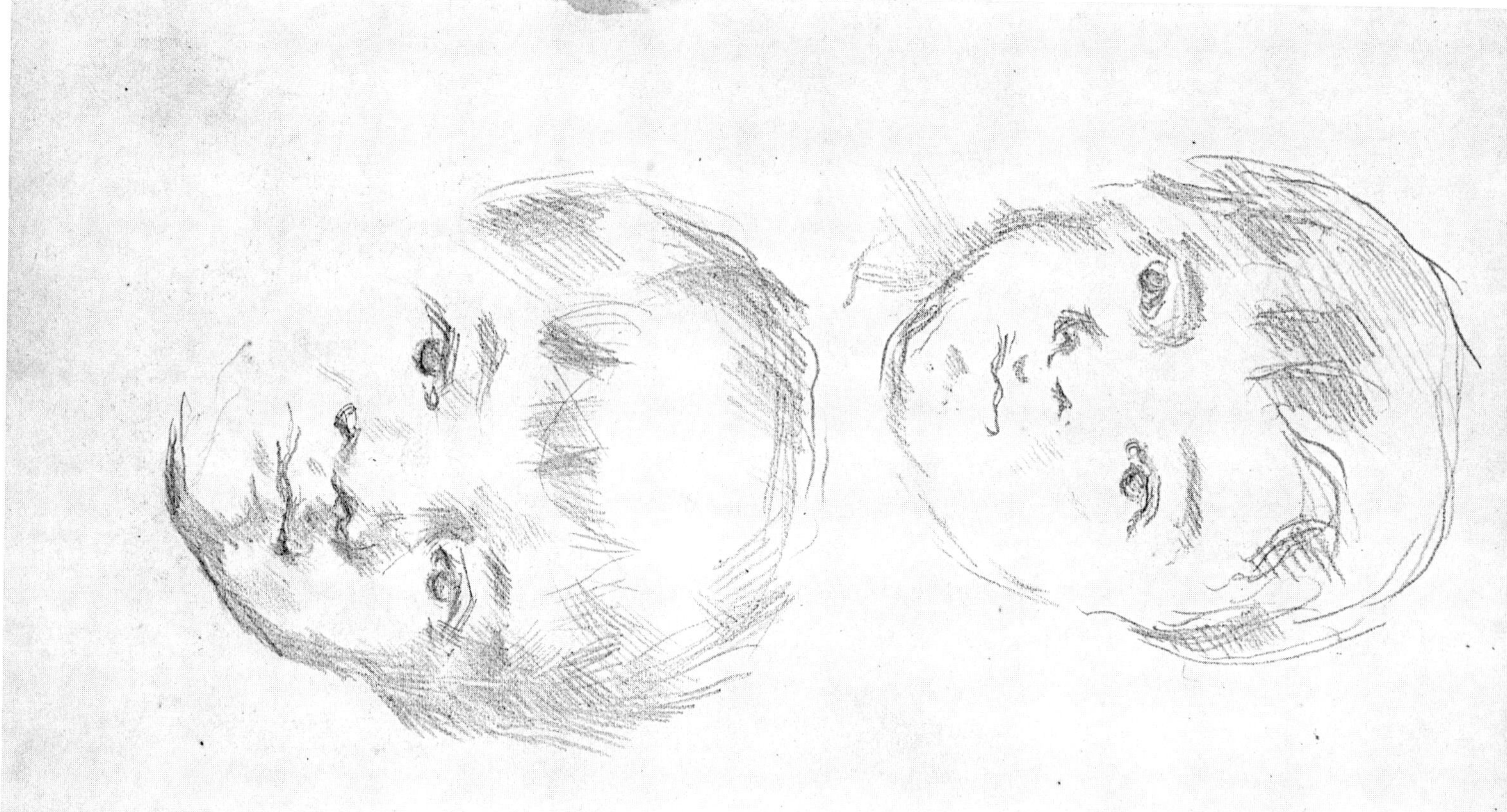

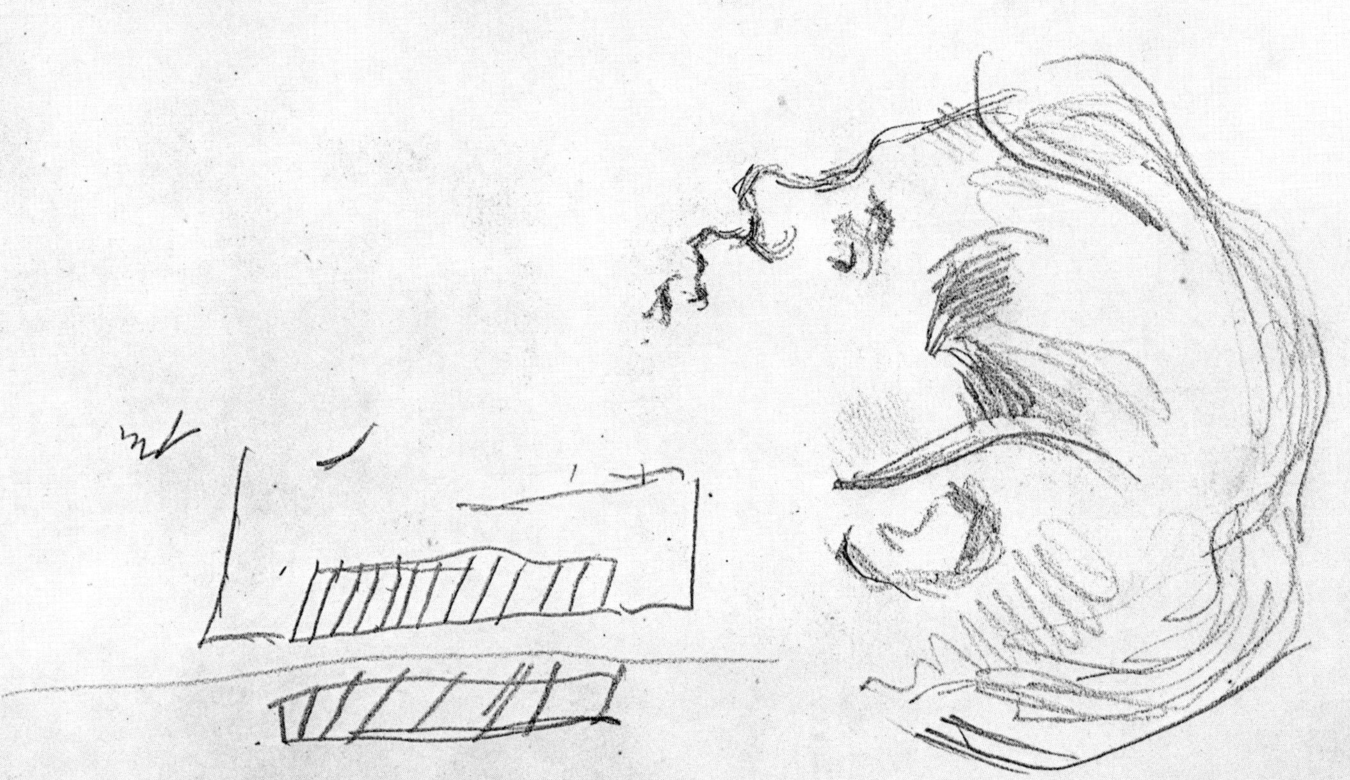

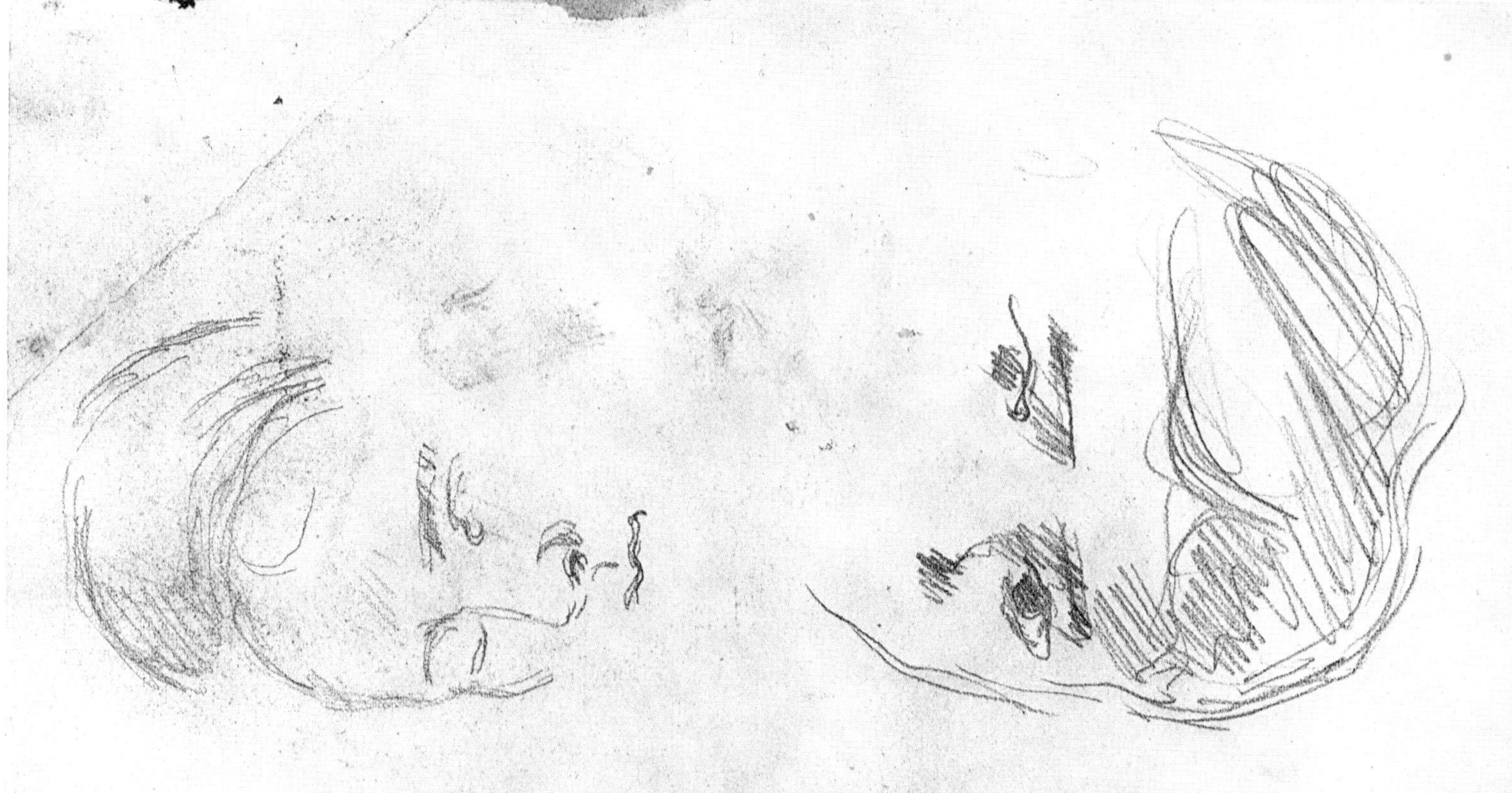

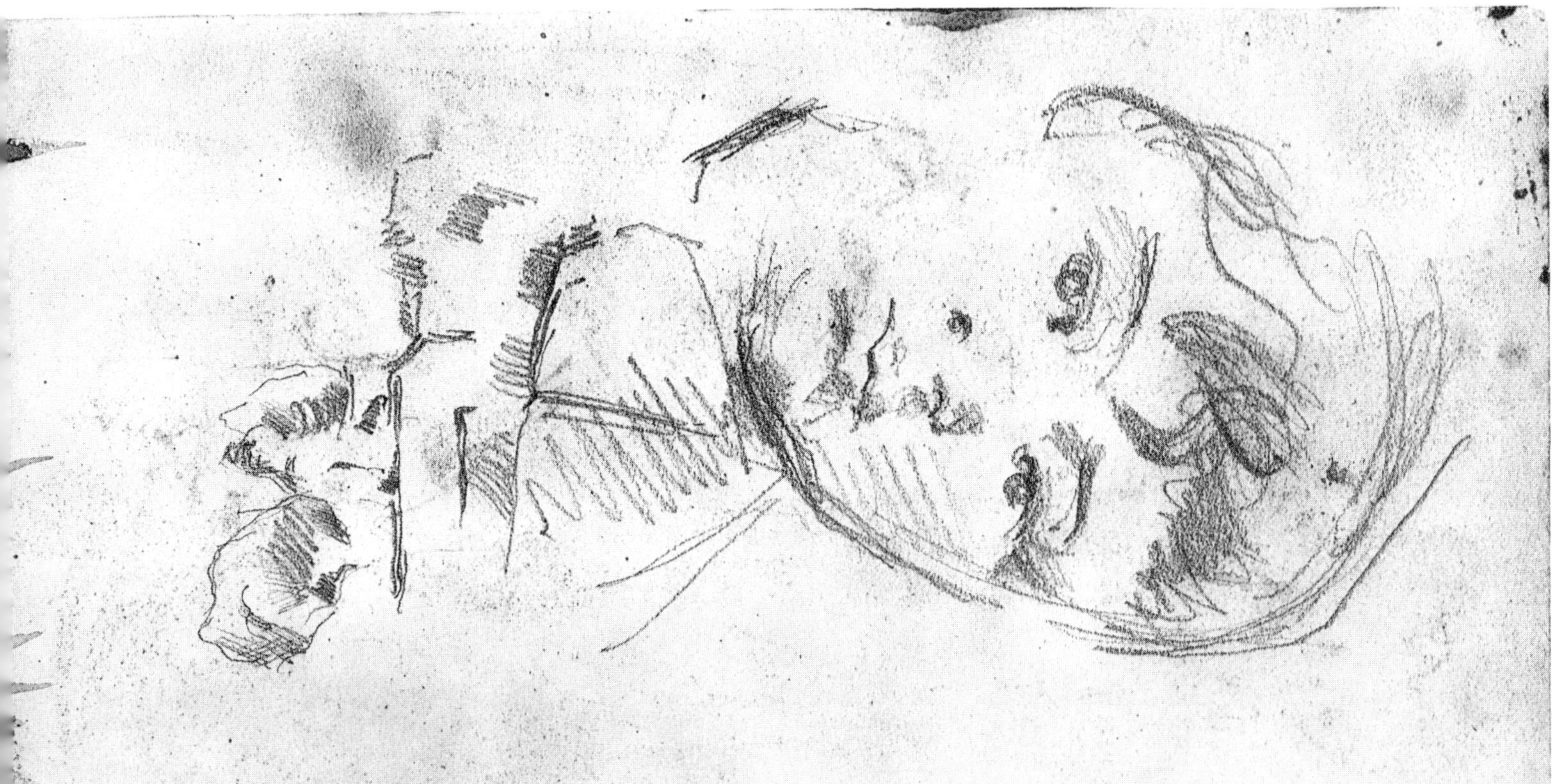

XLI

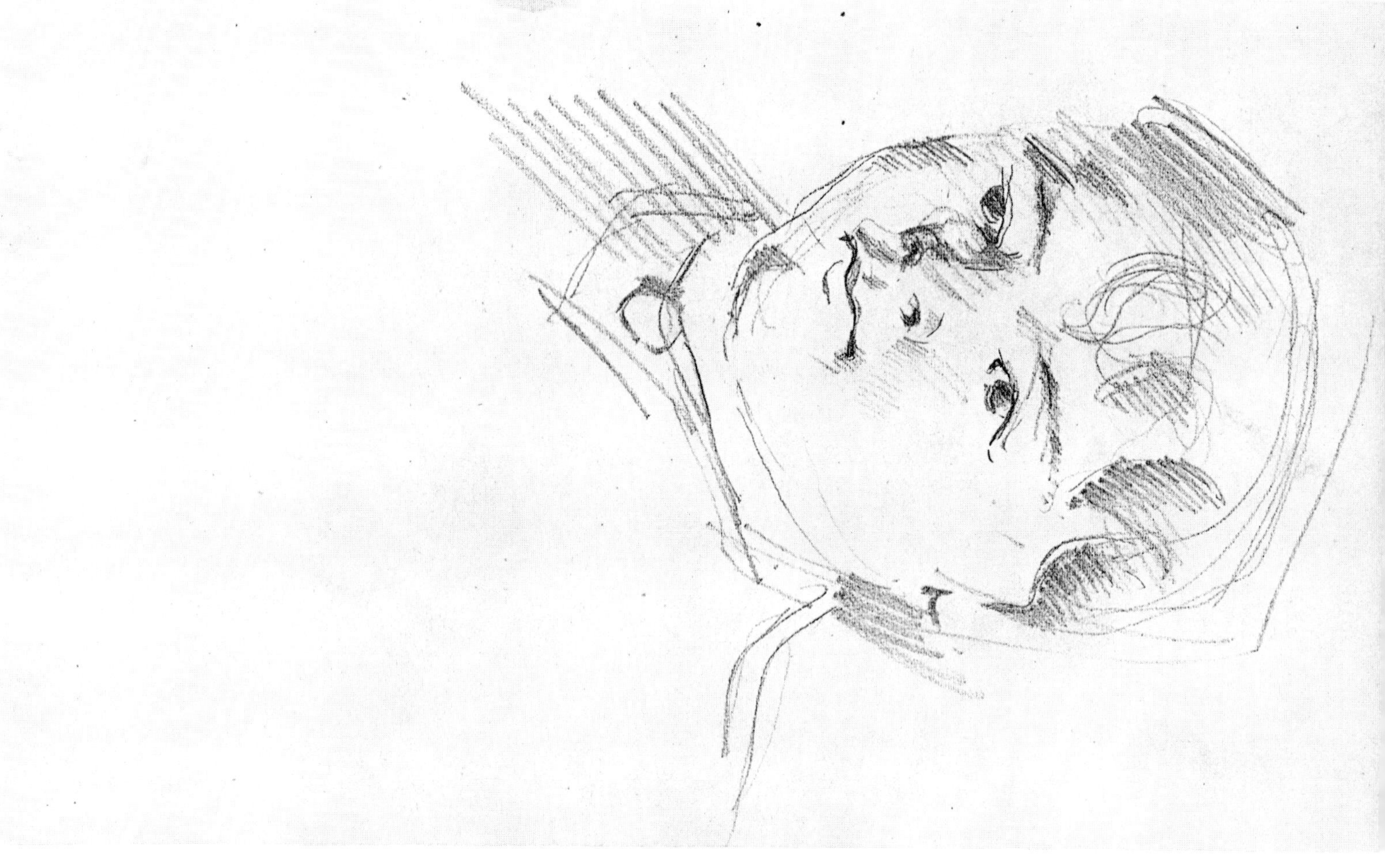

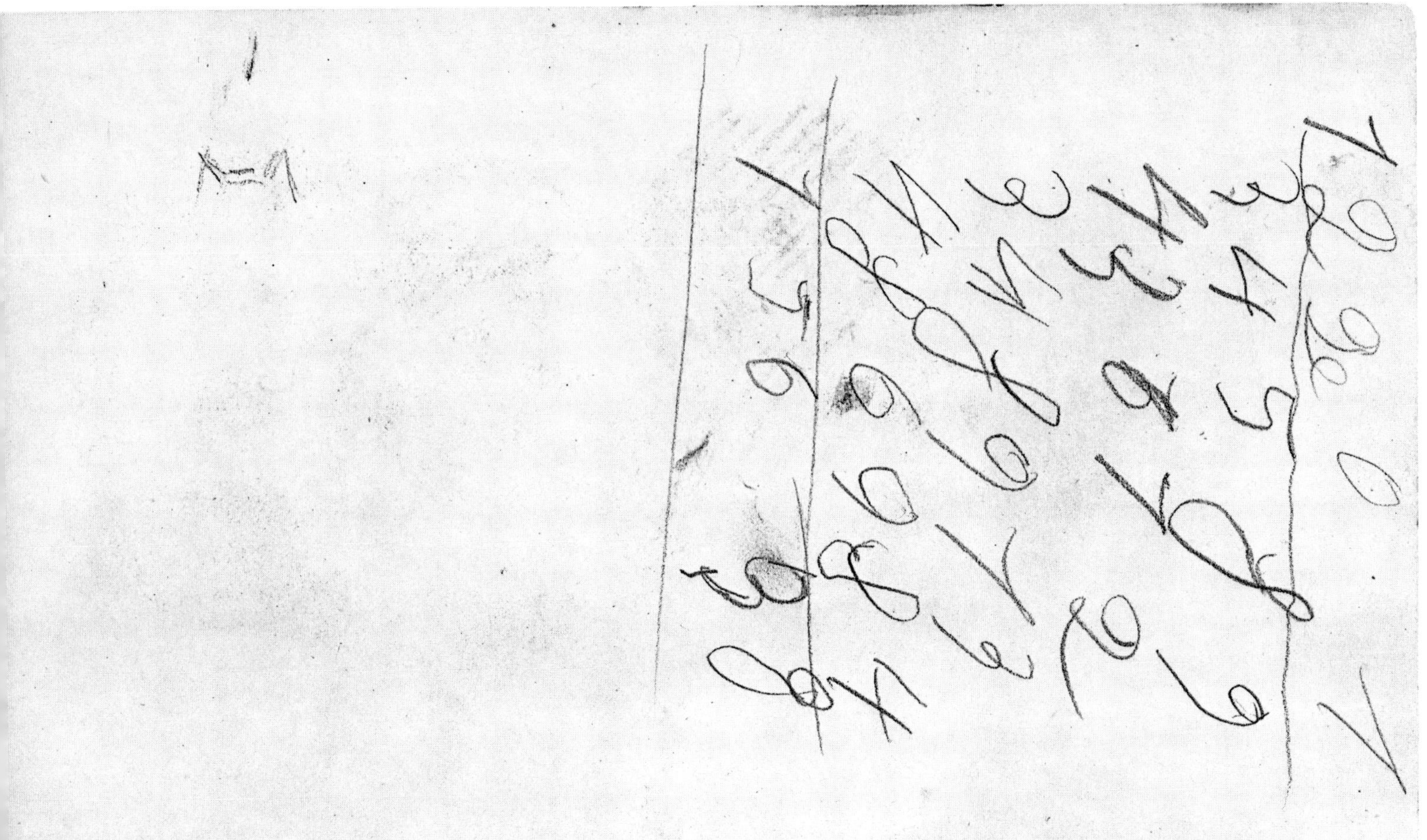

1 2 9 0 1

3 4 5 8 9

4 3 6 7 2

3 4 8 9 7 3

4 8 6 9 8 4

1 5 6 9 8

XLII

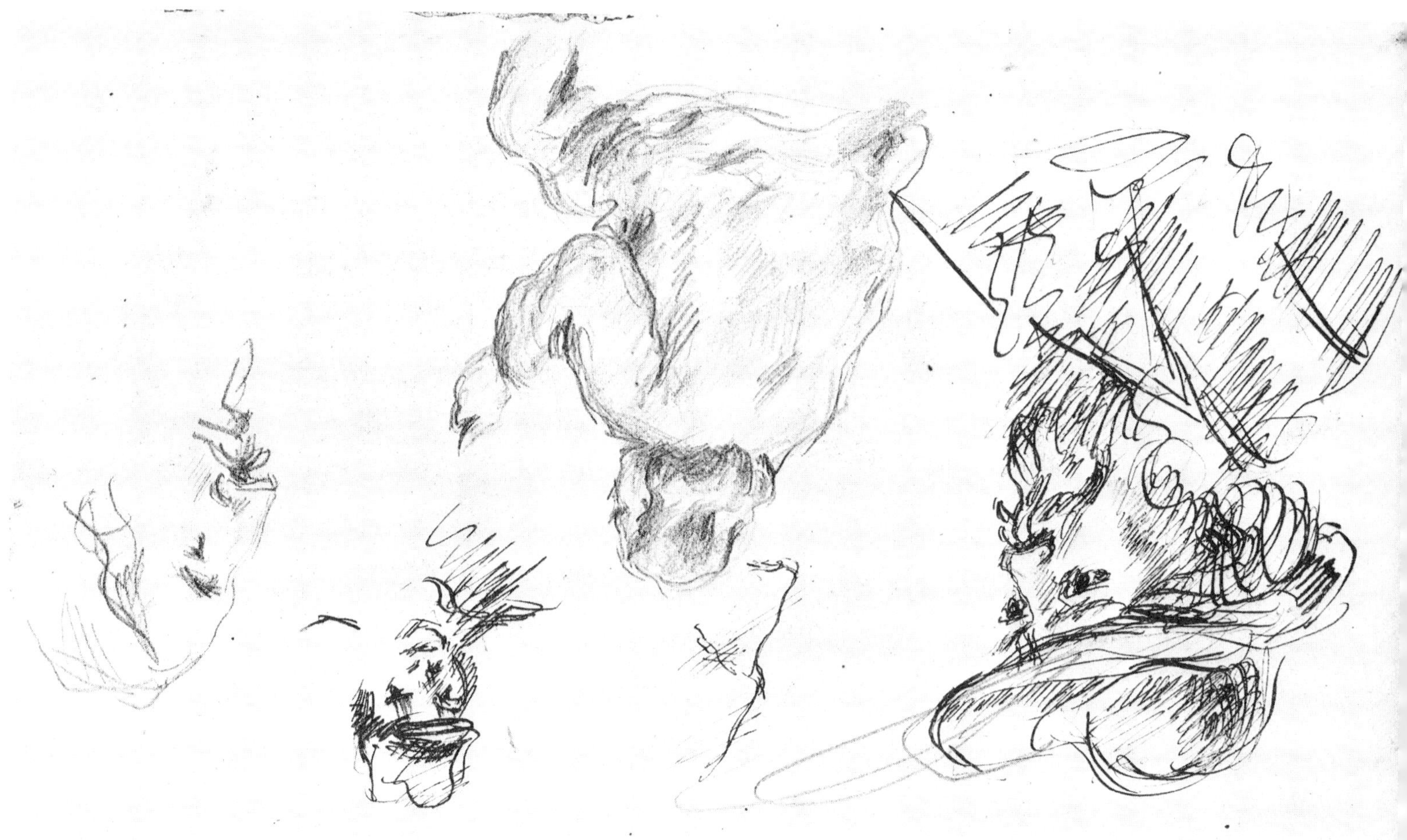

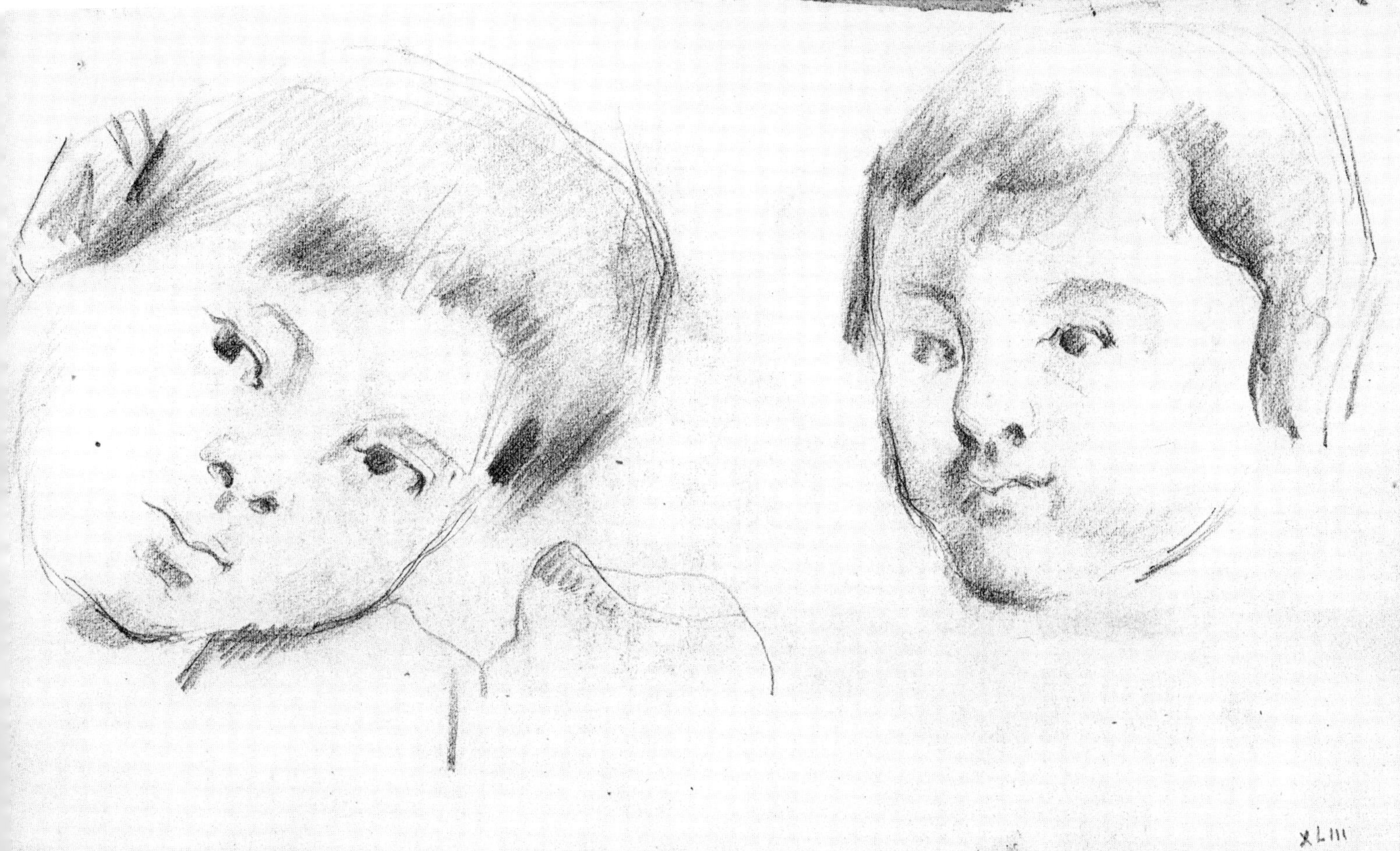

XLIII

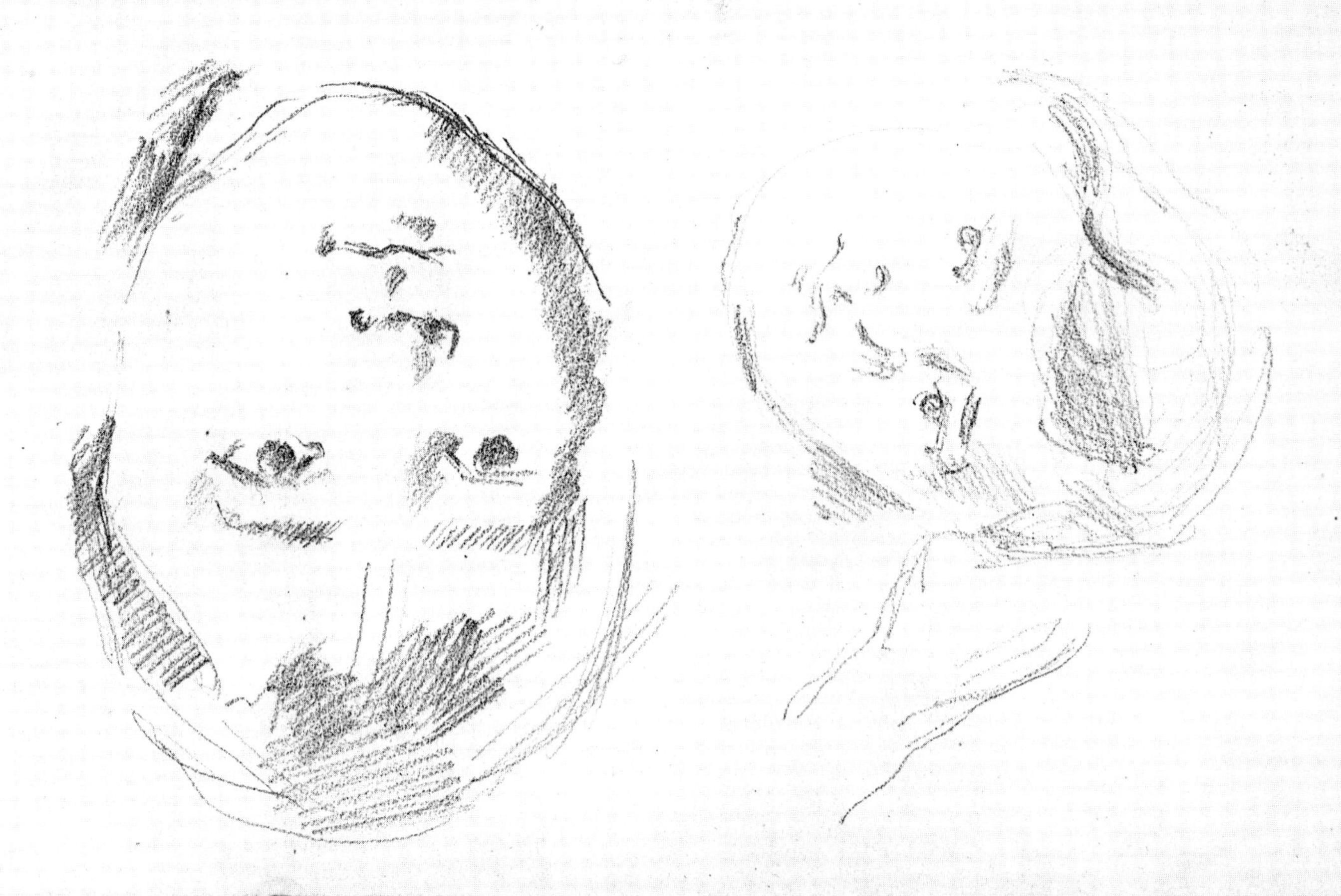

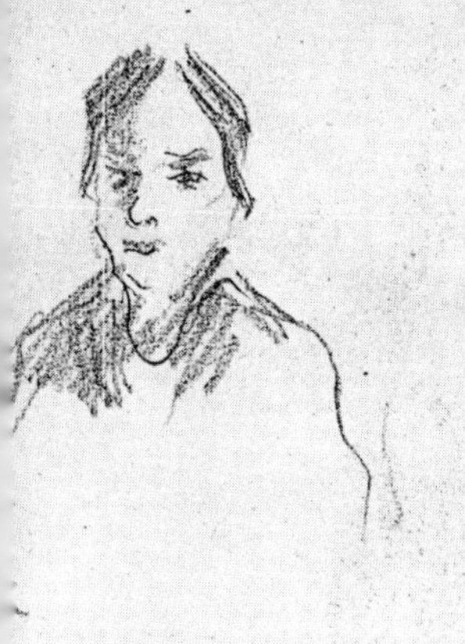

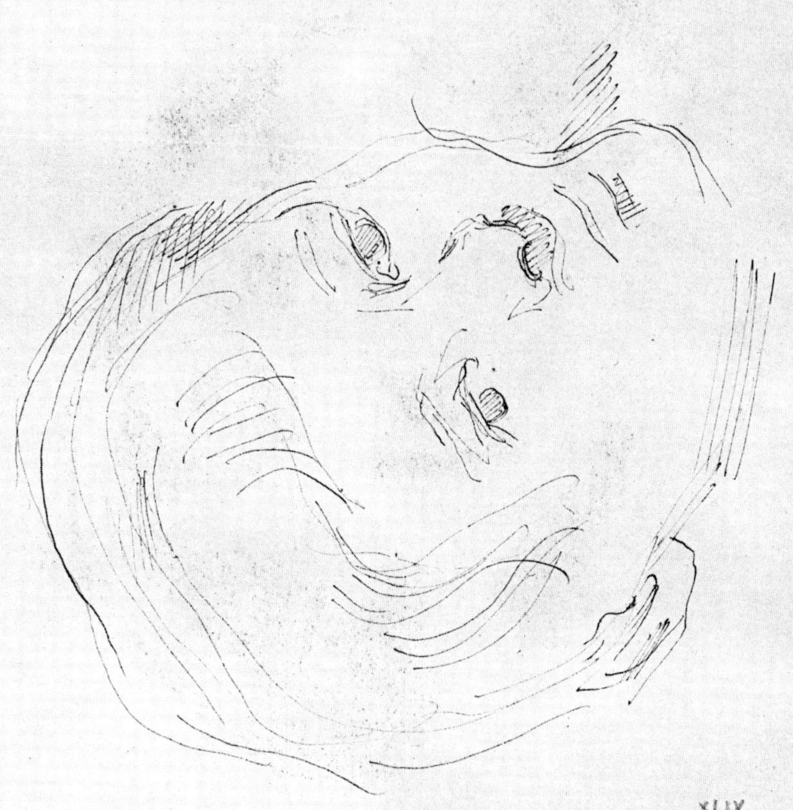

XLIV

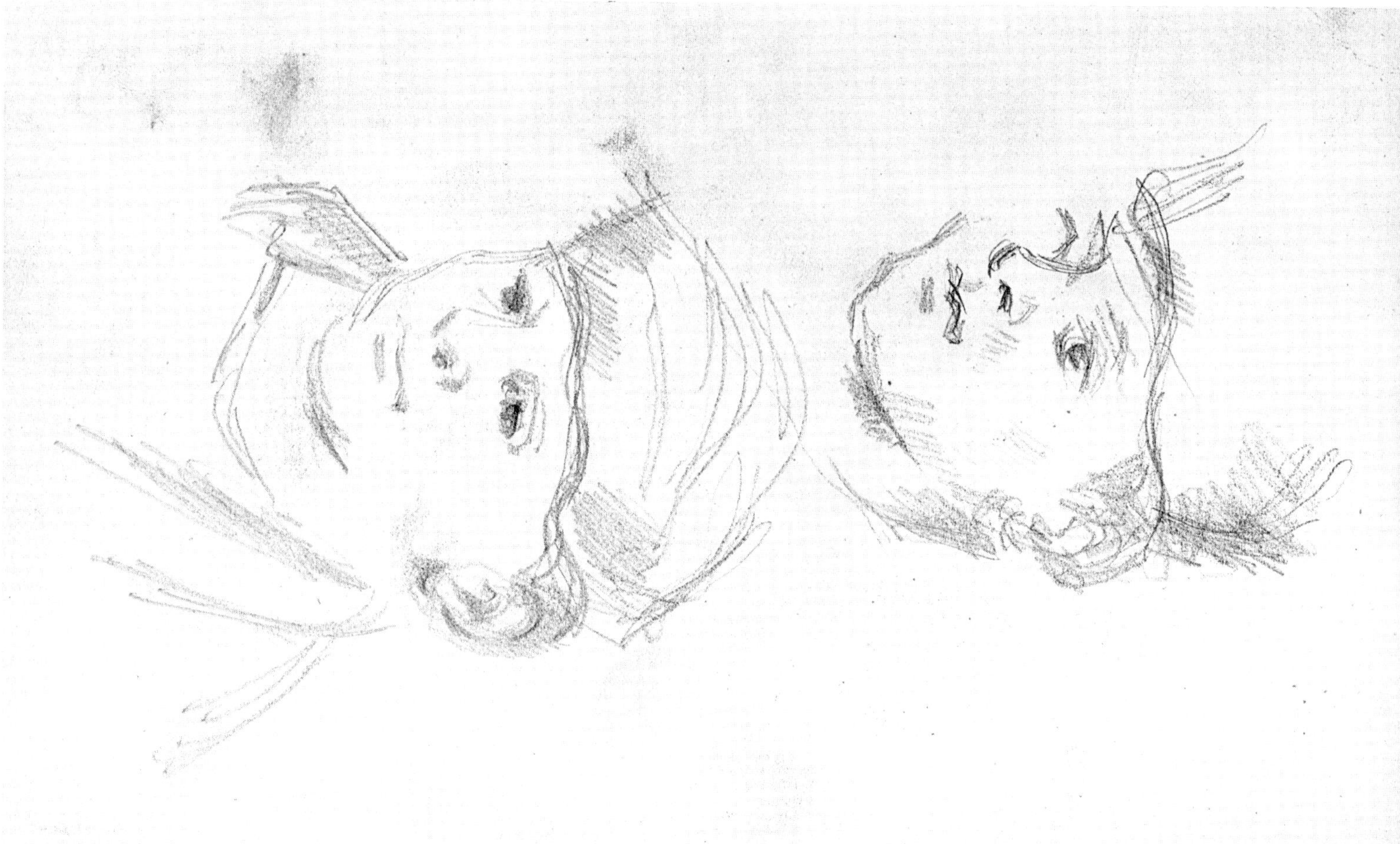

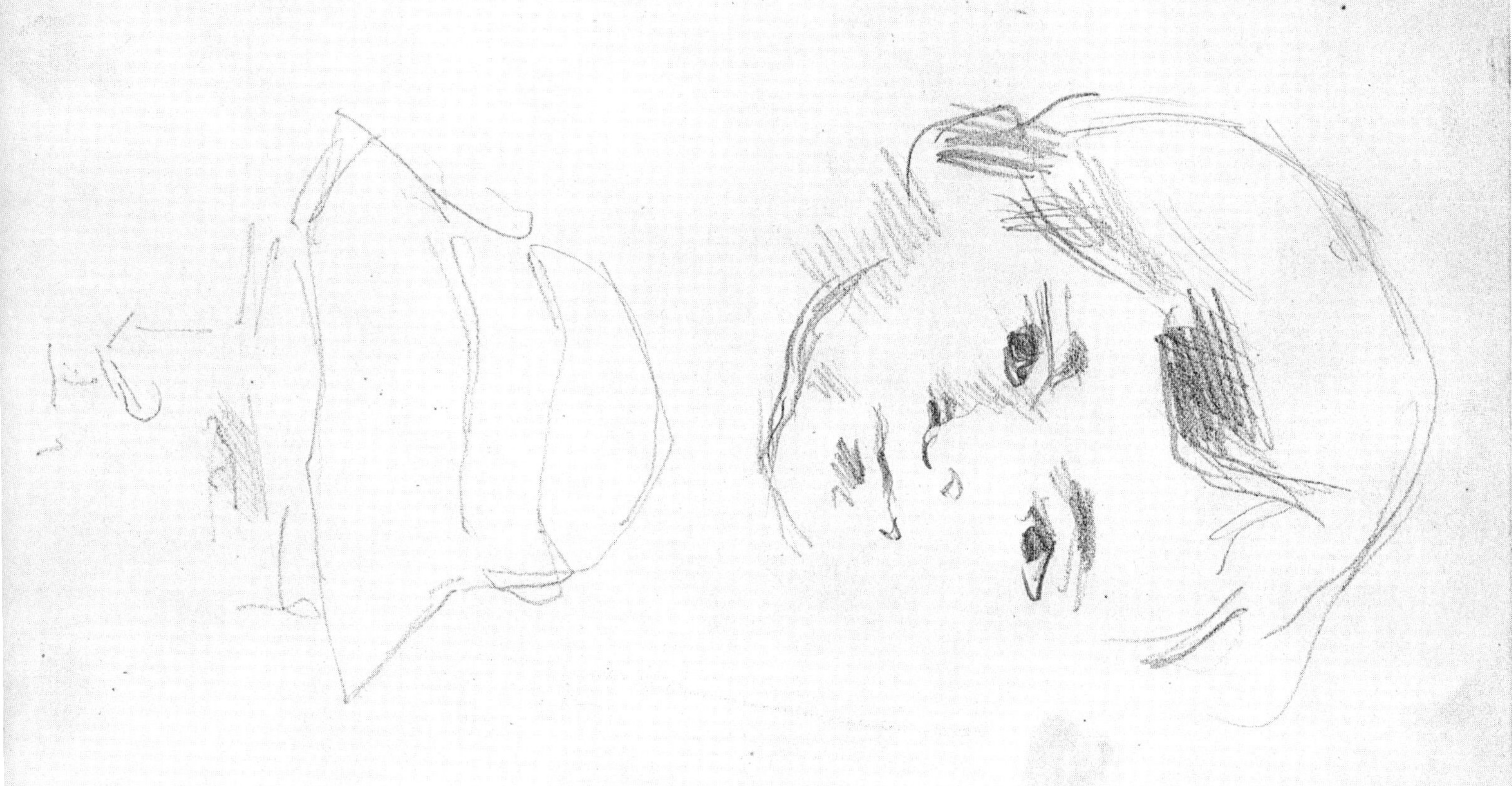

XLV

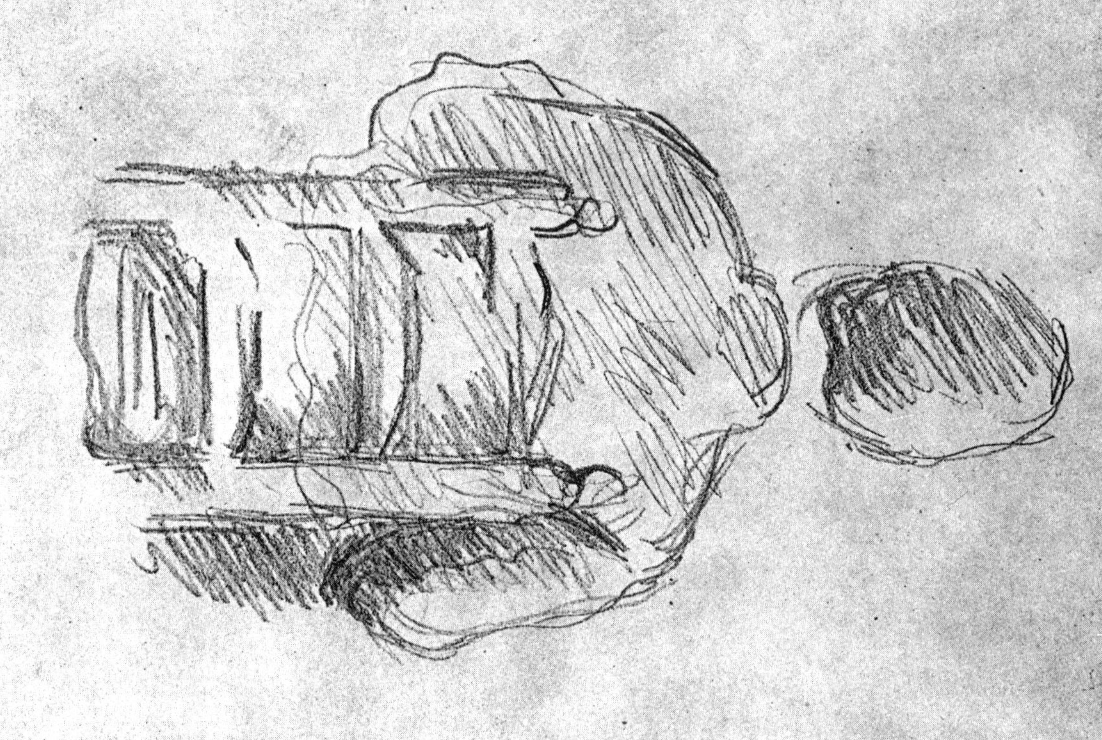

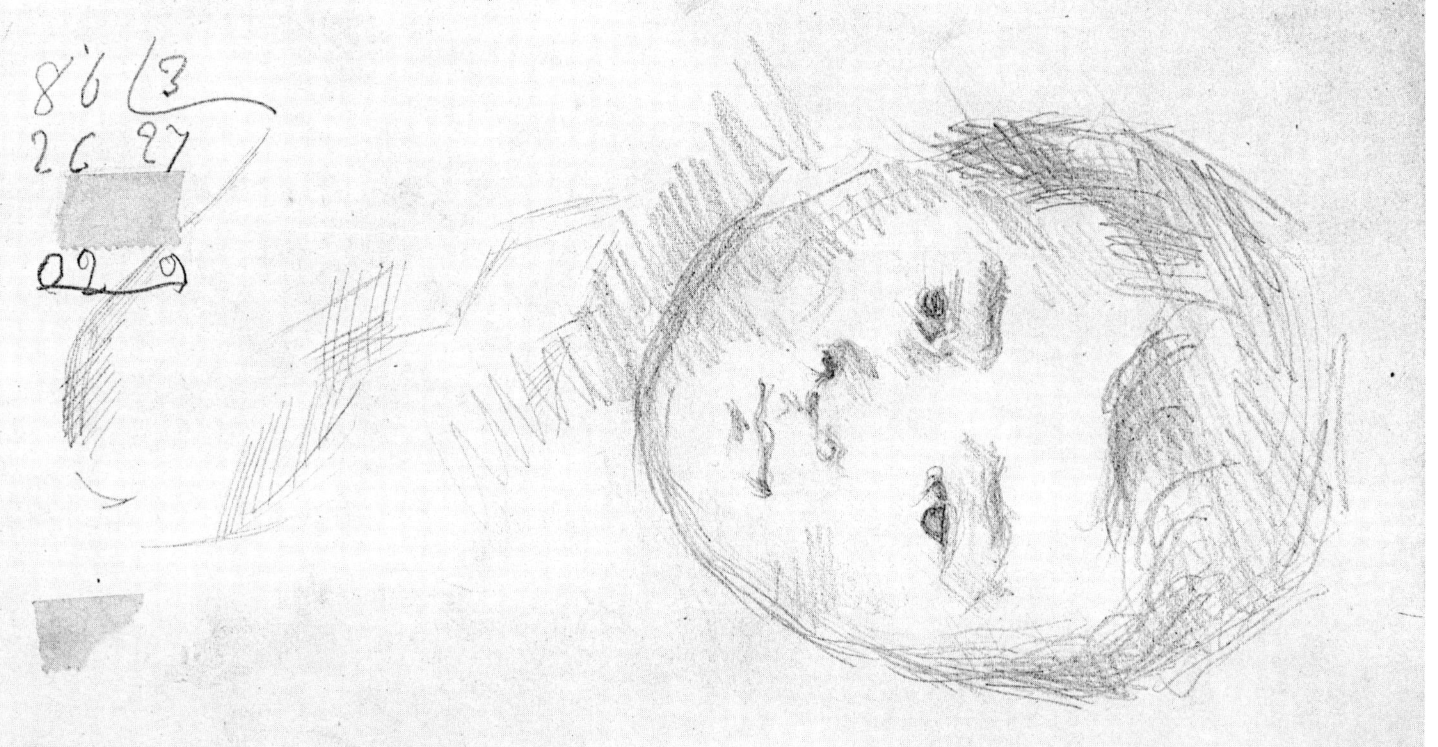

XLVI

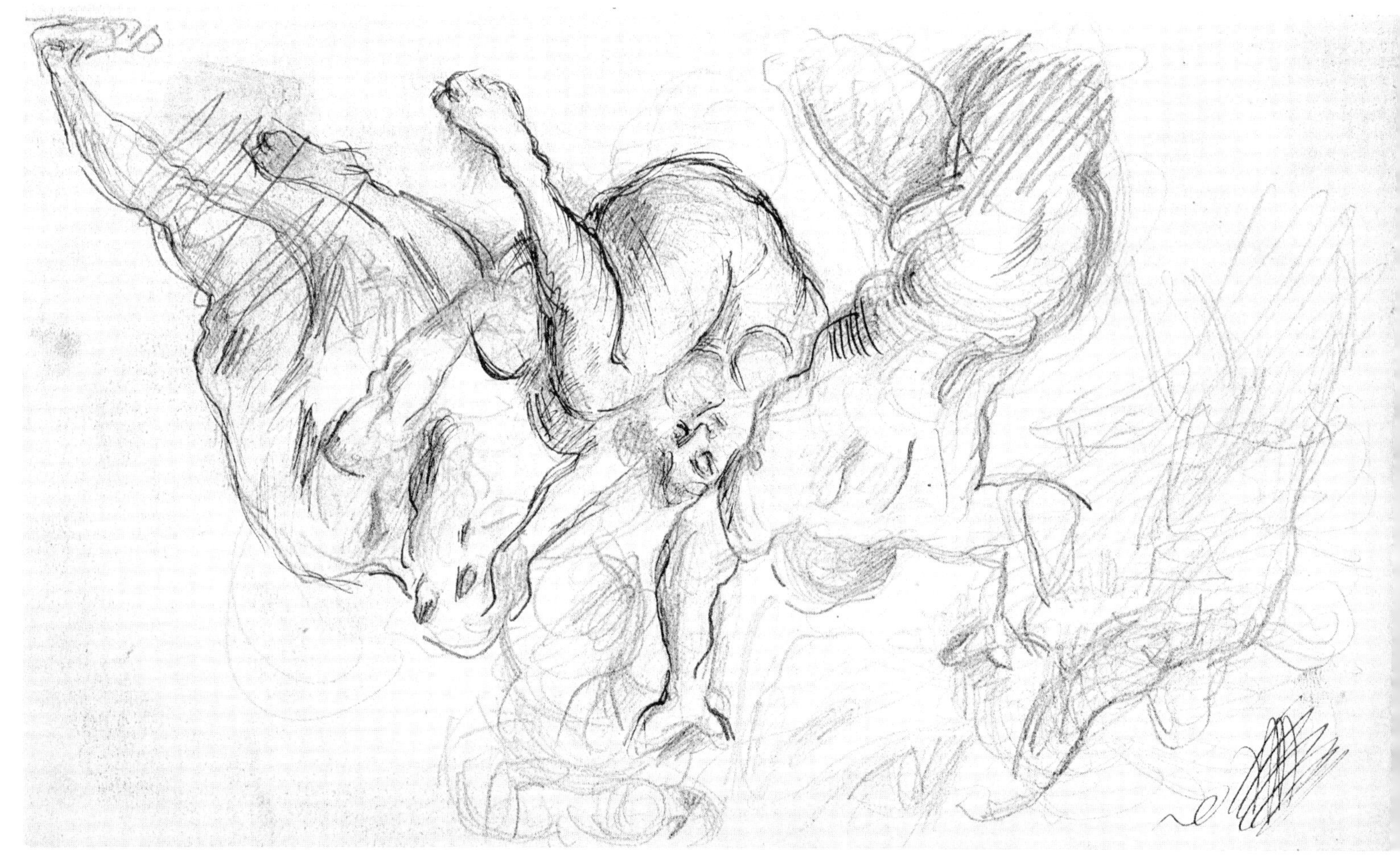

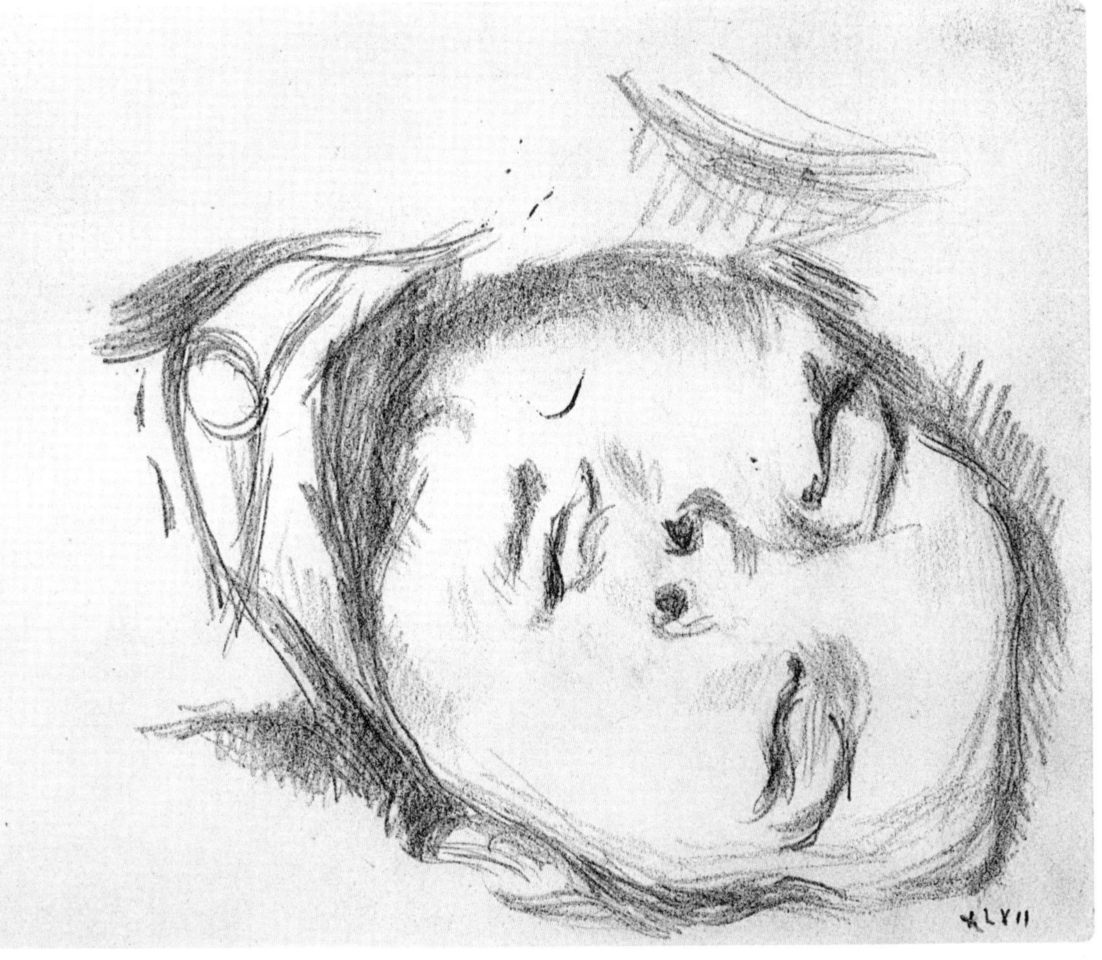

XLVII

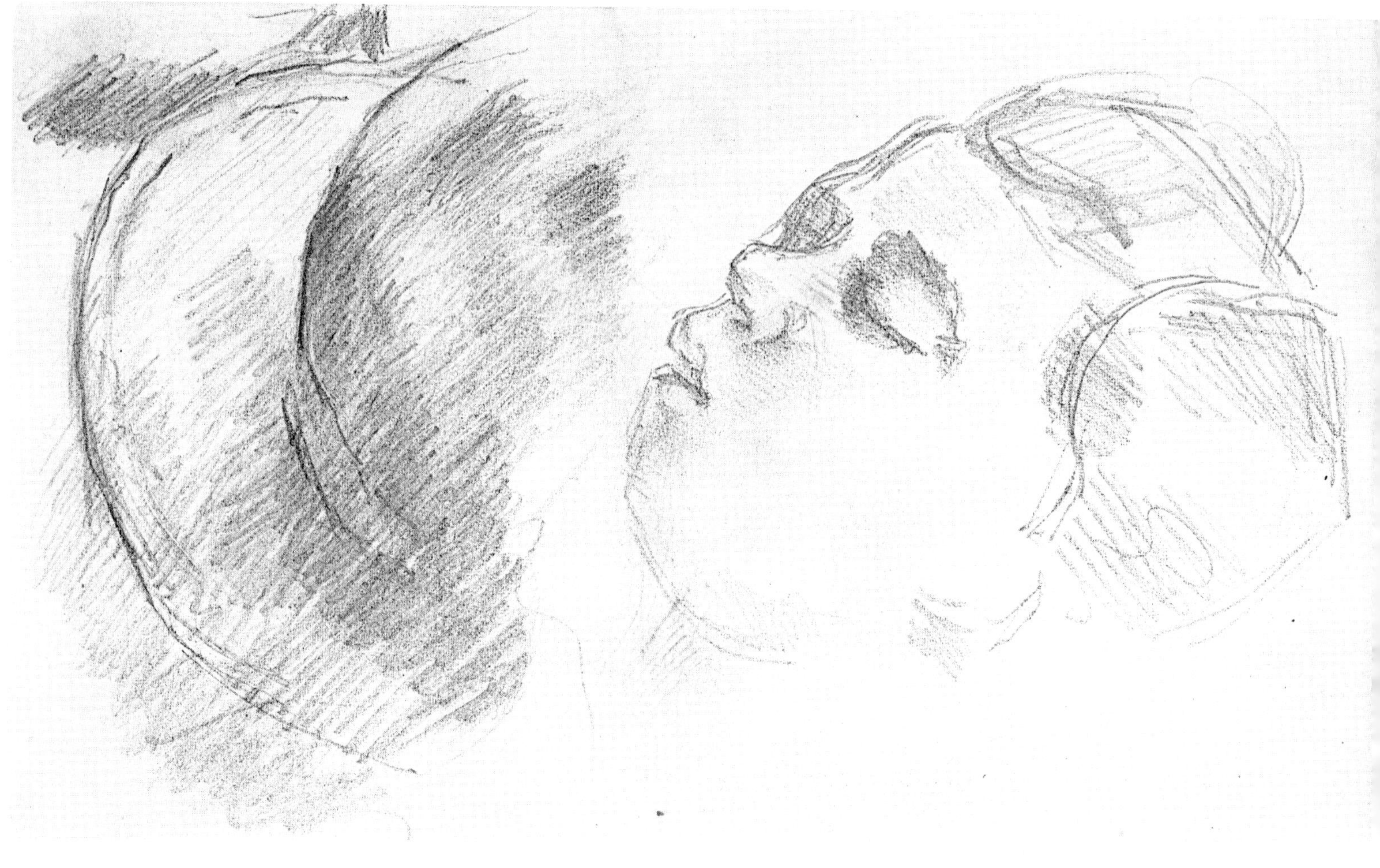

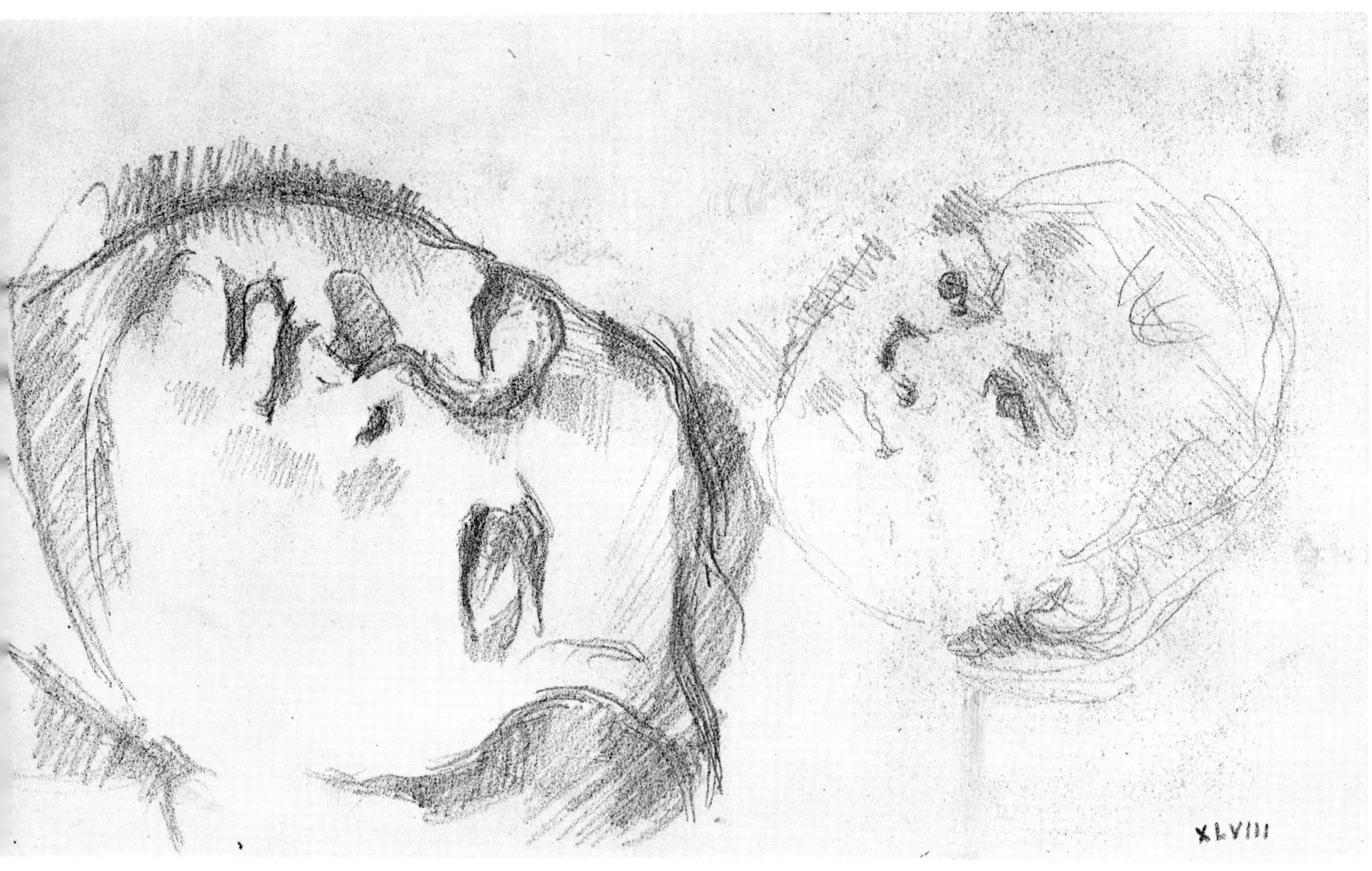

XLVIII

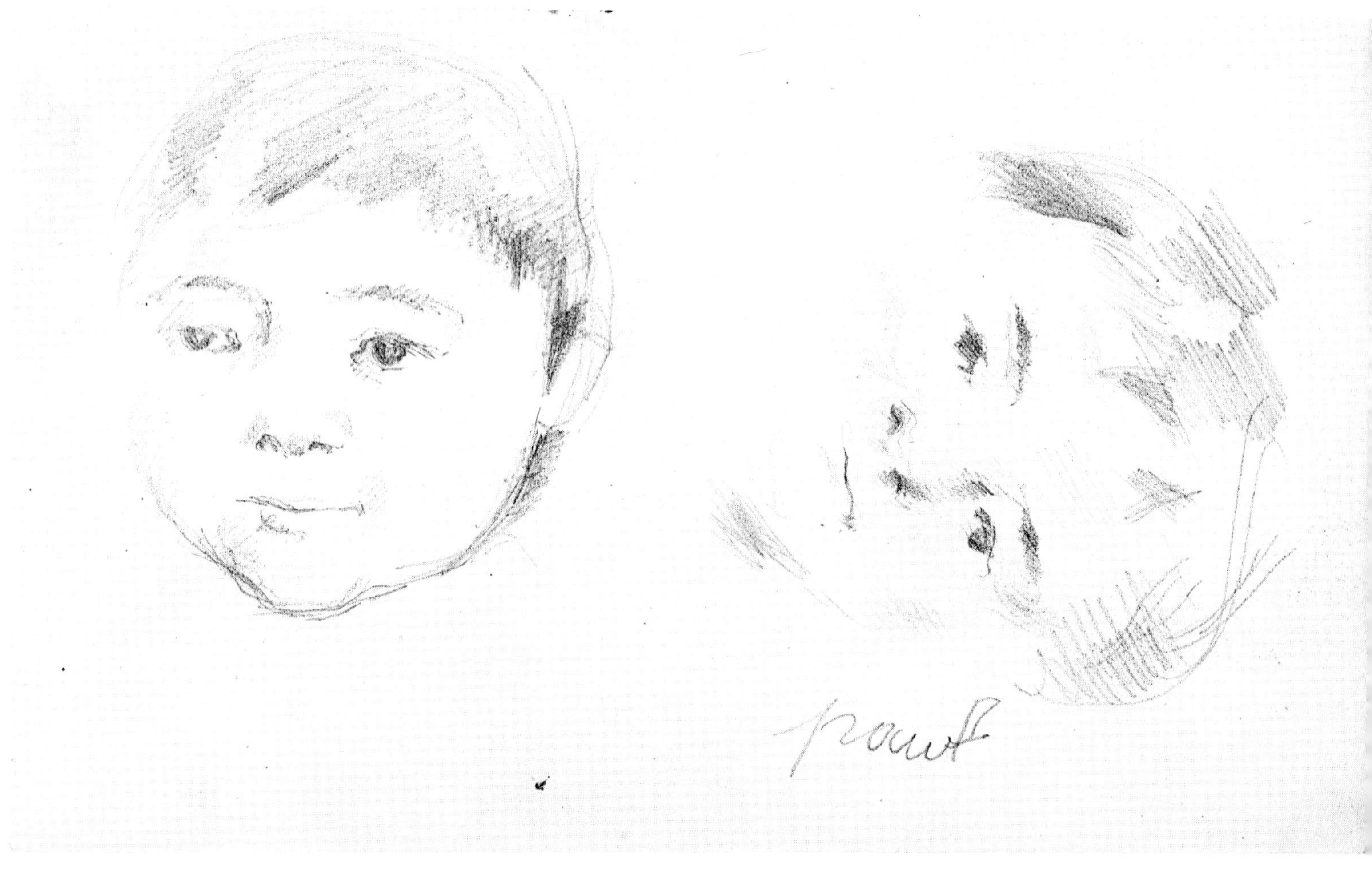

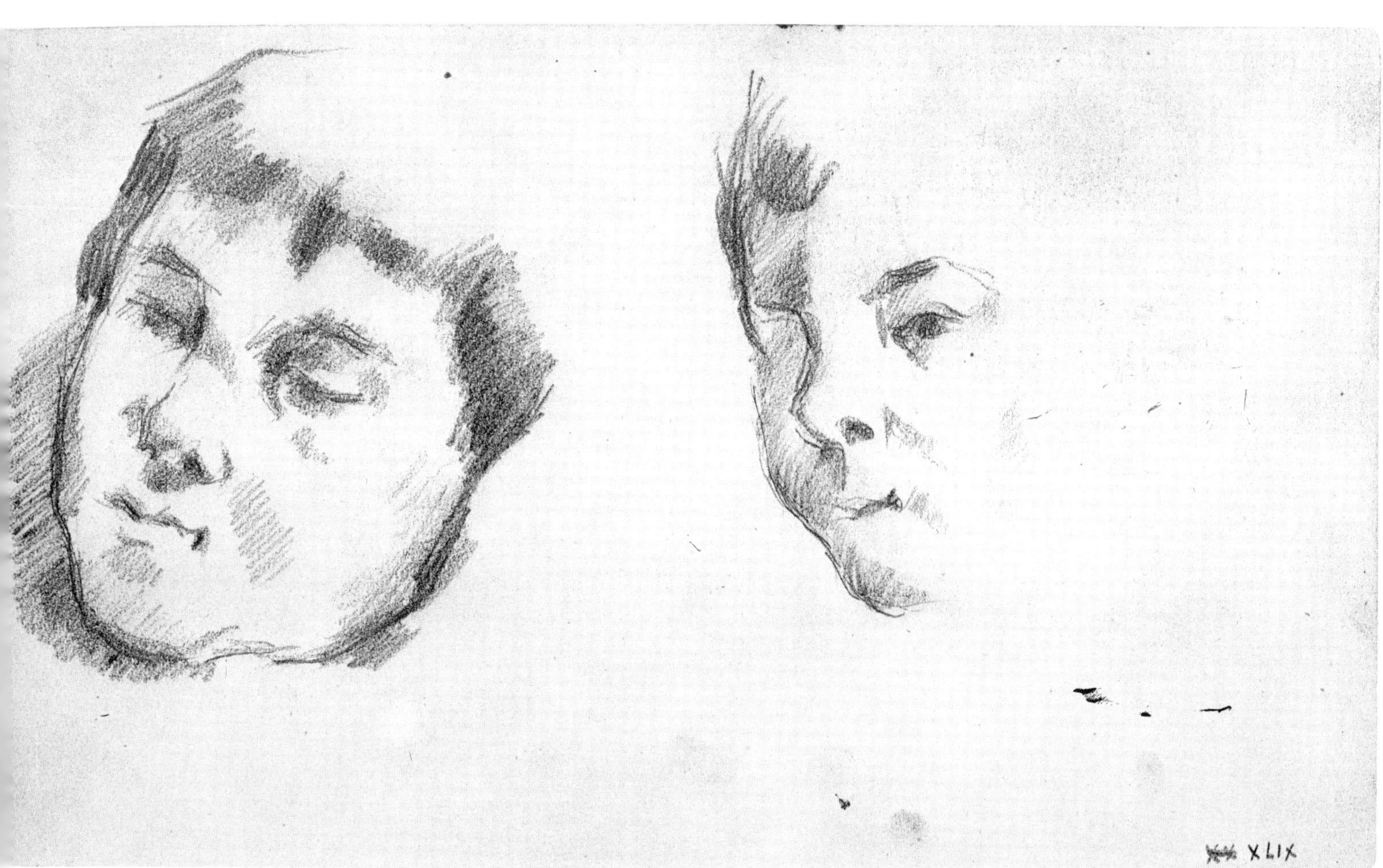
XLIX

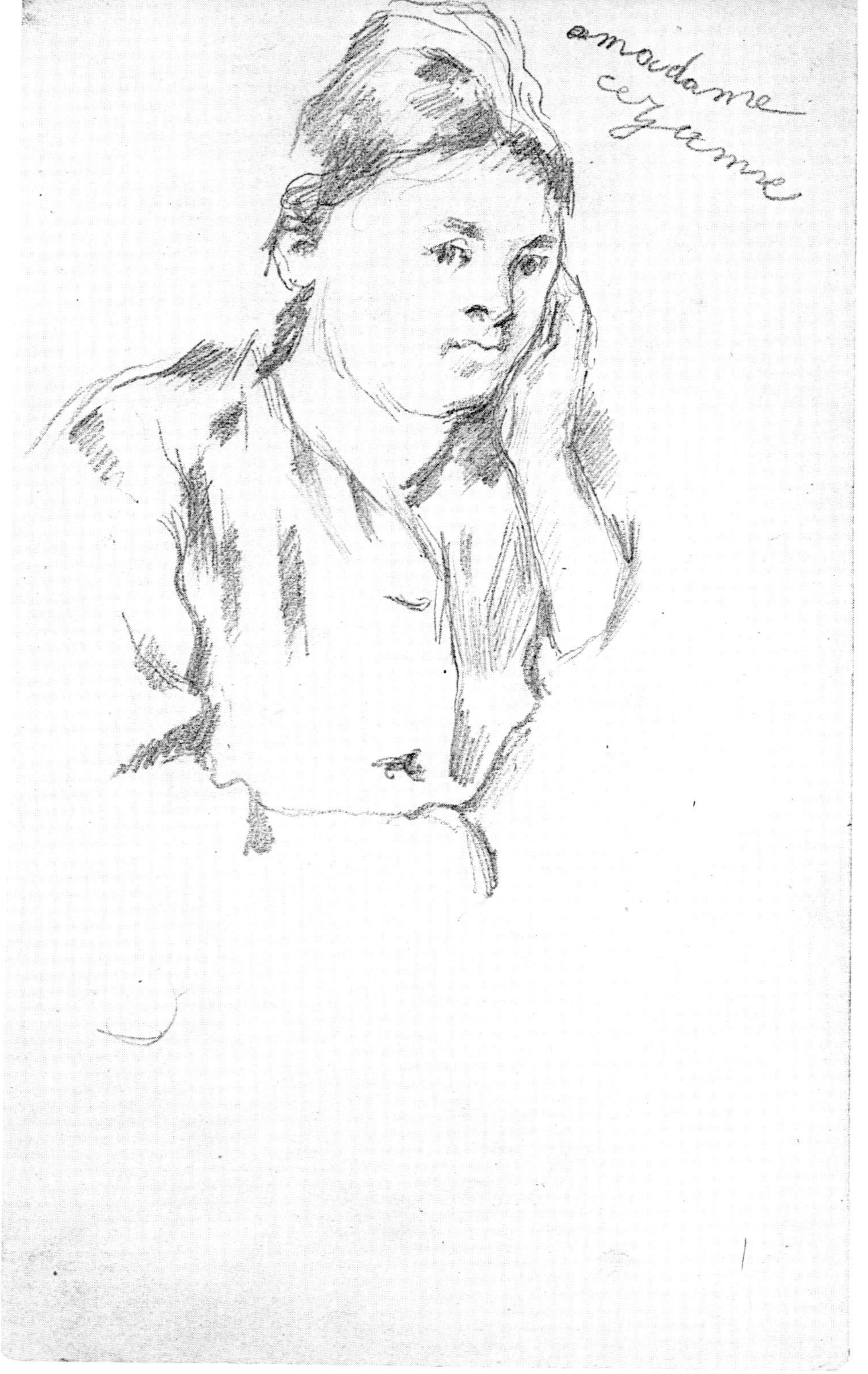
a madame
cezanne

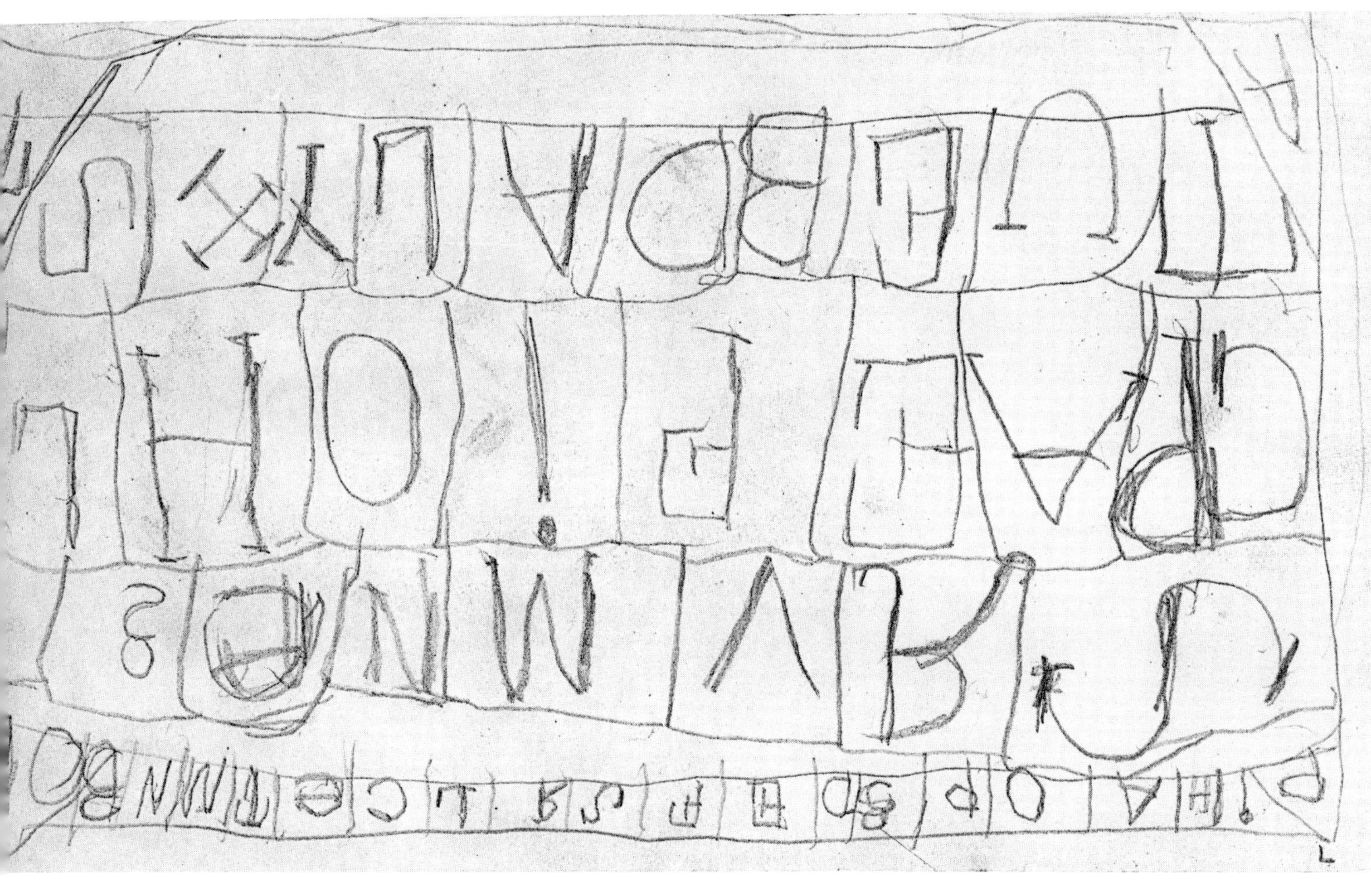

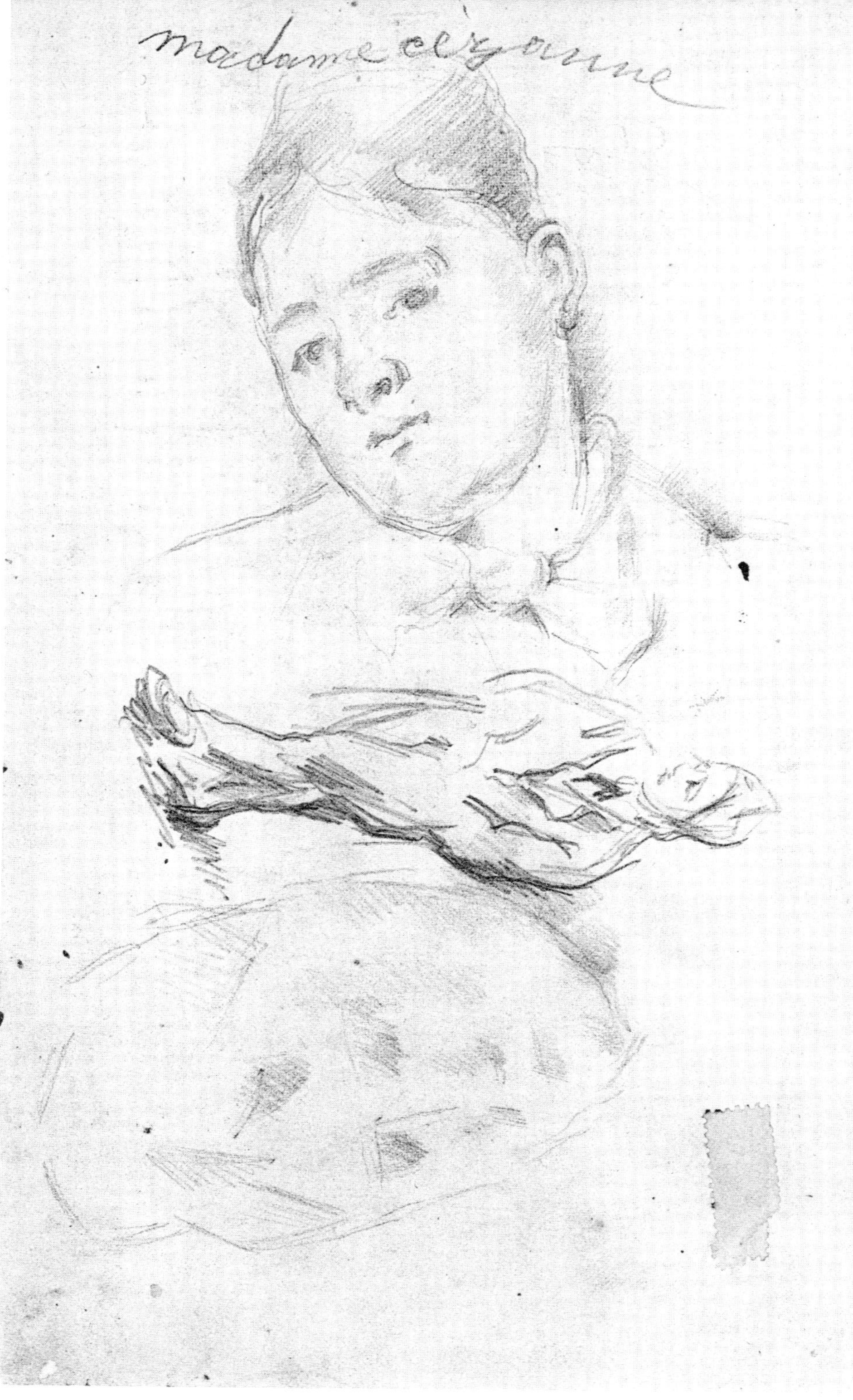
madame cézanne

Pot de fleur, 0,32 c.
boîte de fer blanc chaup
tricot pour Rose
boîte de fer blanc poivre
toile grise
bottines femmes.
Charbon, pour chaufferette
pincette